To Be President

Quest for the White House 2008

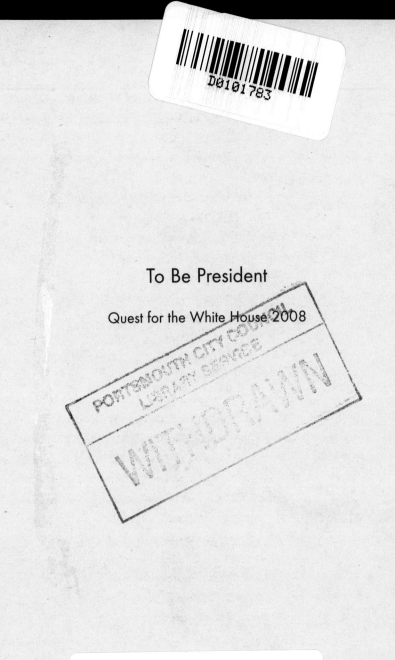

To Be President

Quest for the White House 2008

Ian Leslie

POLITICO'S

First published in Great Britain 2009 by
Politico's Publishing, an imprint of
Methuen Publishing Ltd
8 Artillery Row
London
SW1P 1RZ

10 9 8 7 6 5 4 3 2 1

A CIP catalogue record for this book is available from the British Library.

ISBN 978-1-84275-233-3

Set in Garamond and Futura by Methuen Publishing Ltd
Printed and bound in Great Britain by CPI Bookmarque, Croydon

For my parents

Contents

Acknowledgements

I owe a debt of gratitude to all of the people without whom this book wouldn't have been possible. To the many journalists whose first-hand reports have informed this narrative. To my brilliant agent Nicola Barr, who came up with the idea for this book and a way to make it happen. To my publishers at Politico's, especially to Jonathan Wadman for his scrupulous editing under severe time constraints. To Edward Docx for his inspiration and clarifying advice. To Alice Wignall, for her constant encouragement and emotional support and above all for the countless, invaluable improvements she made to the manuscript.

Introduction

An American presidential election has everything: power and money, race and religion, hubris and humiliation. It is a story that unfolds over many months in the stadiums, town halls, diners and living rooms of a vast and richly peopled land. The candidates are embroiled in a very human drama, their fortunes rising and falling in great swooping arcs. Strengths are revealed, weaknesses mercilessly exposed. At the end, one person stands victorious.

Even by these standards the 2008 presidential race was exceptional. A coincidence of three fundamental conditions made it, quite simply, the most dramatic ever held.

First, a country yearning for change, and not just of president. At a time when the nation faced a deteriorating economy and two foreign wars, Americans had lost faith in their rulers and were fed up with the politics they knew. This year favoured the novel and the different.

Second, a cast of players more compelling than in any election of the modern era. The leading presidential hopefuls were all singular individuals with unlikely life stories and political careers that paralleled and intersected with each other's like railroad tracks.

Third, a wide open field. For the first time since 1928 no incumbent president or vice-president was standing, and there was no gilt-edged front-runner for either party's nomination. As the first primaries came into view in late 2007 a credible case could be made that any one of eight people had a shot at becoming the forty-fourth president of the United States. Three of them stood to make history by winning: a woman, an African-American and a man who, if elected, would be the oldest president ever to serve.

All this made for quite a year.

The candidates

(in alphabetical order)

Hillary Rodham Clinton (Democrat)

By the time she became the leading candidate for her party's nomination, Hillary Clinton was both highly familiar and barely known. Few have had their lives as thoroughly raked over in public whilst remaining opaque to the people's gaze.

This may have had something to do with the manner in which Clinton became famous. A politician's spouse walks an uneasy line between being a private and a public figure, and the role of first lady in particular comes with such heavy expectations that Clinton struggled to adapt to it for most of her time in the White House. Of course, anyone might have difficulty defining themselves as an individual when they're standing next to Bill Clinton. Just ask Al Gore. But Hillary Clinton was never a confident self-expresser like her husband. She learned from a young age the importance of putting her best face on in public, whatever she felt in private.

Hillary Rodham's great-grandparents arrived in Scranton, Pennsylvania in the 1880s after travelling in steerage from Wales. Her grandfather Hugh Rodham began work at the Scranton Lace Company, then the world's biggest producer of Nottingham lace. One of Hugh's three sons, Hugh E. Rodham, attended Penn State University before relocating to Chicago, where he found a job selling drapery fabrics, returning to Scranton regularly to give his mother his paycheque. Hugh Jr married a woman named Dorothy Howell and the couple had a daughter – Hillary, born in 1947 – followed by two sons. They took Hillary to Scranton to be baptised into the United Methodist Church, and she returned to her father's family seat regularly as she grew up, although she was raised in the Chicago suburbs.

It was a conservative, traditionalist household, dominated by her father, a forbidding figure with an epic temper. In her autobiography, *Living History*, Clinton describes him as a 'rock-ribbed Republican'. Hugh E. Rodham was a fervent anti-communist who spied enemies everywhere. Like many children of the Depression, he feared nothing more than the return of poverty and he aggressively instilled a sense of parsimony into his family, forcing Hillary and her mother into lengthy negotiations with him for special purchases like a new dress. Mr Rodham was a fierce disciplinarian who didn't indulge displays of vulnerability, and his daughter learned always to wear her best face and carry on achieving even when everything around or inside her was in turmoil. It was a carapace that was to thicken and develop throughout her adult life.

Both parents encouraged their only daughter to exercise her evident intellectual abilities and aspire to an independent career. It soon became clear that Hillary was fixated on politics, and following the lead of her father she became a Republican. Aged thirteen, furious at Nixon's defeat by Kennedy in the 1960 presidential election, she set off with a friend to investigate possible voting fraud in the South Side of Chicago. She knocked on doors of this poor and mainly African-American neighbourhood to check voter lists, often being yelled at for her trouble. Young Hillary found clear evidence of fraud, and was excited to tell her father – but when he found out where she'd been, he was furious.

Hillary Rodham was a volunteer in Barry Goldwater's doomed

conservative insurgency in the 1964 presidential campaign, although by this time her political philosophy was becoming a compound that included her mother's more liberal instincts and the views of her dashing young Methodist minister, a passionate advocate for black civil rights. Enrolled at the prestigious female college Wellesley to study political science, Rodham became president of the Young Republicans in her freshman year. But as with so many others, her worldview was roiled by the Vietnam War and the struggle for civil rights. In 1968 she supported the anti-war candidacy of Eugene McCarthy in his campaign for the Democratic nomination. When Martin Luther King Jr was assassinated in April of that year she organised a two-day student strike and worked with black students to recruit blacks to the college. Attending the 1968 Republican convention she became fed up with what she perceived as the veiled racism of Richard Nixon's campaign, and left the party for good.

Rodham was a whirlwind of political activity at Wellesley, though socially she felt ill at ease amongst the cosmopolitan, moneyed students the college attracted. She graduated with honours in 1969 and became the first Wellesley student to be given the honour of addressing fellow students at graduation, in the form of a 'commencement speech'. *Life* magazine featured her speech, casting Rodham as part of a new generation of strong, politically aware women. She began to be spoken of as having the potential to become the first female president of the United States.

It was at Yale Law School that Hillary Rodham met Bill Clinton. She'd seen him more than once in the library holding court to groups of students, discoursing on the size of Arkansas watermelons. His gaze would regularly wander over to meet hers. Extending her hand to him one afternoon, she declared that if they were going to keep looking at each other then they might as well be introduced. They soon formed a relationship based on a mutually consuming passion for politics.

What a contrast Bill must have presented to the other man in Hillary's life. Whereas her father was a disciplinarian as tight with affection as he was with money, Bill was chaotic, warm, voluble and tactile. She brought a measure of discipline and order to his unruly life. He had in abundance the easy personal charm she lacked. Both of them met, for the first time, their intellectual match.

Back then, Hillary was the one spoken of as having a great political future. But after graduation she took the difficult and pivotal decision to follow Bill to Arkansas, effectively subsuming her ambitions to his – at least temporarily. After being something of a star ever since her first year at Wellesley, she knew that from now on, the centre of attention would be standing next to her. The couple exchanged wedding vows in their living room in 1975. It was to prove an enduring if chaotic marriage. Neither has ever quite got over their amazement that the other would want to be with someone like them; both believed they had married the most brilliant political mind in the country.

Bill's rise was fast. Within three years he was governor of Arkansas, at the age of thirty-two (he suffered a bruising defeat after his first term, but regained the office in 1982 and held it until 1992). Chelsea, the couple's only child, was born in 1980. Hillary – who worked as a partner in an Arkansas law firm and later took positions on boards of companies including Wal-Mart – had to adjust her north-eastern feminist style in concession to southern tastes and drop her maiden name, the first of many modifications to her public persona that she may have resented but nonetheless made. She also learned to cope with and accommodate her husband's compulsive philandering. How this accommodation came about, and how painful it was, we may never know. But it is clear that the mature equilibrium of the marriage incorporated Bill's infidelities, anchored as it was in their shared love for the great game of politics. Which is not to say, as some imagine, that the relationship was or is passionless. To this day it retains an intensity few long marriages can match.

Hillary Clinton was first thrust into the full national spotlight when the Gennifer Flowers scandal erupted during Bill's campaign for the Democratic presidential nomination in 1992. In an apparently soul-baring interview on television, Bill confessed and Hillary explained why she forgave him, protesting that 'I'm not . . . some little woman standing by my man like Tammy Wynette, I'm sitting here because I love him'. She was vilified for this remark by many who interpreted it as disdainful of millions of 'little women'. It must have been galling for Hillary to find herself coming out of the interview worse than her husband. That interview, together with a remark she made about not wanting to stay home and 'bake cookies', assisted in fixing the image painted by her husband's enemies of an overbearing liberal elitist who looked down her nose at ordinary folks. It didn't help that, sounding like her Wellesley self, she issued a call for a 'new politics of meaning' that would 'waken America from a sleeping sickness of the soul'.

Once in the White House, her husband handed the first lady an unprecedented amount of political power (Bill suggested, rather unwisely, that the country was getting 'two for the price of one'). She was allocated the task of reforming the US health system. Despite working on it for two years, her plan met an ignominious defeat at the hands of Congress. It suffered from Hillary's reluctance to compromise, her instinctive secrecy and her distrust of people not considered intimates. Behind the scenes, the first lady was unpopular with the president's aides, developing a reputation for bawling them out in front of her husband, perhaps as a way of expressing her anger at him. In public she became a figure of irrational hatred and gothic rumour: when a Clinton aide, Vince Foster, killed himself it was whispered that she'd had an affair with him then had him shot.

Although she remained a powerful influence within the White House, Clinton withdrew from the public stage to an extent after the failure of her health care plan and began the project of softening her image. She published a book, *It Takes a Village*, about the welfare of children, made numerous ceremonial trips abroad and spoke on the issues of women's rights. But it was, once again, her husband's infuriating indiscipline that thrust her back to centre stage. In 1998, as details of the Monica Lewinsky affair spilled out into the public realm, the nation viewed her with a mix of sympathy and contempt for her decision to stand by her husband once more.

The conventional political couple, faced with a scandal of infidelity, strives to portray a sense of stability to the outside world whilst keeping any turbulence behind closed doors. For the Clintons, it was the opposite. Despite the stories that Hillary was considering whether to stay with Bill, it's not at all clear that the decision was difficult. A friend later reported seeing them, days after the story broke, hand in hand, laughing and joshing with each other merrily in private. He was taken aback by the contrast with their solemn public demeanour. Perhaps this shouldn't have been a surprise; the fundamental equilibrium of the marriage had not been disrupted. The Clintons had long been energised by a sense that it was them against the world, and the world's disbelief and anger at Bill was transmuted into a fierce sense of defensiveness that only bound them tighter together. The impeachment was, according to Hillary, part of a 'vast right-wing conspiracy', a piece of hyperbole that echoed her father's paranoid worldview.

In early 1999, Hillary Clinton started to plot her own political career after a 25-year deferral. A Senate seat was becoming available in New York, and although she had no ties to the state she and her husband were popular there. Hillary announced her candidacy in 2000, and as Bill served his final months in office (and saw his popularity recover), she was criss-crossing New York state, talking to voters and raising funds. Characteristically, she overcame charges of carpet-bagging through sheer hard work and application. Farmers in rural parts of the state would be surprised by her detailed knowledge of the kinds of local issue national politicians rarely bothered themselves with. She proved to many sceptical voters that she wasn't the left-wing harridan of reputation but a shrewd and capable problem-solver.

It was a reinvention that she continued in her Senate career. Fellow senators, wary of any high-profile newcomer but particularly of a Clinton, were won over by the assiduity with which she learned the institution's arcane rules and procedures and by the way she deferred to senior colleagues rather than use her celebrity status to hog the limelight. She also went out of her way to build relationships with Republicans, defying her reputation as a fierce partisan.

Clinton was considered an effective senator by New Yorkers and won re-election by a large margin six years later, having decided that a run for the presidency in 2004 would be premature. After John Kerry's defeat, it became a virtual certainty amongst the political classes that she would be the Democratic nominee for president in 2008. Clinton was clearly ready, and her husband had decontaminated his own brand by his work towards solving global challenges such as AIDS and climate change. The two of them had dominated their party since 1992 and built a massive network of political and financial support. Not only that, but as late as 2006 no challenger appeared to be a credible threat to her.

John Edwards (Democrat)

John Edwards's life story is so dramatic that it was tempting to root for his accession to the White House on the grounds of narrative satisfaction alone. He knew that, and placed his biography at the heart of his political identity.

Edwards was born in South Carolina in 1953 and raised in the small town of Robbins, North Carolina. Robbins was dominated by a textile industry in terminal decline. Edwards's father worked in the mill and was determined that his children should attend college and find more lucrative careers, though he couldn't afford to pay their fees.

His son John was a good football player: tall, skinny and fast. John enrolled at Clemson University, South Carolina, in the hope of winning a football scholarship. A place of relative privilege, Clemson was just 9 miles from where Edwards grew up but a world away, and he felt out of place amongst the sons and daughters of wealthier families. So he joined North Carolina State University, working nights unloading boxes at UPS to earn money for his tuition fees. Handsome and blond, he was regarded by his classmates as a cocky but essentially good-natured and likeable fellow student.

Edwards's breezy nature concealed a fierce determination to succeed. He was a driven student obsessed with making top grades, attending summer school in order to graduate within three years. He had his sights set on studying law and was accepted to law school at the University of North Carolina at Chapel Hill. It was here that he met a clever, outspoken, passionate law student named Elizabeth Anania, later to become his wife and closest political counsel.

After graduation Edwards joined a law firm specialising in civil trials, representing clients suing companies over alleged malpractice. He quickly became a feared operator throughout the state, making his name representing a five-year-old girl who had been disembowelled by a faulty swimming pool drain; the jury awarded her $25 million. Edwards was renowned for tireless preparation, outworking and out-thinking everyone else, and for the skill with which he employed his boyish charm to devastating effect on jurors. During his legal career he won more than $150 million in jury awards and settlements, becoming a rich man himself in the process.

In 1996 Edwards was forty-three. He was wealthy and blessed with a loving wife and two children: fourteen-year-old Cate and sixteen-year-old Wade. He was eager for a new challenge, and toyed with the idea of quitting law for a career in politics. Wade, who himself had written an essay on voting that won him a trip to the White House and a meeting with Bill and Hillary Clinton, encouraged him to do so.

In April of that year, Wade was killed when his Jeep was over-turned on the highway by a windstorm. Two years later John Edwards ran for Senate. Elizabeth said that he wanted to do work that Wade would be proud of.

Edwards transferred the relentless work ethic and mania for preparation that had made him such a successful lawyer to his run for office. He dispatched his rival for the Democratic nomination and won a contest with the Republican incumbent by painting him as an ineffective representative of the people who had got too comfortable in Washington.

Telegenic, smart, an authentic southerner in a party short on southern credibility and the possessor of an inspiring rags-to-riches life story, Edwards quickly became regarded as something of a star in Democratic circles, and it wasn't long before he was talked of as a presidential nominee. Indeed, in 2004, six years after entering the Senate, he nearly pulled it off, offering himself as the voice of sunny optimism and change against the establishment candidate, John Kerry. In the end Kerry saw off the young challenger, but Edwards had done enough to win a spot on the ticket as vice-presidential nominee.

It proved to be a losing ticket, and shortly after the election Edwards set his sights on 2008. Having resigned his Senate seat to run for vice-president in 2004, he established a think-tank focused on the alleviation of poverty, and began raising money and building support for another run. His wife's breast cancer, discovered the day after the 2004 campaign, returned in 2007, but the two made a joint decision to continue. In a world of competitive personalities, John and Elizabeth Edwards stood out for their ferocious will to win.

In 2004 John Edwards was the voice of optimism; for 2008 he reinvented himself as a pugilistic populist, recounting scraps he got into as a young man, emphasising his battles with big corporations as a trial lawyer, and promising to fight entrenched interests in Washington from the White House. But could he overturn not one, but two better-known and better-funded candidates in the shape of Hillary Clinton and Barack Obama? Given his formidable talents, nobody was writing Edwards off.

Rudy Giuliani (Republican)

For most of 2007, a twice-divorced Catholic New Yorker with a liberal record on abortion and guns was the front-runner for the Republican presidential nomination. That such an unlikely scenario was possible was evidence of the disarray in the Republican Party. It was also testament to the power of Rudy Giuliani's political brand.

Giuliani was born in 1944 and raised in Brooklyn and later Long Island by the children of Italian immigrants. His father was a small-time crook and mafia shark. Rudy, however, was a studious young man who did well at his Catholic school, and after gaining a degree in political science he considered becoming a priest.

In the end he opted for the law and built a successful career in federal prosecution, starting in the district attorney's office in New York before going to Washington in 1975 to work for Gerald Ford's administration and later as the third-highest-ranking official in Ronald Reagan's Justice Department. He returned to his home state in 1983 as United States attorney for the Southern District of New York, the most prestigious such post in the nation. Here he made a name for himself as a vigorous, driven and street-smart 'crimebuster' who took on mafia dons, Wall Street titans and corrupt politicians. The *Daily News* proclaimed 'Good News for the Bad Guys' when he stepped down.

Giuliani cultivated a strong relationship with the press. With their help, he crafted an image of a profane tough guy possessed of aggressive moral certitude, a shark on the side of the people. He tells the story of seeing, in 1992, smoke coming from a historic church, and of how, when he rushed in to save the priest, he saw crooks lifting a candelabrum off the altar. 'Put that fucking stuff down,' he yelled.

Giuliani used his renown to launch a campaign for mayor of New York. He lost his first run in 1989 but in 1993 overturned the Democrat incumbent to become the first Republican mayor of the city in nearly thirty years. He took over at a time when many had come to regard New York as essentially ungovernable: a crime-ridden town in permanent political deadlock. Giuliani's great achievement was to dispel that notion. He set about his task with tremendous energy and imagination, adopting an innovative approach to crime reduction known as 'broken windows' that focused on pursuing minor offences vigorously, to send a message that order would be maintained. Although it is disputed how much of the subsequent reduction in crime was down to his policies, there is little doubt that Giuliani's dynamism restored confidence in the office of the mayor itself. He was elected to two further terms, though he always divided opinions. Not one of life's natural compromisers, Giuliani relished his enemies and loved to humiliate them. He wasn't interested in being liked, and it showed.

It took the attacks of September 11 2001 to turn Rudy Giuliani into a true people's hero. During press conferences immediately after the World Trade Center towers collapsed, Giuliani displayed an unflustered determination to prevail that did much to convince New Yorkers and Americans that the world as they knew it was not about to end. He became a potent symbol of America's stubborn determination to carry on in the face of terror. From that moment on he was talked about as a future Republican president.

For Republican activists, Giuliani's New York-style liberalism on the cultural and social issues that matter so much to them was hard to take. But his status as a national hero, and the promise that he would take on Islamic extremists with the same relentless vigour with which he took on New York's criminals, looked as if they might be enough to overcome all other considerations. He toured the country throughout 2006, speaking to Republican crowds, telling and retelling the story of his finest hours, displaying formidable communication skills in the process. Amongst a pack of candidates who all suffered from major flaws, Giuliani forced himself to the head. By the summer of 2007 he was leading in the national polls. If there was ever a year in which the Republican Party might choose a pro-choice New York Catholic as its candidate, it was this one.

Mike Huckabee (Republican)

Mike Huckabee was the joker in the Republican pack. Whilst few considered him a serious contender to begin with, it became clear during the summer of 2007 that his idiosyncratic combination of scriptural references and stand-up jokes was attractive to many Republican voters dissatisfied with the choice of candidates arrayed before them.

Born and raised in Hope, Arkansas (the small town that Bill Clinton comes from), Huckabee became active in the local church at a young age. He gave his first sermon as a teenager and was later ordained as a Baptist minister. He used his seniority within the Arkansas church and his popularity as a preacher to launch a career in politics. Already lieutenant governor, he was running for the Senate in 1996 when the then governor had to resign after being convicted of fraud in the Whitewater scandal (a property deal in which the Clintons were also embroiled). Huckabee dropped his Senate run to fill the vacant position, and in 1998 was elected to a full four-year term. He proved to be a bold and innovative governor, working with Democrats to push through a series of changes to Arkansas's education and health systems. In 2002 he was re-elected to a second term. Three years later *Time* magazine named him one of the nation's top five governors. Leaving office at the end of his second term in 2006, he began to plan a presidential run.

Huckabee also gained a measure of celebrity for his successful efforts to lose weight. Whilst governor he shed nearly 8 stone as the prelude to a statewide drive to reduce obesity, a feat he chronicled in a book called *Quit Digging Your Grave with a Knife and Fork*.

John McCain (Republican)

Something about this election year demanded unconventional candidates, and John McCain fitted the bill. One of the best-known and most influential politicians in the country, McCain achieved his pre-eminent position through his reputation as the Republican Party's dissenter in chief: a fiercely independent voice given to dangerous candour, a man who never toed the party line if he thought it poorly drawn. Preparing for what he knew was his last chance to win the ultimate prize, McCain softened his edges in the years leading up to 2008, reining in his non-conformist instincts. But he never seemed entirely at ease with the compromises that a bid for the presidency demanded.

Despite coming from a military family, McCain has always seemed to chafe at authority. The son and grandson of four-star admirals, he was born in 1936 on a US military base in Panama. His early years were spent following his father to various naval postings across the United States and the Pacific. McCain attended around twenty schools before taking up the family trade, entering the United States Naval Academy at Annapolis, Maryland. A decent wrestler and boxer, McCain was a cocky kid who was nonetheless well liked by his classmates for his willingness to stand up to authority and his brazen disregard for rules he considered petty. The academy yearbook described him as a 'sturdy conversationalist and party man. John's quick wit and clever sarcasm made him a welcome man at any gathering. His bouts with the academic and executive departments contributed much to the stockpiles of legends within the hall.' Never a conscientious student, McCain graduated in 1958 near the bottom of his class. He then enrolled at flight school in Pensacola, Florida, where he excelled above all at partying. After graduation McCain was stationed on aircraft-carriers in the Caribbean and Mediterranean seas. He was a skilful though somewhat erratic pilot, on one occasion flying his plane into power lines and plunging a whole region of southern Spain into darkness.

In 1964 McCain became friendly with Carol Shepp, a long-legged former swimwear model, who he'd been introduced to while at Annapolis. Since they had first met, Shepp had got married to the friend that introduced them and had given birth to two sons. But the marriage ended in divorce. This time around McCain and Shepp began dating, and a year later they were married. McCain adopted Shepp's children, and they soon had a daughter of their own. But the family was not long together. As the Vietnam War escalated, McCain requested and received a combat assignment.

He was flying a bombing raid over Hanoi in 1967 when his plane was shot down. After parachuting into a lake he swam to shore despite having broken both arms and one leg. He was immediately captured by Vietnamese soldiers and was stabbed and beaten, his shoulder crushed by a rifle butt, before being taken to Hoa Lo prison (unaffectionately known by American prisoners of war as the 'Hanoi Hilton'). In an attempt to force false confessions from him, McCain was tortured regularly, even as his wounds were left to heal untreated. When the Vietnamese learned that he was from a famous military family – McCain's father was at that time commander of US forces in the Pacific – they offered him an early release in the interests of scoring a propaganda victory. McCain refused, choosing to obey the US military code that prisoners ought to be released in the order in which they were taken. His captors were displeased. He spent much of the remainder of his captivity in solitary confinement, subjected to an intensified programme of torture, including rope bindings and regular beatings. In desperation he signed a confession of 'criminality' but afterwards was so ashamed that he attempted suicide. He was stopped by the guards.

McCain was in prison for five and a half years. When he finally limped home in 1973, sporting severe injuries and a shock of white hair, it was to a hero's welcome, his family name giving him a celebrity most fellow soldiers did not enjoy. McCain was told by doctors that he would never fly again. But he was determined to prove them wrong, and after a long and gruelling period of rehabilitation he got his flight licence back. Shortly afterwards he was awarded command of the Navy's largest aviation squadron, based in Florida.

Meanwhile McCain's marriage, which appeared happy to the outside world, was ailing. Whilst he was in prison Carol had broken both her legs and her pelvis in a car crash, and after several operations had lost 4 inches in height. On his return, McCain told friends that she was not the woman he had married. The marriage gradually fell apart, and McCain spent many nights out on the town indulging in a series of infidelities. In 1979 he met Cindy Hensley, a wealthy Arizonan heiress, and began an affair with her. She was twenty-four, he was forty-two. The relationship endured, and McCain left his wife for his new girlfriend. McCain later expressed deep regrets for his behaviour during these years. He remains on amicable terms with his first wife.

At the end of the 1970s McCain retired from the navy and filed for divorce from Carol. He had set his sights on a new life with Cindy (to whom he was married in 1980) and a new career. In 1977 he had been appointed the navy's liaison to the US Senate, and it was then that he first 'heard the music', as a friend put it, of Capitol Hill. His new wife was able to fund his political ambitions, and it was in Cindy's home state of Arizona that McCain ran for Congress. Answering a rival candidate who accused him of 'carpetbagging' in a debate, McCain reminded him that as the child of a peripatetic military family, 'the place I have lived longest in my life was Hanoi'. McCain's Vietnamese imprisonment was already beginning to inform his political identity, although at this time he maintained that he didn't want to be a 'professional PoW', and avoided the topic of his torture in public.

After four years in the House of Representatives, McCain was elected to the Senate in 1986. He won the respect of colleagues across party lines, cultivating strong relationships with influential Democrats as well as those on his own side. He soon established national security and deficit reduction as two of his signature issues. In 1988 he was spoken of as a potential running mate for George Bush Sr. But McCain's promising career hit turbulence when he became enmeshed in a financial scandal. He was one of five senators who had lobbied in defence of a failing savings-and-loan company owned by Charles Keating (they were to become known as 'the Keating Five'). The company was under investigation for fraud, one of the S&L scandals that damaged the US economy during this time. Keating had made large campaign contributions to the senators, including McCain. However, McCain was less involved than the others and received only a minor rebuke for his conduct from the Senate Ethics Committee.

The scandal was a turning point for McCain. As a man who valued his reputation for integrity, he was mortified at the thought that he had allowed his to be sullied, however unintentionally. From then on, he pursued the reform of campaign finance, pushing for a ban on the unlimited contributions to political parties that were used to bankroll campaigns. He took on the powerful tobacco lobby when he sponsored a bill that would raise cigarette taxes in order to pay for anti-smoking campaigns. He also campaigned against 'pork barrel' spending (or 'earmarks'), which refers to the way in which legislators divert federal funds to their own constituents by attaching extra spending commitments to bills in return for their vote. In the process McCain created more than a few enemies on the right of his own party – and started to become known as a 'maverick' within the Grand Old Party (GOP, otherwise known as the Republican Party).

In 1999 McCain published a memoir entitled *Faith of My Fathers*, which formed the cornerstone of his mature political identity. The year before, he had complained, in a magazine interview, that being introduced as a war hero 'made his skin crawl'. But encouraged by his publisher to place his story in the context of his father and grand-father's heroism, and assisted by his co-author and speechwriter, Mark Salter, McCain produced a book that put his years in captivity at the centre of his public persona for the first time. He recalled his experience of imprisonment as transforming him from selfish playboy to responsible patriot, eager to 'serve a cause' larger than himself.

It was McCain's insurgent bid for the presidency in 2000 that made his political brand nationally famous. He faced his favourite type of struggle: an uphill one, against the ultimate establishment candidate, George W. Bush. The scion of a political dynasty and well-funded darling of the right, Bush was the firm favourite to win the Republican nomination, and his campaign positioned him as the 'inevitable' candidate in the hope of wrapping up the race early. Despite having little money, McCain dared to challenge this idea. Running as the crusading reformer of a corrupt and dishonest political establishment, he travelled the country on his Straight Talk Express bus, charming every reporter on board with his disregard for the protocols of political communication. 'Ask me anything,' he would say, and in his conversations – expansive, indiscreet, self-lacerating – he appeared to hold nothing back. In the town halls of New Hampshire he took the same approach, revelling in the unscripted back-and-forth of voter Q&As whilst his opponent stuck tightly to his scripts.

McCain quickly became a phenomenon. His face stared out from the covers of *Time* and *Rolling Stone*. He was magnetic, not just to Republicans, but to voters with no party affiliation and even to some Democrats. He spoke out forcefully against the dominance of money in Washington when nobody else was doing so, and in his town hall meetings he seemed to cut through the layers of fakery surrounding most political discourse. People with little interest in politics, especially the young, were drawn to McCain for his reckless honesty and swash-buckling style. He seemed different. Cynics rediscovered their idealism and the jaded fell in love again. Here was a politician for people who didn't like politicians (the writer David Foster Wallace called him 'the anti-candidate').

By drawing thousands of new voters to the polls, McCain scored an improbable, spectacular victory in the New Hampshire primary, making Bush's coronation as the Republican nominee suddenly appear highly tenuous. Startled by this unexpected reversal, the Bush campaign and its allies in the party establishment reacted with unbridled ferocity. In the lowlands of South Carolina, where the next primary was held, McCain's candidacy was assailed by wave after wave of vicious attacks. Bush stood by as a surrogate accused McCain of forgetting about fellow veterans on his return from Vietnam, and his supporters frequently implied that McCain had an unreliable temper. But it was what happened under the radar that made South Carolina 2000 go down in presidential campaign lore as the most brutal primary ever fought.

Every day at McCain headquarters, reports would arrive of phone calls and flyers spreading toxic rumours about the senator's mental stability, his sexuality, his wife and, most notoriously, a black child he had supposedly fathered out of wedlock (the rumour was a distorted version of the truth: the McCains had adopted a Bangladeshi orphan in 1993). The onslaught worked: Bush won a crushing victory. Karl Rove, Bush's chief strategist, denied involvement in the dirty tricks, though McCain didn't believe him and went down railing against not only his opponent but the religious right, elements of which he believed had conspired in the smears. He described the religious leaders Jerry Falwell and Pat Robertson as 'agents of intolerance'.

McCain, now a national figure, exited the 2000 race bruised and bitter, and disillusioned with his fellow Republicans. For a while he drifted, disconsolate, and considered leaving his party. The attacks of September 11 changed all that. Like a soldier springing into life at the sound of a bugle call, he rediscovered his political *raison d'être* – and his ambition to be president. He believed himself to be the only man capable of facing down the threat of Islamic terrorism. As the ranking member of the Senate Armed Services Committee, he established himself as one of the country's foremost foreign policy hawks and became a leading supporter of the Iraq War.

McCain also began the difficult process of reconciliation with the party establishment. He knew that to win his party's nomination in 2008 he would need to build some bridges, starting with one to Bush, whose re-election he endorsed publicly and, so it seemed, whole-heartedly. He reversed his initial opposition to Bush's tax cuts, and his connection to the president was strengthened when he stood with him on the decision to send more troops to Iraq in 2007 (the 'surge') in the face of almost unanimous dissent.

By the time the 2008 election came into view, McCain was considered the front-runner for the nomination. Although elements of his party still viewed him warily, he retained an ability that the party sorely needed to attract independent voters and even Democrats. But in 2007 McCain, with typical perversity, supported an immigration bill that he knew was massively unpopular with the right of his party. He polling numbers went into seemingly terminal decline, and his funding all but dried up. In the summer of 2007 his campaign faced bankruptcy. McCain was forced to sack most of his campaign staff and slash his costs. The media declared that his last stand was over.

Not for the first time, McCain contemplated an impossible task – and decided to go for it.

Barack Obama (Democrat)

This was always likely to be a memorable election. There were weighty issues of war and peace for the nation to consider, and no safe bets for either party's nomination. But there is little doubt that the decision of Illinois's junior senator to enter the race made this a truly extraordinary year.

Rarely has there been such a spectacular collision of man and moment. By the colour of his skin, but also by his background, name and youth, Barack Obama was a vivid embodiment of difference at a time when the country thirsted for something new. Rocketing to national fame after his speech at the 2004 Democratic convention, Obama's name and face soon resonated beyond politics. He became a cultural phenomenon in a way few politicians ever do, adorning magazine covers, T-shirts and websites before he'd even announced his candidacy.

As the presidential contest got under way, commentators raced to assess the man behind the phenomenon. They had to compete with Obama himself. In an autobiography written in his early thirties, entitled *Dreams from My Father*, Obama had displayed an unusual degree of self-reflection. But his heritage and upbringing had forced him, more than most, to consider the question of who he was and who he wanted to be.

Stanley Ann Dunham (her father wanted a boy) of Wichita, Kansas was studying anthropology at the University of Hawaii when she met and fell in love with a fellow student named Barack Obama, in 1960. Obama Sr was a graduate student from Kenya and, as the first African to attend the University of Hawaii, something of a local celebrity, a status he rather enjoyed. He is remembered as a charismatic personality, who had a habit of turning every conversation into an excuse to orate. Months after meeting, the two were married in Maui,

with Ann – she'd dropped her first name – already three months pregnant. Barack Jr was born in August 1961. But the family was together
only briefly. Less than two years later, Barack Sr left for Harvard to
study for a master's degree in economics. He never lived with Ann
again. Two years later the couple were divorced, though they stayed
in touch.

Back at college, Ann – clearly something of a romantic – met
and fell for an Indonesian student named Lolo Soetoro. She
became Ann Dunham Soetoro in 1967 and, together with her six-
year-old son, followed her husband to Indonesia later that year.
The young Barack lived in Jakarta for four years, where he got used
to being seen as an oddity, being not only foreign and a 'negro' but
chubbier than the locals. When he was ten years old his mother,
determined that he should have a first-rate education, sent him
back to Hawaii to live with her parents, so that he could attend an
elite prep school. Ann followed a year later, having left her husband –
from whom she was drifting apart and was later divorced – behind.
She enrolled at the University of Hawaii again, this time to study
the anthropology of Indonesia. After three years Ann decided to go
back to Indonesia to do fieldwork, and invited her fourteen-year-
old son to accompany her. But Barack told her he wanted to stay
behind this time. He was tired of being the new kid, and he was
happy enough living with his grandparents. Ann reluctantly
agreed.

After graduating from high school, Obama attended college in
Los Angeles for two years, before enrolling at Columbia University in
New York to study political science. He was fascinated by the successes
of the US civil rights movement, and on graduation in 1983 he wrote
to civil rights groups offering himself for work. Receiving no reply, he
took a corporate job in New York. But it felt like a stop-gap. Bored
and dissatisfied, Obama longed to find more meaningful work, and

to put down roots somewhere; he didn't want to be a wanderer like his mother.

In 1985 he found a solution to both quests. He took a job in Chicago as a community organiser, helping poor, mainly black communities in the city's South Side to campaign for better services from the authorities (working on the same streets that a thirteen-year-old Hillary Clinton had explored in the aftermath of John Kennedy's election to the presidency in 1960). Here he also found a place to call home and a community to call his own. Previously agnostic, Obama joined the Trinity United Church of Christ under the guidance of its pastor, Rev. Jeremiah Wright. Obama's spiritual hunger was inextricable from his yearning to belong. He wanted to feel fully part of the local African-American community, for which the church played a central, binding role.

Obama refers to these years as formative to his political outlook, though eventually he became frustrated by the small scale of the changes he was able to achieve as an organiser. He doesn't say so, but it may have been during this time that he began to take the idea of becoming a national politician seriously; certainly he heard people tell him that he might one day become the first black president of the United States.

In 1988 Obama left Chicago to enrol at Harvard Law School. He was an excellent student, and in his second year he was elected president and editor in chief of the *Harvard Law Review*. As the first black person to attain this position, Obama gained a small degree of celebrity, becoming the subject of national newspaper profiles and the recipient of a publisher's advance for what was to become *Dreams from My Father*.

Whilst still at Harvard Obama returned to Chicago during summer breaks to work as an intern at various elite law firms, and it was at one of those that he met Michelle Robinson, who was assigned to him as a mentor. Although she refused to date him at first, citing professional propriety, he eventually persuaded her otherwise, and the two were married less than three years after meeting. Robinson, quite apart from her personal qualities, represented for Obama the embrace of authentic African-American life. The descendant of slaves, she had grown up in the South Side of Chicago amongst the communities in which Obama had done his organising work. Her father was a pump-operator for the city's water department, her mother a secretary. Supported by parents keen on self-improvement, Robinson worked her way into Princeton to read sociology and later Harvard to study law.

After graduation Obama returned to the city he now called home, taking up a teaching post at the University of Chicago. Having established a base and the beginning of a stable family life, Obama began to focus on developing his public profile. His peripatetic child-hood had taught him how to make friends quickly, and as an adult Obama proved a consummate networker, building relationships with the city's political, religious and educational elites. He was appointed to direct Illinois's Project Vote in 1992, and used his organising skills to register 150,000 new voters. This achievement made him something of a player in Chicago, and a career in elected politics beckoned. In 1996 Obama won a seat in the state senate, having got his only opponent removed from the ballot by challenging the legitimacy of her petitions. His first daughter, Malia, was born in 1998, his second, Natasha ('Sasha'), in 2001.

Obama positioned himself as an independent in Chicago politics, beholden to neither Mayor Richard Daley's 'machine' nor old-style African-American race politics. Having declared his intention to restore the public's faith in politicians, he found it difficult to achieve much in practice, because he wasn't a fully paid-up member of any faction. Personally, he divided his colleagues: some found him unbearably arrogant, others succumbed to his powerful charm and charisma. All could see that he had his sights set on higher office.

In 2000 he challenged Bobby Rush, an African-American and veteran Chicago player, for his congressional seat. Rush used every lever of his political machine to outspend and outmanoeuvre Obama; some of Rush's supporters even portrayed Obama as a secret envoy of 'the white man', sent by the Jews to steal black votes. It worked. Obama suffered a humiliating defeat, the first setback in a seemingly effortless rise. It knocked any naïveté out of him, and when he returned to state politics he determined to master the machine for his own purposes.

Obama used the prerogative of the majority party to preside over his own redistricting, creating a constituency that started with his own home patch (the liberal enclave of Hyde Park) and stretched south into the poor black communities he'd got to know as an organiser and north into the city's richest and most influential neighbourhoods. He knew that a coalition of blacks and affluent, liberal whites was a strong base from which to raise support and money for a second bid for national office, and that his mixed-race background and political gifts made such a coalition plausible. In mid-2002 he enlisted the help of Chicago's foremost political operative, David Axelrod, to put together a strategy for winning election to the US Senate in 2004.

By this time, Obama had been noticed by Democrat Party leaders. Here was a talented young black politician who held a powerful appeal to white voters. He was cut from a different cloth from previous generations of African-American politicians, and embodied the promise of a new, post-racial future for the party. At the Democratic convention of 2004, the senatorial hopeful was picked to make the keynote speech, an honour often reserved for rising stars. High-profile convention slots can be a poisoned chalice (Bill Clinton introduced the nominee in 1988, and made a speech so memorably dull that his reputation took years to recover) but Obama seized his moment with aplomb, delivering an electrifying address that made the self-described 'skinny kid with a funny name' a national figure before he had achieved national office.

Obama's Republican opponent in that year's Senate race, a self-made millionaire named Jack Ryan, was forced to drop out after an ugly divorce case. Facing a weak last-minute replacement, and with his own standing immeasurably enhanced by his speech, Obama won the election with 70 per cent of the vote, the largest electoral victory in Illinois history. He became only the third African-American in history to be elected to the Senate.

Obama joined an institution whose members were suspicious of celebrity freshmen. One of his first moves was to sit down for a chat with Hillary Clinton, who had had to deal with similar wariness when she joined the Senate in 2000. Her advice to Obama was: keep your head down, don't showboat, focus on building relationships, and show humility at all times. Obama was too impatient to heed her counsel. In 2006 he let it be known that he was considering a presidential run, generating exactly the kind of publicity Clinton had advised him to avoid. But other Democrats, within and beyond the Senate, were quietly encouraging Obama to go for it. Despite not having completed one term in national office, and having only a thin legislative track record, he took up the challenge.

Obama's 2007 announcement sent shockwaves through the political world. Everybody was expecting him to run for president – but in four or eight or twelve years' time. Was he moving too soon? Many thought so. Clinton exerted such a grip on the Democratic Party machine, and was such a formidable candidate in her own right, that she was unlikely to be dislodged from her position as front-runner for the nomination. But everyone agreed it would be fascinating to watch the young man from Illinois give it a shot.

Mitt Romney (Republican)

Willard Mitt Romney draws more than his fair share of scorn. He is, in obvious ways, an irresistible target: fastidious about his personal appearance and scrupulous of every public utterance, he can appear vain, synthetic and calculating. Yet as a businessman and governor, he has a record of achievement few can match, and former colleagues, as well as every member of his large family, attest to a man of talent, application and decency.

Mitt Romney's father, George, was a wealthy self-made businessman, a senior member of the Mormon church and Republican governor of Michigan. Born in 1947, the youngest of four children, Mitt developed a particularly close relationship with his father, whom he idolised. He attended the elite private Cranbrook School, where he did well but not exceptionally so. He was often ribbed about his famous father. After spending a short time at Stanford University, Romney travelled to Le Havre in France to begin a Mormon mission that lasted two and a half years. Here, out of the shadow of his father, he came into his own. He was spotted as a leader early on by the mission president and put in charge of fifty missionaries, proving to be good at raising the morale of his often-homesick peers. Here also, Romney was at the wheel of a car when it crashed, killing one of his passengers. Though he was blameless, the incident imbued the young man with a seriousness that was to mark his adult life.

Returning to the United States, Romney studied business and law at Harvard, where he overlapped with George W. Bush. But as Bush coasted through on the strength of his family's reputation, Romney studied hard, finishing near the top of his class. On graduation, he had his pick of jobs and took one at Boston Consulting Group (BCG), a firm in the then-new field of management consulting. Within a few years he joined a group of BCG partners to form a new firm, called Bain (he later spun off an operation from within called Bain Capital). Romney developed something of a legendary reputation in the business community as an inspiring and canny leader, who based his decisions on diligent research and analysis of the data rather than on prejudice or gut instinct. It seemed to work: he helped to turn around a string of failing businesses, making his own considerable fortune in the process.

Romney first ran for office in 1994 at the age of forty-seven, losing out in a race for Ted Kennedy's Senate seat, a close-to-impossible challenge that for a while he made look feasible. Kennedy killed him off with the still-devastating indictment 'He's not pro-choice, he's not anti-choice. He's multiple choice.' After losing, Romney swore never to run another race he wasn't certain of winning. He went back to Bain Capital, but in 1999 was asked to take over the organising committee of the 2002 Winter Olympics in Salt Lake City. The games were in dire trouble: way over budget and tainted by allegations of corruption which forced the incumbent managers to resign. It was thought the event would have to be drastically scaled back to remain solvent.

Romney set to work with furious endeavour, cutting costs, revamping the organisation's management and policies, and finding new sources of funding. In the end the games were declared a great success and generated a $100 million profit. Romney later wrote about the experience in a book called *Turnaround*.

He used his success as a springboard for another run at political office, this time as governor of Massachusetts. He defeated the Democratic candidate decisively, in this traditionally liberal state, by pitching himself as a can-do manager that people on all sides of the political spectrum could feel comfortable voting for. Romney proved an innovative governor, acclaimed for an approach that put results before ideology. He gained a reputation for hiring experts based on ability rather than partisan affiliation, and drove through Massachusetts's most widely applauded health care reforms in a generation.

Despite healthy approval ratings, Romney declined to run for a second term, and in the last years of office he began to exhibit a more socially conservative ideological bent, taking a harder line on issues such as abortion, stem cell research and gay marriage. He had set his eyes on higher office, and his audience was no longer Massachusetts voters but Republicans around the country. Romney decided that if he was to win his party's nomination for president, being seen as a results-oriented manager wasn't enough; he needed to reinvent himself as a true believer, a right-wing warrior fighting for conservative values. The tough part would be convincing voters that he meant it.

Fred Thompson (Republican)

Throughout the summer of 2007 conservative Republican voters looked at their menu of presidential candidates and couldn't see anything they liked. They yearned for a true conservative champion. For many of them Fred Thompson was that person, but though he hinted heavily that he was considering a run, something seemed to hold him back.

Thompson started his career as a district attorney in Tennessee and made a name for himself as minority counsel to the Republicans on the Senate Watergate Committee (it is said he helped to frame the famous question 'What did the president know and when did he know it?'). As well as being a successful lawyer, Thompson took up a second career in acting after being asked to play himself in a fictionalised TV version of a case he was involved in. A tall man (6 feet 5 inches) with an authoritative drawl and a reassuringly unhurried manner, he was often cast in legal dramas, becoming famous as a star of *Law and Order*.

Thompson pursued a political career in parallel. In 1994 he was elected to Al Gore's vacant Senate seat in Tennessee, where he stayed until 2003. He was much admired by conservatives for his firm stands against abortion and government expansion.

When Thompson finally declared his presidential candidacy, in September 2007, questions lingered about why he took so long to make up his mind. Was his heart really in it? He had never looked entirely at ease amidst the circus of a political campaign; for an actor he wasn't very good at pretending to enjoy himself.

Other candidates

The Democratic tail included some serious players: Bill Richardson, the governor of New Mexico and former ambassador to the United Nations; Senator Joe Biden of Delaware, one of the nation's foremost foreign policy experts; Chris Dodd, an experienced and senior senator from Connecticut. Dennis Kucinich, the eccentric, very liberal congressman from Ohio, also stood.

Republican candidates included Congressman Tom Tancredo of Colorado, who ran on an anti-immigration platform; Kansan senator Sam Brownback, the ultra-conservative Christian evangelist; and Ron Paul, a Texan congressman who loudly opposed the Iraq War and gained a substantial following on the internet. Candidates from beyond the two main parties included the environmental activist Ralph Nader, a perennial presidential hopeful, running as an independent; and Bob Barr, nominee of the Libertarian Party.

November 2007

The Democrats: game on

It is a Saturday night in Des Moines, Iowa. In an arena that has hosted Elvis Presley, Neil Diamond and Ozzy Osbourne, 9,000 Democrats see five of their party's presidential candidates lay out why Iowans should vote for them in the first primary of the season, now less than two months away. The event is Iowa's Jefferson-Jackson dinner, a fixture in the Democratic primary calendar.

John Edwards, the boyishly handsome former senator from North Carolina, tells the crowd how, as the self-made son of a millworker, he has been driven by a lifelong passion for fighting poverty and injustice. He promises that, as president, he will combat the corrupt corporate interests that dominate Washington politics, and stand up for working people. Bill Richardson, the jocular governor of New Mexico and America's most prominent Hispanic politician, flatters Iowans by thanking them for embodying democracy at its best. He appeals to Iowa's affection for the underdog and implores fellow Democrats not to 'tear each other down'. Senator Joe Biden begins with a joke about the leading Republican candidate, Rudy Giuliani: every Giuliani sentence seems to contain nothing but a noun, a verb and '9/11'. But now that the right-wing preacher Pat Robertson has endorsed Giuliani, Biden says he'll add 'an amen' in there. He goes on to outline his plan to end the war in Iraq and ensure that America regains its reputation in the world. Chris Dodd, the silver-haired senator from Connecticut, declares that his first priority will be to 'restore the US constitution' after what he says are the abuses of the Bush years.

All of the speeches are solid, as you'd expect from candidates who have been honing and developing their stump speech in town halls, churches and rallies across Iowa for months. Different sections of the crowd cheer loudest for their favourite candidate, waving banners and chanting slogans in the intervals between speeches. But it is a long night, and the cheers become more muted as the evening goes on. Nancy Pelosi, the House Democratic leader, and officially neutral in the race, is a slightly awkward master of ceremonies. She takes care to be even-handed, introducing every candidate as 'the next president of the United States'.

The last candidates to speak are the two leading contenders for the nomination, and the crowd are eager to hear them.

Hillary Clinton, the senator from New York and front-runner for the 2008 Democratic nomination, is up first. Suffering from a cold, her voice is pitched lower than usual. She begins by pointing out that on 20 January 2009 somebody will raise 'his or her' hand to be sworn in as the next president. Rarely can this familiar formulation have raised such a cheer. After laying into the 'incompetence' of the current administration, she goes on to explain her plans for comprehensive health care and an end to the war in Iraq. Clinton's emphasis throughout is on her ability to get things done. Change is just a word, she says – in implicit reference to her main rival – unless you have the strength and experience to make it happen. Americans need a president who is 'ready to lead on Day 1'. Clinton's speech is well received. It is a persuasive pitch from the woman most observers judge to be the likely winner of this race.

By the time the last candidate gets his turn, the event is running an hour over time. It is shortly before midnight, and most of the audience has been sitting for at least four hours, hearing speech after speech cover familiar ground. But as Barack Obama, junior senator from Illinois, makes his way through the arena, a current of energy surges through the auditorium. He is almost physically pulled up the steps to the stage by the noise of the crowd. His campaign has packed the hall with more supporters than anyone else. But the cheering is coming from every corner. It is hard to escape the impression that tonight, the previous candidates – even Clinton – were support acts, and that the headliner has arrived.

Voters in Iowa are fascinated by the young man who is challenging Clinton for the presidential nomination. They've heard that he can give a great speech. But perhaps they're wondering which Obama is going to turn up. His appearances on the campaign trail in recent weeks have been lacklustre, long on policy detail but short on passion. It's almost as if he's been rebelling against his own charisma. But tonight, after sitting through hours of worthy speeches, the crowd desperately want some excitement – and that is what Obama delivers.

He thanks the hosts, and in the pause before he begins his speech a lone female voice from the arena cries out: 'I love you!' Without missing a beat he says: 'I love you back,' flashing a megawatt grin.

Obama starts with an easy applause line about how, in November, the name George W. Bush will not be on the ballot. 'Neither will my cousin Dick Cheney.' (A recent story in the press had found an obscure genealogical connection between Obama and the vice-president.) 'Everybody has a black sheep in the family,' he deadpans.

He looks at ease, entirely comfortable on the big stage. Physically he is less than graceful. He gangles. His suit seems to hang off him. He has a boyish face, a small head and protruding ears. But his voice, a deep rich baritone, is powerful and he uses it artfully, rhythmically layering sentences on top of each other with beats in between, building to a series of climaxes each of which yields noisy applause from the crowd. Holding the microphone with his left hand, he strolls around a small area of the stage, emphasising words with his free hand, occasionally unfurling a long index finger to jab a point home as if concluding an argument to the students of his former employer, the University of Chicago.

He lists the broken promises of the Bush administration, winning the ready applause that the other candidates enjoyed for similar litanies. But then he goes further. He uses the audience's dislike of Bush to pivot into an attack on 'old-style politics' and, by extension, Clinton (though he never names her). He declares that the 'same old Washington textbook campaigns *just won't do*', emphasising each of those last words with his right hand, as if knocking three times on a door.

The same three words punctuate a crescendoing riff on the difference between old and new politics. 'That's *why* not answering questions because we are afraid our answers won't be popular *just won't do*. That's *why* telling the American people what we think they want to hear, instead of telling the American people what they need to hear, *just won't do*.' He lets the 'why' lengthen and expand to suggest the cadences of a pastor at the pulpit, before bringing each sentence up sharp with those three raps on the door. It's a compelling mix of teacher and preacher, and the crowd are enthralled.

Obama is himself a mixture of these things: lecture theatre and church, Harvard and Chicago's South Side. Back in his days as a community organiser he knew that if he was to make a name for himself he would have to improve his speaking style, which was too cerebral, too professorial for his audiences. So he studied the preachers in church and made a conscious effort to emulate something of their soaring oratorical flair. As his Chicago friend and mentor Abner Mikva recalls, 'he listened to patterns of speech, how to take people up the ladders. It's almost a Baptist tradition to make someone faint, and by God he's doing it now.'

This evening Obama leads the crowd of Iowa Democrats up the ladder of their party's glorious history. He calls on them to revive the spirit of Jefferson, Roosevelt and Kennedy, each of whom led 'not by polls but by principles'. He declares his intention to summon the nation to 'a common purpose, a higher purpose'. 'That's why I'm in this race,' he says. 'To offer *change we can believe in.*' The audience erupts. One or two of its members faint.

For a candidate who has spent just three years in national politics to position himself as the heir to the party's greatest figures is an act of breathtaking audacity. But then, audacity is something Barack Obama has come to be known for, ever since he seized the opportunity to introduce the party's presidential nominee, John Kerry, at the 2004 Democratic Convention, giving a rip-roaring speech that brought the hall to its feet and his face to the attention of millions of viewers around the country.

In that speech's most famous passage he decried the division of America's political and cultural map into 'red states for the Republicans and blue states for the Democrats', declaring that 'we worship an awesome God in the blue states . . . and we have gay friends in the red states'. The approaching contest between Bush and Kerry, he said, came down to a choice between cynicism and hope:

> It's the hope of slaves sitting around a fire singing freedom
> songs; the hope of immigrants setting out for distant
> shores; the hope of a young naval lieutenant bravely
> patrolling the Mekong Delta; the hope of a millworker's
> son who dares to defy the odds; the hope of a skinny kid

with a funny name who believes that America has a place
for him, too . . . the audacity of hope!

The structure of this ringing passage itself declared Obama's
ambition. By placing his own story last, he managed to suggest that
Kerry and his running mate, John Edwards, were mere supporting
acts to his own pre-destined triumph – indeed, that the whole of
American history would find its apotheosis in the coming of Obama.
The aggressive self-promotion was little commented on at the time,
but the appeal of this new face – who did not even hold national
office yet – was the story of the convention.

Given the vaulting ambition evident in his convention speech, it
was hardly surprising that Obama, after becoming a senator, would
consider a run for the presidency. Few expected when he moved into
his Senate office that the time would come so soon – least of all
Obama. But the stuffy nature and sluggish pace of the Senate were
not to his liking, and throughout his second year there, Obama was
titillated by the number of Democrats who urged him to consider a
run in 2008. He didn't need any more convincing of his own political
talents. During his Senate campaign he had confided to a friend his
ambition to be president, telling her that he felt he had special qualities
that it would be a shame to waste. 'You know, I just think I have
something,' he said.

By the autumn of 2006, when he went on a national tour to
promote his second book, *The Audacity of Hope* (already the phrase
most associated with him), Obama let it be known that he was
considering a run at the next opportunity. The result was a sustained
wave of publicity. *Time* put him on the cover, with the headline 'Why
Barack Obama Could Be the Next President'.

In November of that year, Obama, his wife Michelle and his team
of advisers crowded into a meeting room in the Chicago offices of his

chief strategist David Axelrod's consulting firm. Michelle Obama was sceptical, concerned about the effect of a long campaign on her children and about her husband's safety. If they were going to run, she wanted to know they could win. 'I want you to show me you're going to do this. You need to show me that this is not going to be a bullshit fly-by-night campaign,' she is reputed to have told the assembled team.

A month later, at an all-day meeting billed as 'The Summit', Barack Obama's would-be campaign manager, David Plouffe, presented a detailed plan for the potential campaign to the senator and his wife. They discussed not only the plan, but why he should run: the basic motivation that would get him and his family through the hard times. They agreed that it was the need for a new type of politics; for change more fundamental than a change of administration or even party.

In December, after an encouraging visit to New Hampshire, second on the primary calendar, Obama met the former Senate majority leader Tom Daschle for a long heart-to-heart at a restaurant in Washington. Daschle, a Democrat from South Dakota, had enjoyed a long career in the Senate but never found the right moment to run for president (he lost his seat in 2004). 'Don't think that you're going to have another opportunity in 2012 and 2016,' he told Obama. 'You might. But – like me – you might not.'

Obama also called and spoke to an old friend and mentor, Rev. Alvin Love, a Baptist minister from Chicago's South Side. 'My dad told me that you've got to strike while the iron is hot,' said Love.

'The iron can't get any hotter,' replied Obama.

In early January, after spending Christmas with his grandmother in Hawaii, Obama called Daschle at home to tell him he'd made up his mind. 'I'm going to run.' With the help of Axelrod and Plouffe, he began to assemble a campaign team. He had a clear idea of the kind of people he wished to be surrounded by: discreet, disciplined and hard-working. Anybody with a high Washington profile who frequently appeared as a 'strategist' on TV news shows was unwelcome. Most of all, Obama sought to create a campaign dominated by personalities similar to his own: 'What I want around me are people who are calm,' he told one early interviewee. 'People who don't get too high and don't get too low, because that's how I am.'

On 10 February 2007, Obama stood in front of the building where Abraham Lincoln had delivered his famous 'House Divided' speech against slavery in 1858. On the steps of the Old State Capitol in Springfield, Illinois, Obama formally announced to the world that he was running for president. In his speech he acknowledged that he hadn't spent a long time in national politics, but that he'd 'been there long enough to know that the ways of Washington must change'. He bemoaned 'the failure of leadership, the smallness of our politics – the ease with which we're distracted by the petty and the trivial'. He declared that his campaign would be the vehicle for the hopes and dreams of 'millions of people calling for change'. Referring to a 'tall, gangly lawyer' who believed that 'we are one people', he self-consciously positioned himself as the heir to Lincoln.

Obama's announcement shouldn't have been a surprise to Hillary Clinton and her team of advisers but somehow it was. Clinton's team had already spent years putting together a plan for her presidential campaign, but they saw John Edwards as their sole credible rival. Obama did not figure in the polls that Mark Penn, Clinton's chief strategist, had been conducting amongst the electorates in Iowa and New Hampshire.

It was only in January 2007, when the Clinton team got word that several of the party's top fundraisers had pledged loyalty to Obama, that they began to wake up to this potential threat. They rushed forward the announcement of Clinton's candidacy. In a video emailed to her supporters and the media, a relaxed-looking Clinton made the announcement that everyone had been expecting for at least the last four years.

Obama's entrance was worrying to the Clinton team for two reasons. First, it disrupted the assumption that Clinton's nomination was a certainty. The Clinton strategy, modelled after George W. Bush's successful nomination campaign in 2000, was to persuade the party's donors and key players that her victory was assured and that they should get behind her as quickly as possible or risk missing the bus. The media and the party had so far concurred. Obama's entry threatened this consensus and slowed her momentum.

Second, it undermined Clinton's ability to represent change. With a massively unpopular incumbent president, a war in Iraq that dragged on with no victory in sight, and an uncertain economic future, the country wanted to start afresh. Clinton's advisers hoped that the possibility of electing the first female president would help overcome her associations with the past. But now along came somebody whose ability to symbolise change was as great if not greater.

Unsurprisingly, Obama made 'Change' the theme of his campaign. His strategy was to tie Clinton and Bush together as part of the 'failed politics' of the last twenty years. Building on the theme he'd established so resoundingly at the 2004 convention, he promised to reach across partisan divisions and unite the country.

Obama knew that he couldn't rely on the early support of the party's establishment. He aimed instead to build a popular movement of ordinary voters behind his campaign. His novelty and appeal as a candidate made this viable. Volunteers rushed to support him in large numbers, enabling his campaign team to set up operations in primary states across the country with unprecedented speed. Thousands turned up to hear him speak at major rallies in Iowa and New Hampshire, and their names were added to mailing and email lists.

The most impressive manifestation of Obama's 'movement' was its unprecedented fundraising capacity. Within months, drawing on an army of small donors, many of whom contributed via the internet, Obama had raised more than all the other Democratic candidates combined. For the Clintons, who had assumed that their grip on the traditional fundraising levers of the party would assure a big financial advantage over all comers, the news of Obama's ability to raise such sums was deeply unsettling.

But despite this early success, the shine came off Obama's candidacy during a long summer of campaigning. He didn't overtake Clinton in the polls, and by the autumn Clinton had recovered her balance. She seemed to have found the measure of her youthful opponent, winning the first televised debate between all the major Democratic candidates. In response to a question about how he would react to a terrorist attack, Obama rambled on about disaster preparedness, sounding more like a mid-level bureaucrat than a potential president. Clinton, seeing her moment, answered as a commander in chief: 'I think the president must move as swiftly as is prudent to retaliate.'

It was a moment that crystallised the difference between the two candidates' debating skills. Clinton was practised and confident. A close observer of her talented husband and the winner of tough debates during her Senate run in New York, Clinton's command of policy detail and her focus on preparation made her a formidable debater. Obama, on the other hand, often seemed ill at ease on these occasions. He was no fan of debates, disdaining the pressure to come up with soundbites and 'zingers' that would make the morning news bulletins, and he hadn't mastered the knack of communicating his positions in short, clear sentences. As a result he came across as hesitant and ponderous.

Neither was Obama living up to expectations on the stump. In an effort to compensate for the charge that he was all talk and no substance, Obama had been giving defiantly dull speeches at events across Iowa and New Hampshire. Voters ready to be awed by the inspirational speaker they'd heard so much about found themselves listening to a disquisition on the nuances of health care provision, devoid of uplift. Leaving the venue, many concluded that if it was policy wonkery they wanted they could hardly do better than Clinton.

In October 2007, Obama was campaigning in one of the early primary states, South Carolina, when he received a call from the head of his campaign's finance committee, Penny Pritzker. Back in Des Moines, around 200 of Obama's biggest fundraisers were holding a two-day meeting over a weekend and, she informed Obama, there was a sense of anxiety, verging on panic, in the room. Despite the record-breaking sums of money raised by the campaign and the massive crowds drawn by the candidate, Obama remained well behind Clinton in the national polls. Some were calling for Obama to shake up his campaign and switch tack. Surely it was time to drop the lofty 'new politics' stance and go negative against Clinton?

Obama made his way back to Iowa to make an unscheduled appearance at the meeting that Sunday night. He called for a show of hands from his finance committee. 'Can I see how many people in this room I told that this was going to be easy?' No hand was raised. 'We're up against the most formidable team in twenty-five years,' he said, referring to the collection of high-powered talents that Clinton had put together. 'But we've got a plan, and we've got to have faith in it.' To those who called on him to go aggressively negative, he replied: 'That's not who I am.' He asked his backers to be patient. A win in Iowa would launch them on the route to victory, he said. But until then progress would seem slow. At the end of October, Obama had dinner with nine advisers at a supporter's apartment on Chicago's affluent Lake Shore Drive. The old Washington hands present pressed him to hit back hard against Clinton. 'You gotta get down, get dirty,' they urged – or risk being destroyed by a more ruthless opponent. But Obama held his ground. 'If I gotta kneecap her,' he said, 'I'm not gonna go there.' For Obama, this wasn't a question of decency so much as a political calculation: the rationale for his claim to be a transformative leader would disappear, he believed, if he came to be seen as just another politician.

Some of those in the room, and many more in the media, concluded that Obama's candidacy was fated to be a retelling of the same old story of Democratic insurgencies, whose past protagonists included Gary Hart, Paul Tsongas, Bill Bradley and Howard Dean. A young charismatic candidate promises a new kind of politics and builds a 'movement' of voters, many of them young, around him. He enjoys tremendous media acclaim and fundraising success, but is then crushed into dust by a machine politician using standard operating procedures. Clinton was this year's candidate of the party establishment, and once again, commentators talked of her as the almost-certain nominee.

It took one question in a televised debate at the end of October to dispel Clinton's aura of inevitability. That night, in Philadelphia, the other candidates all turned their fire on the front-runner, hoping she would buckle under the pressure. They sensed that unless something happened very soon to change the dynamic of the race, they would all be making an early exit. Obama and John Edwards, but also Chris Dodd and Joe Biden, attacked Clinton from all angles. They repeatedly challenged her on the issues and on her electability, portraying her as a symbol of the Washington status quo. Most damagingly, they began to question her honesty and her character.

Clinton, who had not experienced such a sustained barrage of attacks before, was shaken out of her usual composure by its intensity. She looked grim, turning her head back and forth to respond to attacks from Edwards and Obama on either side. 'I need to rebut that,' she said at one point. 'I don't know where to start.' She didn't quail or lose her temper, however, and for the most part retained her impressive command of the issues. But her response to a question about a minor topic became the story of the night. The moderator asked her if she agreed with Governor Eliot Spitzer's plan to issue driving licences to illegal immigrants in New York, on the principle that if they were going to be on the roads anyway, the government may as well keep track of them. Clinton, stuck between her desire to appear tough on illegal immigration and her need to maintain a working relationship with the Democratic governor of her state, refused to say clearly if she was for or against it.

Dodd, an opponent of the policy, spotted an opening and sharply pointed out Clinton's evasion. In response, Clinton, voice raised and eyes popped wide, affected anger. But she still didn't answer the question, managing only to sound both strident and shifty at the same time. Edwards, who had made millions as a trial lawyer from his ability to expose the flaws in an opponent's argument, followed up with a silky evisceration of Clinton's non-answer, linking it to the question of her character. Obama piled on, questioning Clinton's ability to be honest with the country about the challenges it faced.

The next day, Clinton's trouble with the driving licence question was the story all the news shows focused on. It was the worst part of a bad night for Clinton, because it appeared to confirm what many voters suspected: that she had trouble being straight with people.

From that moment onwards, the Democratic race became a real contest. The other candidates and the media sensed that Clinton might not be inevitable after all. But it was still up to her opponents to prove that they could exploit her sudden vulnerability.

❖

Eleven days later and to noisy cheers at the Jefferson-Jackson dinner in Des Moines, Barack Obama is doing just that. 'Triangulating', he says, referring to the famous Clintonian political strategy, *'just won't do . . .* this party has always made the biggest difference in the lives of people when we led not by calculation but by conviction.' He doesn't mention Hillary Clinton, but then he doesn't have to. Her reputation as a calculating, poll-driven politician is the vulnerability Obama is attacking. Obama explains his decision to take Clinton on in this race with another swipe at the former first lady: 'I am not in this race because of some long-held ambition or because I believe it's somehow owed to me. I am in this race because of what Dr King called "the fierce urgency of now".'

In his closing section, he works the crowd into a frenzy by challenging them to 'stop settling for what the cynics say we have to accept. In this election – in this moment – let us reach for what we know is possible. A nation healed. A world repaired. An America that believes again.' With that, he leaves the stage to wild cheering from all corners of the hall. Iowa's Democrats go home exhilarated, with one name on their lips more than any other.

The next day, media commentators are unanimous in calling Obama the evening's winner. If the Philadelphia debate was the moment when Hillary Clinton stopped seeming inevitable, Iowa's Jefferson-Jackson dinner is the night when an Obama victory starts to seem possible.

The Republicans: anybody's game

As Barack Obama wows Iowa's Democrats in Des Moines, a Republican candidate, also running on a message of change, is preparing his first TV ad of the campaign. It features the candidate exchanging one-liners with Chuck Norris, an action movie star with legendary status in America. 'My plan to secure the border?' says the candidate. 'Two words: Chuck Norris.' Flippant and charming, it is, to say the least, an unorthodox ad. But then, Mike Huckabee is no orthodox Republican candidate.

Unlike with Obama, when Huckabee announced his presidential candidacy at the beginning of 2007, the political world didn't sit up and take note. The Republican field already had an array of well-known figures who were running or expected to run, including Rudy Giuliani, Mitt Romney and John McCain. Huckabee, the former governor of a small, rural state, was not thought to have the resources, fame or breadth of appeal necessary to compete with these heavyweights.

Huckabee had spotted a gap in the market, however. Of the leading Republican candidates, none was fully trusted by the evangelical Christians who make up a large part of the electorate in Iowa, where the first Republican primary would be held. Giuliani was twice divorced, held liberal positions on abortion and gay rights, and was once photographed dressed as a woman. McCain fell out with the party's religious leaders during his fierce nomination battle with George W. Bush in 2000 and had never been considered a true believer. Romney was a Mormon. Huckabee saw that by running as the only authentic religious conservative in the race, he might just cause an upset.

He first captured the media's attention by doing surprisingly well in a straw poll in Ames, Iowa. In a straw poll, each candidate makes their pitch and afterwards voters express their preference. Such polls are tests of organisation, because winning them depends on filling the event with as many of your supporters as possible, often by bribing them to turn up. Huckabee, who had spent $150,000 in the state overall, came a close second to Romney, who had spent $2 million.

'I can't buy you,' Huckabee told the audience. 'I can't even rent you.' His strong showing was the first sign that he might have a surprising ability to generate spontaneous enthusiasm and support.

Now, with Iowa less than two months away, Huckabee is climbing in the polls. It isn't just evangelicals that find him appealing. Huckabee is no stereotypical fire-and-brimstone preacher: he is witty, warm and self-deprecating and comes across more like a jocular neighbour than a zealot. Unlike older Christian conservatives, he doesn't appear to be enraged by modern America. He is a Jimi Hendrix fan and plays bass in a rock band called Capitol Offense, which once opened for Willie Nelson. Huckabee describes himself as 'the conservative who is not mad at anybody'.

In the televised debates, Huckabee excels. He is expressive: his puppyish eyes emote and twinkle, and his thick eyebrows perform a dancing counterpoint to his answers. He is funny: Huckabee specialises in the memorable one-liner. Introducing himself as coming from Hope, Arkansas – Bill Clinton's home town – he says to the audience of Republican voters: 'All I ask is that you give us one more chance.' Referring to the expensively coiffured Democratic candidate, he describes Congress as 'spending like John Edwards in a barber's shop'. He is also a deft debater, fluent and impassioned, with a gift for framing every issue in simple, commonsense terms. Viewers take note, and so do the media. The man treated as an amusing sideshow earlier in the year is suddenly being talked of as a serious contender.

This unexpected development is reconfiguring the whole Republican contest, undermining some candidates and offering renewed hope to others. The man with most to lose from Huckabee's rise is the one currently leading in the Iowa polls, Mitt Romney.

If the nomination were awarded on the basis of who looks most like a president, or who has the most money to spend, Romney would win. Standing over 6 feet tall, he sports a cleanly sculpted jaw, thick dark hair that greys at the temples, and radiant teeth. He is spending a chunk of the vast fortune he accumulated as a venture capitalist on buying more advertising in Iowa and New Hampshire than any other candidate. But the contest isn't decided on money or looks alone, and Romney will have to work hard at convincing sceptical voters that he is the man he claims to be: a true social conservative.

As the former Republican governor of one of the most left-leaning states in the union, Romney had to steer to the political centre. But when the time came to work out a strategy for his presidential campaign, he decided to reinvent himself as the ideological heir to Ronald Reagan and outflank McCain and Giuliani from the right. He wears the mantle of the true conservative uneasily, however, and his opponents love nothing better than hurling past positions and statements at him. He is charged with being that most heinous of things, a flip-flopper.

Huckabee has a direct connection to evangelical voters that Romney, as a Mormon, can't match. Not only that, but Huckabee's ease with himself, the inner belief he exudes, makes for an uncomfortable contrast with the former Massachusetts governor, who finds it hard to project a sense of real conviction on the stump or in debates. Romney's camp is confident, however, that Huckabee's success is the political equivalent of a stock market bubble and that at some point – before the Iowa vote, they hope – it will burst as Huckabee comes under serious scrutiny for the first time.

Huckabee's popularity in Iowa is also undermining the nascent candidacy of Fred Thompson, the former senator for Tennessee and TV star. Thompson, an avuncular southerner, has consistently taken conservative positions during his political career on issues such as abortion and guns. This, along with his age (65), authoritative demeanour and plain-speaking style, convinced many in the party that he was the second coming of Ronald Reagan. But Thompson took a long time coming. After months of flirtation with the idea of running, he finally announced he would stand in September, after all the other candidates had already spent months in Iowa, New Hampshire and the other states.

Now that Thompson is in the race, he gives every impression of not wanting to be there. He is a proud man, and something in him seems to resist the undignified dance of a presidential campaign. He has gained, fairly or unfairly, a reputation for being lazy, which isn't helped when an eyewitness spots him shopping on a day when all the other candidates are campaigning. On another occasion, Thompson makes a trip to the small town of Waverly, Iowa to go on a walkabout, but once there elects to stay on the campaign bus and be driven to the local fire station, where one of the firemen hands him his helmet. After gazing at it ruefully for a few moments, Thompson says, in his slow southern drawl: 'I have a silly hat rule,' and passes it to his wife. In New Hampshire, a TV reporter about to do an interview with Thompson urges his studio to hurry up, saying: 'The next president of the United States has a schedule to keep.' 'And so do I,' mutters Thompson. Such moments reinforce the impression that Thompson's heart just isn't in it.

The candidates with less to lose from Huckabee's rise, and perhaps something to gain, are Giuliani and McCain.

The former mayor is an even more unorthodox Republican candidate than Huckabee. But he has two high-value cards, and he plays them well. The first is his record as mayor of New York. Although there is debate over how much of the steep decline in crime during his tenure can be attributed to his policies, there is no doubt that he oversaw a period of rapid economic and social regeneration for the United States' biggest city. As mayor, Giuliani's aggressive, confrontational style upset many, but he accomplished much. At a time when many voters are in despair about the direction of the country, such forcefulness is attractive. The second card is his status as an American hero. Giuliani's steady leadership in the immediate aftermath of the attacks on the Twin Towers has attained legendary status. It gives him authority with Republicans who might otherwise find him unconscionably liberal. Some Republican observers believe that Giuliani has the potential not just to win the nomination, but to transform the GOP into a broader-based, more socially inclusive party.

Giuliani's campaign strategy is, like his very candidacy, unconventional. Traditionally, candidates aim to win Iowa or New Hampshire or preferably both and ride the resulting wave of exposure and acclaim into subsequent primaries. But Giuliani's advisers have calculated that his brand of urban tough will never play well in these rural states. By effectively conceding both before they've been held, and pinning his hopes on a win in delegate-rich Florida, Giuliani is placing a big bet against the conventional wisdom that momentum is all-important. He stands a much better chance of winning his bet if no clear winner emerges from Iowa and New Hampshire – so by unsettling Romney and generally sowing confusion, Huckabee has done Giuliani a favour.

Huckabee's rise has also raised the hopes of the senator from Arizona. In the space of six months, McCain has already won and lost this nomination. As the best-known Republican in the country after the president and probably the best liked, most observers felt that 2008 would finally be McCain's year, and up until February 2007 he was firmly established as the front-runner in national polls. It seemed likely that McCain would at last gain dominion over a party he nearly walked away from following his painful defeat in 2000.

But McCain, perhaps uneasy with being anything but the

underdog, contrived to throw away his early lead. He sponsored a legislative effort to pass comprehensive immigration reform, creating a 'path to citizenship' for undocumented aliens. Few issues were guaranteed to anger the Republican Party's core voters more. He also fervently supported the president's decision to send more troops to Iraq, in the face of near-universal opposition in his own party as well as across the political spectrum.

During 2007, Giuliani overtook him in national polls, and McCain's fundraising plummeted until, in July, his campaign seemed to have come to a premature end, weighed down by debt . Nearly all his staff deserted him or were fired. The press wondered only when he would announce his withdrawal from the race.

But McCain, knowing that at the age of seventy-one this was his last shot, resolved to stay in. As a fighter pilot, he lived by the maxim that no plan survives contact with the enemy, and he still relished the need to improvise in the face of unexpected adversity. He didn't pretend to be optimistic. 'I'm a dead man walking,' he told his closest aide and friend, Mark Salter. 'I know it. I'm a dead man walking. I'm going to lose this campaign.' In a way, though, he was back in his idiosyncratic comfort zone. A connoisseur of lost causes, McCain is always at his happiest when written off (his favourite film is *Viva Zapata!*, in which the eponymous hero, played by Marlon Brando, walks out into the village plaza alone to meet his certain death). He told Salter and his other remaining aides that he would carry on, no matter what. 'I'm going to go to New Hampshire and tell people the truth,' he said.

McCain took out a loan and got back on the bus, embarking on what he termed the 'No Surrender' tour. The allusion was to the issue he cared about most – the Iraq War – but also, unmistakably, to his own campaign. Unlike the other candidates, he had no money to spend on advertising and barely any campaign staff. But if this was a disadvantage it was also a liberation. Without an army of consultants writing his speeches, or an elaborate campaign structure to oversee, McCain was thrown back on the resources of his own instincts and political wits, just as he had been in 2000. He could speak his mind on Iraq and other issues without having to worry about the consequences: he had nothing to lose now.

In the early autumn of 2007 McCain held one town hall meeting after another in New Hampshire and Iowa, often speaking to just twenty or thirty people at a time. For the advisers who had stuck by him, it was deeply uncomfortable to watch the man they revered addressing such small audiences. But McCain seemed to be enjoying himself. Helped by his friends in the media, word spread that McCain's events were the most interesting of any of the candidates', and the crowds began to grow. At the same time, McCain's political luck was coming good. Immigration receded as an issue after the failure of the White House's bill, and it began to be recognised that the military 'surge' of troops in Iraq was bringing a measure of stability to the country. McCain's poll numbers moved upwards, and the money started to return. People were taking his candidacy seriously again.

With the first primary less than two months away, the Republican race, already open, has been turned into an experiment in chaos theory by the emergence of Mike Huckabee as a serious contender. The front-runner in Iowa, Mitt Romney, is losing ground. Rudy Giuliani, making only occasional visits to Iowa and New Hampshire, lurks down in Florida hoping to spring an ambush. Fred Thompson's supporters urge him to light a fire in his belly. John McCain is back in the game. This is now the most unpredictable battle for the Republican nomination that anyone can remember.

Front-runners under attack

If Mitt Romney is looking vulnerable in Iowa, so is Hillary Clinton. Barack Obama has gained momentum from his strong performance at the Jefferson-Jackson dinner, whilst Clinton has stumbled into a couple of mishaps that, though trivial, have confirmed the impression that there are unresolved questions about her character.

Anita Esterday, a waitress at a diner in Toledo, Iowa, gave a radio interview in which she claimed that when Clinton and her team came to visit in October, they didn't leave a tip. Following the visit, Clinton had namechecked Esterday – a single mother of two with two jobs – in her stump speech as an example of the kind of voter she was standing up for. Esterday was annoyed that Clinton was using her name without permission.

Within twenty-four hours, Esterday's interview became a national story, ricocheting around the blogs and being replayed on the cable news shows. What had actually happened – whether or not a tip had been left – was unclear. The story turned into whether Clinton was an honest person or an unscrupulous politician cynically using other people's predicaments for her own advancement.

Days later a nineteen-year-old student who had asked a question about global warming during a Clinton Q&A session in Newton, Iowa revealed to CNN that she had been instructed to ask the question by a Clinton staffer. These sessions are supposed to be forums for authentic candidate–voter interchange, undistorted by the media prism. For Clinton to be seen as abusing this process by planting questions was for many another sign that she was untrustworthy and cynical.

The stories of the missing tip and the planted question ought to be insignificant. But in the political pressure-cooker of Iowa in November, every day's news cycle counts, and these stories, reflecting badly on Clinton, take up valuable airtime. Worse, they play to an underlying suspicion amongst some voters that Clinton is an unscrupulous politician of dubious character who plays the same old political tricks. Obama's promise of a new type of politics ('the politics of hope') is designed to take advantage of precisely such perceptions.

Clinton halts the slide in her campaign by turning the spotlight back on her opponents in the forum in which she excels: a debate. On 15 November, in Las Vegas, she gives a commanding performance, demonstrating once again her unrivalled grasp of the issues. She accuses Obama of favouring a middle-class tax increase by the back door, a thrust he fails to parry, before laying into his health care plan. Obama flounders on the question that had tripped Clinton up a couple of weeks previously – driving licences for illegal immigrants – and has to be pressed by the moderator into giving a straight answer. When Clinton is asked if she favours it, she simply answers 'No'. The Clinton team are jubilant. The debate seems to have repaired much of the damage caused by the last two weeks.

Days later, Robert Novak, a prominent conservative columnist, pens a piece in which he claims that Clinton 'agents' have been spreading the word that she holds 'scandalous information' on Obama but has decided not to use it. The Clinton team deny this, but not immediately. Obama, rather than letting it pass, holds a press conference at which he attacks Clinton for being slow to deny the story, and declares that he will not tolerate 'slime politics'. The Clinton team accuse him of overreaction, but Obama has already succeeded in moving attention away from his inglorious debate performance and back to Clinton's tactics. The 'scandalous information' never materialises.

In the closing weeks of November the two leading Democrats square up to each other more and more. They use tougher language, attacking each other at their strongest points. Obama challenges Clinton's main claim – to be the most experienced candidate in the race. He notes that she did not hold executive office in her husband's administration: 'I don't think Michelle would claim that she is the best-qualified person to be a US senator by virtue of me talking to her on occasion about the work I've done.' At other times he does concede her the experience claim, but points out, to enthusiastic applause on the stump, that she joined other 'experienced' politicians such as Dick Cheney and Donald Rumsfeld in supporting George W. Bush's decision to make war on Iraq. Clinton's team say that Obama has 'junked the politics of hope' and is acting like a run-of-the-mill politician. Like two boxers in the early rounds of a fight, they are seeing what they can get away with, searching for their opponent's weak spots.

The other contenders hope that these two will knock each other out. John Edwards in particular rates his chances of a stealth victory in Iowa. He knows the state better than any other candidate, having campaigned there four years ago and spent much time cultivating contacts and voters ever since. In 2000 he ran on a platform not unlike Obama's, as a sunny optimist keen to reach across divides. This time around he has reinvented himself as a fiery Democratic partisan, economic populist and angry critic of the war (having apologised for his Senate vote to authorise it in 2003). Although some are unconvinced by this transformation, many find him and his highly intelligent, likeable wife Elizabeth an attractive proposition.

The month draws to an end with the insurgent candidates on either side gaining momentum and working out how to maintain it. Mike Huckabee is now within striking distance of Mitt Romney. He is adjusting to the fact that he is no longer considered a novelty but a serious contender, subject to serious scrutiny and serious attacks. Obama is working out how to take on Clinton more directly without undermining his claim to be practising the politics of hope.

Romney and Clinton are, to lesser or greater degrees, the candidates of their party's establishment. Both are favourites to win their party's nomination, particularly Clinton. But in Huckabee and Obama they face two candidates, running as agents of change, who cannot be written off as mere distractions. Romney and Clinton face similar questions: will attacking their chief rivals bring them down or make them stronger? If they do attack them, how should they do it? Only one thing is for certain: nobody is predicting the outcome of Iowa with any confidence.

At around 12.30 p.m. on the last day of November a man claiming to have a bomb strapped to his chest walks into Clinton's campaign headquarters in New Hampshire and takes two staff members hostage. Who he is and what he wants are unclear. Police surround the building, and the cable news channels send their helicopters to the scene. For a few hours, the entire election is on pause as the public watch to see what happens. Clinton cancels an event in Virginia and heads back to her home in Washington amid fears for her safety. Later in the afternoon, the hostages are released, though the hostage-taker holds out until the evening. He is identified as a local man with a history of mental illness. He makes calls to CNN from the office, apparently to protest against the mental health care system in the United States. Eventually he is detained and arrested by police without incident. Clinton emerges to hold a press conference in which she thanks her staff for their courage under pressure. It is a surreal, unsettling end to an intense month on the campaign trail.

December 2007

Organise, organise, organise

A man knocks on the door of someone's house in Carroll, Iowa. The door is opened, and the man says: 'Hi, I'm Bill Clinton, and I'm campaigning for John Edwards.' The name, he later tells a reporter, gets a lot of conversations started.

The former president's namesake is one of thousands of volunteers working for a candidate in Iowa. He is a local man; many others have travelled in from out of state. In Carroll, Audubon, Muscatine and Coralville, and right across every town and county in the state, people are hearing a knock on the door and upon opening are being asked if they have decided on a candidate yet. In the evenings when their phones ring they know it is probably either a person asking them to hear about a particular candidate, or a pollster, or – if they're lucky – Scarlett Johansson calling on behalf of Barack Obama. Voters are offered plenty of enticements to volunteer for one of the candidates: a ride in Edwards's bus if they join his campaign, or a special place in the audience at Hillary Clinton's next event if they sign up to hers.

Iowans are the most intensively courted electorate in the world. By an accident of history, they have ended up having a disproportionate say in who becomes the next leader of the free world. The voters get to see the candidates close up, to examine the bearing and demeanour of famous faces, venerable senators and buzzworthy new names, in town halls and churches, fire stations and municipal libraries. Every four years, journalists at the *Des Moines Register* find themselves at the centre of national attention: their political columns resound across the country; their endorsement is tirelessly sought by some of the most powerful men and women in the land.

It wasn't until 1972 that Iowa received its first-in-the-nation status, when for obscure reasons of party management the state Democratic Party moved its caucus ahead of the traditional first nomination event, in New Hampshire. That same year, a relatively unknown senator from South Dakota named George McGovern organised and campaigned heavily in the state, spotting an opportunity to make a name for himself against better-established rivals who were still relying on their national standing and party connections to deliver the nomination. He came a strong second, and the momentum and media attention he received as a consequence helped him on the way to the nomination.

In 1976 Jimmy Carter, then largely unknown outside the south, launched an intensive effort in Iowa, resulting in a strong showing that made his name and started him on the path to the presidency. If there had been any doubt before, there wasn't any more: Iowa mattered. That year, the Republicans followed the Democratic example and held their Iowa caucuses on the same date. So it was that this small, largely white farm state came to play a key role in the nation's choice of president.

Throughout the 1980s, the state became an increasingly important fixture in the presidential nomination calendar, the focus of intense media attention and effort from the candidates. Throughout all this Iowa Democrats have stubbornly retained their arcane and somewhat anachronistic caucus mechanism, necessitating enormous on-the-ground organisational efforts from the campaigns.

Whereas Republicans hold a swift and secret ballot, the Democratic caucus is a complicated affair. Democrat voters (although registered independents and even Republicans can also participate) attend small meetings in school halls, churches, libraries or private homes. Precinct captains appointed by the campaigns kick off with a short speech on why their candidate deserves support. Voters then split into groups each representing their favoured candidate, and stand in different parts of the room. Heads are counted, and groups not passing a certain threshold are dissolved. The voters in those groups then reallocate themselves to their second choices, amid much horse-trading and deal-striking. This often takes at least a couple of hours to complete. Finding enough voters who are willing to commit a whole evening to the process, and then ensuring they get to the caucus and stand with your candidate, is considered the key to winning Iowa.

Although some Iowans complain about the disruption to their lives every four years, many more seem to cherish their state's unique role in the nation's political life. In this election in particular, Iowa's Democrats are seized by the importance of their choice. They sense that this is their party's year. There are more undecided Democrats than usual at this stage, as voters agonise over a choice between three leading candidates who are all strong, accomplished and, in their different ways, charismatic (the Republicans, by contrast, are dissatisfied with their menu of candidates).

Many potential voters in Iowa have never attended a caucus before, and the Obama campaign in particular is counting on energising younger first-time caucus-goers to boost its candidate's vote. John Edwards has spent years assembling a team of experienced and committed precinct captains expert at getting people to caucus for their candidate. Hillary Clinton's team have created a viral video entitled 'Caucusing Is Easy', featuring a cheeseburger-munching Bill Clinton in comedy mode, that explains the caucus process to her potential voters.

In Carroll, Brian Albert, an Obama volunteer, tries to persuade supporters to attend a mock caucus, where people practise by choosing which they like best: beer, wine or soda. In Lake View, in the west of the state, a Clinton campaign worker sets out to rally her troops by encouraging them to get to know one another over coffee at her house; it's important to make voters feel that the caucus will be fun, a party where they'll see familiar faces. Susy Bates, an Obama staffer from Denver, works with six new precinct captains, explaining the caucus process in detail to them. At the end she asks how everyone feels about it: 'Excited?' One of the first-time caucus-goers and precinct captains speaks up. 'I feel dumb,' she says. 'Do I have to make a speech?'

No amount of organisational prowess will deliver victory to a candidate who does not excite the imaginations of Iowan voters. This relies, in part, on the local and national media getting excited about them too – and at the right time. The way to win Iowa, say old hands, is to 'organise, organise, organise, and get hot at the end'.

Republican front-runners run into trouble

Mitt Romney is pondering how to tackle what he refers to as 'the comma problem': journalists always follow his name with two commas, in between which they write 'a Mormon'. For months, Romney's advisers have argued about how to address the issue of his religion. Mormonism is viewed with suspicion and incomprehension by many Americans, including the evangelical Christians that Romney is having trouble winning over. Hence his dilemma: should he discuss his faith openly, or by doing so will he risk making it into more of an issue than it needs to be? Those urging him to speak on his religion argue that this isn't just about religion: it's about him. By opening up about his faith, Romney will allow voters an insight into the core of his character.

Romney looks and sounds the part of a Republican nominee for president. He is happily married to his high-school sweetheart and has five improbably good-looking sons, all of whom adore him. He takes conventional conservative positions on just about every political, economic and social issue. He has an authoritative command of detail, and rarely flubs or fumbles in debates or on the stump. But despite the money and resources he has poured into Iowa, voters aren't convinced. They wonder about the man behind the politician. It's hard to tell who Romney really is. He never seems to loosen up, to show his true colours. He seems artificial, constructed, too good to be true. As a result, Romney is acutely vulnerable to the relaxed, authentic folksiness of Mike Huckabee, who seems, by contrast, eminently knowable.

Huckabee, smelling blood, is attacking Romney aggressively, presenting himself as the little guy up against a well-funded political machine. He credits his surge in support to 'an army of ordinary people who are out there not because somebody's paying them to love me' but because 'they'd like to have a president who didn't buy his way into the White House but earned it'. That he manages to attack Romney without damaging his reputation for being likeable is a tribute to his considerable communication skills.

Romney realises that unless he acts, he is in danger of losing Iowa and being knocked off his path to the nomination. His political positions aren't the problem: he knows this because his team have researched them intensively, just as any good business person would research their product. But a presidential contest is as much about the character of the man or woman who wishes to be president as it is about their policies. Romney hasn't convinced voters on that crucial criterion.

As Romney finds himself overtaken in the Iowa polls by Huckabee, he concedes to those urging him to tackle the question of his religion head on. A decision is taken to address Romney's faith in a set-piece speech, on the model of John Kennedy's successful address about his Catholicism to a gathering of ministers in 1960. This may be the most important speech of Romney's career. It is his chance to convince the voters of Iowa that conservatism is not just a philosophy that he wears in public, like one of his well-cut suits, but a deeply felt creed, rooted in his faith. Romney needs people to look into his eyes and feel that they have glimpsed his soul.

His campaign team find a suitably presidential venue: the George Bush Presidential Library, at College Station, Texas. Introduced by the former president himself – who once faced similar questions about the authenticity of his conservatism – Romney speaks from behind a podium with an American eagle emblazoned on it, framed by two US flags. Echoing Kennedy, he says there should be no religious test for the presidency: 'A person should not be elected because of his faith, nor should he be rejected because of his faith.' But, reassuring the evangelical Christians to whom the speech is in part addressed, he also says that he resists the idea that the United States should become a 'nation of secularists'. He doesn't discuss his Mormonism in any detail, noting only that 'my church's beliefs about Jesus Christ may not all be the same as those of other faiths'.

Romney links his religion to his character by reminding voters of his long and successful marriage. Quoting from the Bible to a crowd that includes his wife of nearly forty years, he says:

> My faith is grounded on these truths. You can witness
> them in Ann and my marriage and in our family. We are

a long way from perfect, and we have surely stumbled along the way, but our aspirations, our values, are the self-same as those from the other faiths that stand upon this common foundation. And these convictions will indeed inform my presidency.

At the end of the speech, the invited crowd stand and applaud, and Romney allows emotion to show on his face. His eyes mist up as he says: 'God bless this great land, God bless the United States of America.'

The speech is respectfully received by the media and most Christian leaders. It is acclaimed as well written and nuanced. But it doesn't appear to have a marked impact on Romney's relationship with the electorate or the media. He has provided an intellectual explanation of his religious beliefs without dispelling the sense of emotional distance between him and the voters. Huckabee maintains his lead in the Iowa polls.

Rudy Giuliani, observing Romney's struggle to connect with conservative voters, ought to be optimistic. The fact that nobody has pulled away from the field in the early states' polls means that his strategy of arriving late to the party remains viable. But Giuliani has problems too. In recent weeks he has received a battering at the hands of the media. Stories have emerged detailing the cost to New Yorkers of his trips to the Hamptons, where, accompanied by a security detail, he wooed the woman who would become his third wife. There are also stories about the impending trial on fraud charges of Bernard Kerik, Giuliani's former police chief, business associate and close friend, and questions about whether he exploited his tenure as mayor to make money from his security and legal businesses.

As a result Giuliani has been sliding in the national polls and in Iowa and New Hampshire. Whilst the early states do not, in theory, matter to him, it is important that he finish respectably there. If he places too poorly he risks looking like a loser, and will have trouble establishing any kind of momentum going into Florida at the end of January. His campaign decides to engage in damage control. By consenting to a long interview on one of the country's leading news shows, *Meet the Press*, Giuliani hopes to put a bad couple of weeks behind him.

Wearing a dark, sombre suit, Giuliani parries a long series of probing questions from his interrogator, Tim Russert, on the recent flurry of stories about his past. He employs some tried and tested damage control techniques – questioning the assumptions of the interviewer whilst admitting to some errors of judgement. ('I don't make many mistakes,' he says, 'but when I make them, they're big ones.') But he never gets off the back foot. What surprises many observers is his lack of fighting spirit. Rather than responding to Russert's questions with the feisty, occasionally abrasive tone for which he is known, he seems strangely subdued.

This is the first time since Giuliani assumed the status of national front-runner that his candidacy has run into real trouble. Seasoned Republican-watchers recall that in the early stages of his contest with Hillary Clinton for a Senate seat (from which he had to drop out owing to health concerns) there were faint suspicions that he didn't seem quite hungry enough to endure the rigours of a long campaign. After the Russert interview, the question is asked: does Giuliani have the stomach for this fight?

Bill and Hillary back on the road

One man who undoubtedly does is Bill Clinton. Time and again, ever since he won and lost and won the governorship of Arkansas, he has proved himself to be perhaps the most tenacious campaigner of modern times. Clinton thrives in a political battle, the tougher the better.

Retired from electoral politics himself, this year he finds himself in a position that is not only new to him but unprecedented: a former president supporting the presidential campaign of his wife. Usually, ex-presidents are expected to keep a stately distance from nomination battles, rarely endorsing one or other of the candidates. But Clinton makes no pretence that he is anything but his wife's most passionate advocate.

Up to now, however, the former president has not been closely involved with her campaign. With a few exceptions, Hillary has not hired any of his advisers because she wanted to build a team in her own image, even if it meant working with a less experienced group of operatives. She didn't want people to think she was running for her husband's third term. Understanding this, Bill has kept his distance. But as December comes around and Hillary is still losing ground to Barack Obama in Iowa, he can stand it no more. Blowing through her campaign headquarters like a tornado, he tells her advisers forcefully that by focusing only on Hillary's track record, they are making her look like an incumbent in a year when everyone wants change. Instead, he says, they should be using her record to argue aggressively that she is the only person who can bring change to Washington. This also means that it is time to take on Obama far more directly.

It's not just behind the scenes that Bill Clinton is causing a stir. His colourful language and penchant for making statements that beggar credibility are drawing much media attention – attention that might otherwise be available to his wife. He remarks during an interview that he 'opposed the Iraq War from the start', an assertion that turns out to be demonstrably untrue. He claims that when she is president Hillary will send him and George Bush Sr on a joint diplomatic mission to repair America's image in the world, forcing his presidential predecessor to issue a statement saying that no such mission has been agreed or even contemplated.

In a long TV interview with Charlie Rose, Bill Clinton argues that the media have been too soft on Obama, and suggests that a vote for the inexperienced Illinois senator would represent a 'roll of the dice'. This is strong stuff from a former president, and he is criticised by many in his own party for implying that his fellow Democrat isn't up to the job of commander in chief.

The humanity show

Meanwhile, Bill Clinton's influence behind the scenes is manifested in his wife's new willingness to attack Barack Obama directly. In an interview, Hillary Clinton explains her new approach as retaliatory, saying that she is sick of being a punching bag: 'After you've been attacked as often as I have, you cannot just absorb it. You have to respond.' Asked directly whether she intends to raise questions about Obama's character, she replies: 'It's beginning to look a lot like that.' She says she is relishing a good fight, declaring, with a flash of her rather mordant humour, that 'now the fun part begins'.

Clinton's new approach backfires almost immediately, when some on her team overenthusiastically interpret her declarations of aggression. The co-chair of the Clinton campaign in New Hampshire, Billy Shaheen, brings up Obama's former drug use in conversation with a reporter (Obama wrote about taking drugs as a young man in his autobiography). Shaheen says this will be a problem in any general election. 'It'll be: "When was the last time? Did you ever give drugs to anyone? Did you sell them to anyone?"'

Shaheen's comments set off a storm of criticism: Clinton's campaign is roundly condemned by people across the party for raising the issue, and Shaheen is forced to resign. This incident comes shortly after two Clinton volunteers have to be fired for forwarding to reporters emails that suggest Obama is a Muslim intent on destroying the United States.

It's not just volunteers and surrogates who are crossing the line. A press release issued by Clinton's chief strategist, Mark Penn, attacks Obama for claiming not to have nurtured long-term presidential ambitions. Part of Penn's evidence that Obama's ambitions go a long way back is an essay, entitled 'I Want to Become President', that Obama wrote in kindergarten, aged three. After his memo is widely derided, Penn claims that the kindergarten reference was a joke. But it's too late: the reference smacks of desperation. (Obama has fun with it: 'I know that folks were rifling though my kindergarten papers. I'm going to be disclosing them tomorrow. It will show that I experimented with colouring outside the lines. I was pulling on pigtails. I liked it.') Penn then compounds the Shaheen mishap by using the explosive word 'cocaine' in reference to Obama's youthful drug habits, during a live TV interview.

None of these incidents is disastrous in itself; overzealous surrogates and misjudged memos are a feature of every campaign. But taken together over the course of a couple of weeks they generate coverage of the Clinton campaign's troubles and missteps, when the intention had been to turn the scrutiny on to her opponent. Worse, they compound an already existing caricature of Clinton in the public's mind as a devious, cynical politician stuck in her old ways. Obama's stump speech now includes mocking reference to Clinton's determination to investigate his kindergarten papers. He criticises her for supposedly describing such attacks as 'the fun part'.

This run of rebounding stories is doubly unfortunate because it comes at a time when the Clinton campaign is finally making efforts to humanise its candidate. Senior Clinton advisers such as her campaign manager, Patti Solis Doyle, and her advertising consultant, Mandy Grunwald, have been saying for weeks that although voters respect Clinton's ability and experience, many find her too cold and remote to vote for. They argue that the campaign needs to warm her up.

Penn has resisted these entreaties. A large, uncomfortable-looking man with lank hair and devastated fingernails, he is the most influential voice within Clinton's campaign, despite being disliked and distrusted by his colleagues. He helped Bill Clinton win re-election in 1996 and has had the ear of the Clintons ever since. Now the global CEO of a massive public relations company, Penn is known for his faith in polling data and for the jealousy with which he maintains his prime position in the Clintonian hierarchy.

Penn repeats to Hillary Clinton advice he says he once gave Bill Gates: 'being human is overrated'. His polls, he says, show that the 'soft stuff' has no effect on people's voting intentions. 'People don't care if you're warm and fuzzy about your mother,' argues Penn; they care about your policies – on health care, the economy, education. Grunwald and Solis Doyle disagree, unsurprised that a man they regard as lacking all human empathy should take such a stance. They think that negative perceptions of Clinton's character are a big problem, and they want to address them. Senator Clinton, far more comfortable discussing policy than she is her personal life, has until now readily agreed with Penn.

But as Clinton continues to lose ground to Obama she finally consents to taking a more personal approach. Her mother Dorothy and daughter Chelsea join her on the campaign trail. Grunwald produces an ad that features an interview with Dorothy talking about what a good daughter Hillary is. Just in case viewers need any more convincing, a title appears on the screen: 'Hillary's mom lives with her'. A new website is rolled out, called The Hillary I Know, with thirty-eight videotaped testimonies from friends and colleagues.

Clinton embarks on a 'Get to Know Hillary' tour, appearing with her husband and friends like Magic Johnson, the basketball player, in diners and groceries around Iowa.

Although it's clearly not something she's entirely comfortable with, Clinton makes an effort to speak about her life at these events. 'I was raised in a middle-class family,' she says at a stop in Ottumwa, speaking softly. 'My dad believed in people fending for themselves and taking whatever they could to get a better life. And my mother believed in reaching out and helping people and being compassionate, and so I was lucky that I got all those values.' Moments later she retreats to safer ground: 'Thank goodness for the children's health insurance programme!' Pulling out a piece of paper with policy proposals on it, she plunges gratefully into the list.

Hillary Clinton is not the only candidate making efforts to show her human side. Mitt Romney has begun crying in public.

Romney rarely makes a mistake or veers off message before an audience. But the flipside of his self-discipline as a candidate is that he can seem like an automaton. Voters may be forgiven for suspecting that, when he leaves the podium or the TV studio, he is reprogrammed for the next event. Romney is self-aware enough to realise the problem, but, like Clinton, he is reluctant to address the question of his personality directly, even as he loses ground to a rival acclaimed as more likeable. Coincidentally or otherwise, Romney starts to show signs of deep emotion in public. After misting over at the end of his religion speech, he wells up again when recalling that African-Americans were only admitted to the Mormon church in 1978. 'I heard it on the radio and I pulled over and I literally wept,' he says.

At a meeting in Londonderry, New Hampshire, Romney tells one of his stock stump stories about witnessing the return of a dead soldier from Iraq at Boston's Logan airport. But this time his eyes fill up, and he adds: 'I have five boys of my own. I imagined what it would be like to lose a son in a situation like that.' When questioned by reporters about these uncharacteristic displays, Romney replies: 'I'm a normal person. I have emotions. I'm not ashamed of that at all.' The newsroom cynics are not convinced, nor are the voters. People suspect that Romney is managing his outbursts of humanity just as carefully as he manages every other aspect of his candidacy.

A Massachusetts politician and former colleague of Romney's claims that Romney's reputation for restraint is down to his background in business: 'In the business world, you don't really show your emotions.' But Romney's tightly controlled public persona owes at least as much to his upbringing as to his career.

Mitt was the youngest son of George Romney, a successful businessman and former governor of Michigan. After his elder siblings left home, Mitt and his father grew particularly close. They developed a loving and intensely intellectual relationship, discussing the issues of the day around the dinner table. By running for president, Mitt is following in the footsteps of George, who died a year after his son's failed run for the Senate in 1994.

Mitt Romney is keenly aware of how his father's political career came to an end. Following Barry Goldwater's disastrous defeat to Lyndon Johnson in 1964, George Romney emerged as the front-runner for the Republican presidential nomination in 1968. Romney Sr was admired as a proven achiever who cared little for political partisanship. He was not a natural campaigner, however. Governor James Rhodes of Ohio remarked that 'watching George Romney was like watching a duck try to make love to a football'. In public, he rarely stuck to an agreed form of words, preferring to talk off the cuff. But he had limited verbal felicity and often made mistakes that were seized on by the press.

He made his career-ending mistake at the end of the summer of

1967 when discussing the Vietnam War, which he had initially supported but came to oppose. Asked by an interviewer why he had changed his mind, he replied that he had been 'brainwashed' by the military. The remark made George Romney sound like a dupe. His poll numbers plummeted, and though he carried on for a few months they never recovered. He withdrew from the race in February 1968 and never ran for elective office again.

Having seen his beloved father's political career destroyed by verbal indiscipline, it is little wonder that Mitt Romney controls every aspect of his public utterances with such care, rarely allowing the emotions of the moment to distract him from his internal script: he is desperate not to follow in his father's missteps.

Huckabee faces scrutiny

One man in particular has profited from the perception of Mitt Romney as an overly stage-managed politician. Mike Huckabee's effortless authenticity forms an attractive contrast to his better-financed rival. But now that he finds himself at the head of the pack, Huckabee is experiencing some of the discomfort that comes when people start taking you seriously.

His opponents raise an episode from his time as governor of Arkansas to cast doubt on his record on law and order. Huckabee had asked a prison board to consider the early release of a convicted rapist, Wayne Dumond. Dumond had become a born-again Christian and the board judged him to be a reformed man. A year after he was released, he murdered a young mother of three children. (The full story makes for gruesome reading: Dumond had first been charged with the rape he was convicted for in 1984. Free on bail, he claimed that local men had come to his house and castrated him, though it was suspected that he inflicted the injury on himself in a bid for sympathy. The local sheriff acquired Dumond's testicles and kept them in a fruit jar on his desk. Dumond later sued the sheriff over that humiliation and won a $100,000 award. The sheriff went to prison in an unrelated extortion case and died there.)

As Huckabee is having his judgement questioned over this case, he is also exposing his somewhat sketchy knowledge of foreign policy. In an article in the heavyweight journal *Foreign Affairs*, he lays out his grand vision of America's role in the world, using the suitably formal name of 'Michael D. Huckabee'. In one part of the essay he sombrely declares that 'Sun-tzu's ancient wisdom is relevant today: "Keep your friends close and your enemies closer."' As one commentator points out, this ancient piece of wisdom is attributable not to Sun-tzu but to Michael Corleone.

When asked about the US intelligence report on Iran's nuclear programme, newly published and headline news around the world, Huckabee admits ignorance. In a press conference he rattles off a list of foreign policy 'advisers', several of whom fail to confirm that they've had much to do with him other than a handshake at a conference or the odd email. The overall impression is of a man winging it, and not very convincingly. But so far none of this appears to be hurting him. His neighbourly charm seems to make him immune to the usual rules of political gravity.

As Christmas nears, some of the candidates release ads tinged with a festive theme. Huckabee's eschews any political message at all; he just wishes voters a happy Christmas. As he addresses the camera, behind him in shot is a white bookcase, the joints of which appear to form a cross. Immediately, the chatter in the blogosphere is that Huckabee is sending a subliminal message to Christian voters. Asked about it at a press conference, Huckabee says it is pure coincidence, adding: 'I will confess this: if you play the spot backwards it says:

"Paul is dead, Paul is dead, Paul is dead.'" His response demonstrates once again his ability to appeal not just to Christian voters, but to anyone with a sense of humour. As Romney is finding out, that makes him a very difficult candidate to attack.

The long shots

Written off as a serious candidate only a few months before, John McCain is once again being spoken of as having a real chance, albeit a slim one, of winning the Republican nomination.

He is focusing on New Hampshire, scene of his famous victory over George W. Bush in 2000. McCain's campaign runs on a shoe-string budget and a skeleton staff. He can't afford to advertise nearly as heavily as his rivals, especially Mitt Romney. He is running an oddly old-fashioned campaign that relies on voters seeing him in person and then spreading the word, and on getting favourable coverage in local newspapers and cable TV stations.

He doesn't hold big rallies. His speciality is the town hall meeting, an event he has made his own. The meeting doesn't actually have to be in a town hall. McCain will speak anywhere there's enough room for a hundred or so people: a veterans' lodge, a company's headquarters, even a microbrewery. Dressed informally, often wearing a baseball cap, McCain stands on a raised platform in the middle of whatever space he's in, and plays to his audience in the round.

He hosts as many as four of these events every day, travelling from venue to venue in his Straight Talk Express bus. He always starts with several minutes of jokes so old that his aides have the punchlines printed on their T-shirts. Then he makes a brief speech about why he's in the race, before discussing whatever is in the news at the moment – when Benazir Bhutto's assassination is dominating the headlines just after Christmas, McCain addresses the United States' relationship with Pakistan. Before long he is into the meat of the meeting, the part he clearly enjoys most: questions and answers.

Whereas most presidential candidates shy away from spontaneous conversations with voters, preferring friendly venues stuffed with supporters, McCain relishes the unpredictability of unscripted debate. He invites questions on any area of policy. After giving his initial answer he usually goes back to the questioner, teasing out their point of view, seeking a genuine dialogue. If questioners attack his positions angrily, he says: 'I respectfully disagree,' and gently explains why, without condescension.

Not that he likes being agreed with. Whatever his questioner's stance, McCain seeks to inject a sense of dramatic conflict into the conversation, probing for areas of difference rather than consensus. For instance, he goes out of his way to tell environmentally minded questioners that he is a supporter of nuclear power when he could easily bask in his record as a supporter of action on climate change. Most candidates avoid questions from voters who look like they're associated with a particular cause or pressure group. McCain readily calls on those wearing an 'I Am a Health Care Voter' sticker or a 'Stop Global Warming' T-shirt. He has a habit of inviting anyone on stage who turns up in a costume. 'You look like a chicken,' he teases an environmental campaigner dressed as a snowman. At another meeting, a young man asks with a notable lack of tact if McCain might die or develop Alzheimer's in office. After explaining that he is in excellent health, McCain finishes his answer with a grin and an insult: 'Thanks for the question, you little jerk.'

Incredibly, McCain's low-fi approach to campaigning seems to be working. He is moving up in the New Hampshire polls and doing well in Iowa too. He's helped enormously by the chaos of the Republican field. Mike Huckabee's rise has knocked Mitt Romney from his perch, although few think the Arkansas governor has the gravitas to go all the way. Rudy Giuliani has had to take a few days out of the campaign after falling ill; the symbolism is resonant, and ominous for him. Fred Thompson still hasn't managed to convince people that he wants to be president. Amidst this confusion, McCain might just do better than anyone would have thought three months ago.

On the Democratic side, the candidate considered to be a smart outside bet has just appeared on the cover of *Newsweek* above the headline 'John Edwards: The Sleeper'. Like McCain, Edwards doesn't have as much money to spend as his main rivals. But he has spent the last three years – ever since finishing second to John Kerry and running as Kerry's vice-presidential candidate – plotting a win in Iowa, 2008. For most of that time Edwards assumed he would be in something like a two-person race with Hillary Clinton. The entrance of another major candidate, especially one as well funded and charismatic as Barack Obama, means that Edwards is struggling to even be considered a viable contender.

But many in Iowa and elsewhere are tipping him to pull off an upset. Over the last few years, Edwards has been rounding up support in Iowa's rural areas, winning over potential voters in towns like Sac City (population 2,189). He expects to lose to Clinton and Obama in the state's bigger cities, but hopes to win the state by dominating these far-flung pastoral precincts. He's also been carefully cultivating and training loyal staff and supporters in Iowa, who can help him reach voters otherwise reluctant to caucus. The polls underestimate his support, they say. Come 5 January all that patient preparation will pay off and 'the sleeper' will surprise the pundits. And if he wins Iowa – who knows?

It's a long shot but, as Edwards would no doubt say, his whole life has been a series of long shots.

Getting hot at the end

For the time being, however, the media are fixated on the battle between Hillary Clinton and Barack Obama. As Christmas approaches the two are still locked into a neck-and-neck race in the polls. The last debate before caucus day is sponsored by Iowa's most influential paper, the *Des Moines Register*, and is uneventful save for one moment that seems to signal Obama's growing confidence. The moderator asks him how he intends to make a 'break from the past', given that so many of his advisers are former Clinton officials. Before he can start his answer Clinton laughs noisily, calling out: 'I wanna hear that!' With a gleam in his eye, Obama replies: 'Hillary, I'm looking forward to you advising me as well.'

Shortly after the debate, Clinton receives a boost from the editorial board of the *Register*. The paper declares that though it's very attracted to Obama, it believes America needs a more experienced president in a time of war and economic uncertainty. The Clinton campaign hopes that Iowa voters will reach the same conclusion.

Both the Clinton and the Obama campaigns are engaged in a furious effort in these final days to persuade first-time caucus-goers to get out and vote for them. The scale and scope of this effort is unprecedented. Both campaigns use sophisticated computer models to identify potential voters, and send out repeated mailings to their targets. Clinton's team focus on female voters, whilst Obama's focus on the young. Sitting in Clinton's Iowa headquarters are hundreds of green shovels waiting to be distributed to volunteers who will clear the pathways of older women wary of going out in the snow. The Obama campaign has promised free baby-sitting to any parent who needs it on caucus night. The Clinton campaign has printed doorknob hangers with caucus locations in extra-large type, and has mailed refrigerator magnets carrying the caucus date to potential first-timers.

Both campaigns employ hundreds of staff to phone voters and knock on doors. Thousands of volunteers are ready to help people get to their local caucus. The Clinton campaign alone has 4,900 drivers for caucus night (compared to the 350 that Kerry had in 2004). The volunteers and staff come from around the state and from all over the country too. The Obama campaign has been far-sighted enough to recruit people who share the agricultural background of most Iowans. The team believe that Iowans are much more likely to listen to people who know the price of a tractor than to students from New York or professionals from Washington.

The candidates themselves make their final appeals to the voters, in sharply contrasting styles.

Clinton's events are meticulously planned and orderly. She is accompanied by Chelsea, who often stands with her on stage and joins her to work the crowds afterwards. Clinton's speech contains a long list of accomplishments: all the things 'I've worked for'. She speaks confidently of what will happen 'when I am president'. Rather than expanding on her vision of America, she focuses on policies aimed at easing the economic anxiety of the middle classes, just as her husband did in 1992. She is the candidate of action, accomplishment and solutions. After her speech, Clinton spends a long time meeting supporters, having her photo taken with them, signing autographs and shaking hands.

Obama is zigzagging his way across the state on a 'Stand for Change' tour, reprising the themes that he communicated so power-fully at the Jefferson-Jackson dinner. Compared to Clinton's, his events are rag-tag affairs: homemade banners are waved, spontaneous chants break out and toddlers run riot. He presents himself as a fresh face, untainted by the Washington 'experience' that Clinton touts as an asset. He is less likely than she is to use the first person singular. He prefers to speak of 'we' and 'us', meaning all those who wish to change the political system rather than 'play the game' – an allusion to the Clintons' mastery of conventional political warfare. Drawing on his days as a community organiser, he seeks to create the sense that he is merely riding the wave of an irresistible grassroots movement for change.

But Obama rarely hits the rhetorical heights of Jefferson-Jackson. It's as if he keeps his best game in reserve for the big occasions. For the most part, he is more teacher than preacher. He holds his opponent's arguments up for examination before dissecting them, sounding like the law professor he used to be. 'That's the experience argument,' he instructs patient listeners in Muscatine. 'We're hearing another argument now.'

As 2007 becomes 2008, the eyes of the nation are on Iowa, and in particular on the toe-to-toe, eyeball-to-eyeball battle between Clinton and Obama. It is almost impossible to determine who is winning. Christmas is never a good time to poll, and Iowans have stopped answering their phones (some report being called fifteen times a night by different campaigns). Not only that, but nobody knows how many will vote. Turnout is expected to soar, because the enthusiasm amongst Democrats here, like everywhere else, is so high this year. Four years ago it was 124,000. This time, who knows? Some are speculating it could even be as high as 200,000.

Given this uncertainty, the major campaign teams are thinking ahead, constructing elaborate gameplans for various Iowa scenarios. It is likely there will be two, possibly three, truly viable candidates emerging from the Hawkeye State, although minor candidates like Bill Richardson may carry on in a bid to raise their national profile and bargaining power with the remaining candidates. Behind the scenes, the Clinton campaign team are no longer confident of victory. They think it's possible that Obama, or more likely John Edwards, will come out on top in Iowa. But as Clinton says in a radio interview: 'I'm in it for the long run.' Though it's not a very long run, she continues, predicting that the race will be over by 5 February, otherwise known as Super Tuesday, when twenty-two states have their vote.

Just before New Year Rudy Giuliani makes a surprise visit to his campaign headquarters in Iowa. He is trailing badly in the polls here. His campaign is suddenly panicked that if he performs abysmally in Iowa and New Hampshire he might lose touch with the contest altogether. He has recovered from his illness, but the former Republican front-runner cuts a diminished figure. He makes three campaign stops, drawing small crowds to small venues.

It is quite a comedown for the man who dominated the Republican field only a few months before. Over the summer, many predicted that Giuliani, despite his unconventional background, would win the nomination, transforming the Republican Party, and hence US politics, in the process. But Giuliani and his team badly underestimated the extent to which the media carnivals of Iowa and New Hampshire would suck the oxygen from their campaign. Now Giuliani just looks tired: defeated before a single vote has been cast. When things are going badly, some candidates seem to gain energy. Rudy Giuliani isn't one of them.

In a bakery in Indianola, Iowa, a voter asks Giuliani why he has so rarely visited the state. He replies vaguely that he has 'spent time everywhere'. He says thank-you to those who turned out and travels back to the airport, where he will take a plane to New Hampshire.

January 2008

In the final days before Iowa votes, people across the state, the nation and the world are trying to discern who is getting hot at the end.

On the Republican side, Mike Huckabee still has the momentum, and Mitt Romney hasn't recovered his stride. But Huckabee is having a last-minute wobble of his own. After disavowing negative attacks, he has been persuaded by his new adviser Ed Rollins – a gnarled veteran of Republican campaigns who once boasted that he'd bribed African-American ministers to suppress the black vote – to respond to Romney's attacks on him. Two days before caucus day Huckabee calls a press conference to unveil a new commercial that drives home his case against Romney.

But he surprises the assembled reporters by renouncing his own ad. He says that he has had a change of heart, and quotes from the Bible: 'If you gain the whole world but lose your own soul, what does it profit you?' Huckabee declares that the ad will never air. Then he plays it anyway, before live television cameras, 'just to prove that it existed'. Reporters are amused at this seeming attempt to have it both ways, and wonder if it will undermine Huckabee's reputation for straight talking. But it seems only to highlight the attractively improvisational, seat-of-the-pants nature of Huckabee's campaign.

More attention is focused on the Democratic race, for which Iowa – due to the greater efforts required to organise for its caucus process – is more pivotal than for the Republicans. Some think that Hillary Clinton may have done enough to fight off her challengers. Clinton's strength amongst older voters may tell in her favour, as they are more likely to get out and caucus. Others think Barack Obama might pull off an upset, but only if younger voters turn out for him in unprecedented numbers. Nobody is writing off John Edwards, who has stayed close enough to Obama and Clinton in the polls to make this a true three-way contest. Others point to Joe Biden, Bill Richardson and Chris Dodd, predicting that they will make stronger showings than expected.

The Democratic candidates make their final pitches with hoarse voices, trying not to let their tiredness show or to sound too desperate, on a bitterly cold day. John and Elizabeth Edwards are on a non-stop 36-hour campaign marathon across the state, ending up at a rally in Des Moines alongside the singer John Cougar Mellencamp, a blue-collar hero. Clinton speaks to a crowd of about a thousand at a rally in Cedar Rapids. 'You don't run for office to feed your ego, you don't run for office to get your name in the headlines,' she says, in a final attempt to stir the suspicions of some Iowans that Obama is a shallow glory-seeker. 'You run for office to help other people.' In Coralville, near the University of Iowa, Obama challenges his young crowd to act on their declarations of support: 'They say a lot of you will never show up. Are you gonna prove them wrong? I can't hear you. *Are you gonna prove them wrong?*' If he's going to win, he needs them to.

Everybody has a theory about who has the edge. But trying to work out what's going on is like trying to plot a course through one of the snowstorms that sweep through Iowa around this time of year. The polls give an idea of where the race stands. They can't predict who will actually turn out to caucus, or indeed what they will do when they get there. Many Iowans say they walk in undecided and make their choice on the spot. The day before caucus day, the *Des Moines Register* publishes its much-awaited final poll. It shows Obama with a seven-point lead. But a third of voters say they might change their mind.

Finally, Thursday 3 January arrives. Across Iowa's 99 counties and 1,781 precincts, caucus meetings are held in church basements, school gyms, fire stations, libraries, town halls and homes. What unfolds is a long way from the polite discretion of a private ballot; each meeting is a rowdy and convivial marketplace for votes. Precinct captains marshal their candidate's supporters into their designated corner of the room – some try to tempt undecided voters with cookies and cake. Speeches are given, pitches made and impassioned arguments conducted. Waverers are implored to switch sides. Husbands and wives stand together or apart. Groups are formed and re-formed amid last-minute deal-brokering. Finally, there is a counting of heads, and the results of each meeting are reported to party officials.

The first thing that amazes the officials is the number of people who have turned out to vote. The boldest predictions estimated that up to 200,000 might attend the caucuses. But tonight an astounding 239,000 Iowans declare their preference for a Democratic candidate, nearly double the number that did so in 2004.

The second thing that amazes them is the result.

Iowa rolls the dice

The party's officials aren't the only ones in shock. This small farming state has produced an upset that shakes the country, and the world. Barack Obama has scored a decisive victory. John Edwards lags nine points behind and Hillary Clinton is forced – just – into third place.

A few months ago it was almost unthinkable that she would be beaten here at all.

Whatever happens next – even if this is the last victory Barack Obama wins – history has been made today. A newcomer to national politics who four years ago was a lowly state senator has defeated the best-known brand-name in American politics, by taking on and besting the most feared election-winning machine in the country. What's more, he has done it as a black man in largely white, rural Iowa. African-Americans have won Democratic primaries before. But only in states with high African-American populations, and none stood a realistic chance of attaining the nomination. This time is different.

Obama's victory speech tonight hits the heights he attained two months beforehand at the Jefferson-Jackson dinner. 'They said this day would never come,' he declares, alluding to the historic nature of his victory without explicitly mentioning his race. 'They said our sights were set too high. They said this country was too divided – too disillusioned to ever come together around a common purpose.' He skilfully winds together his campaign themes of change and unity with the larger historic story. 'We are one nation,' he says. 'We are one people. And our time for change has come.' One day, he declares, the American people will look back on the 2008 Iowa caucuses and say: 'This was the moment when it all began.'

The result is a tribute to the Obama campaign's power of organisation. It won the Iowa ground game hands down, persuading more first-time caucus-goers to the polls than Clinton and her formidable team of experienced Iowa operatives. It is also testament to Obama's capacity to inspire enthusiasm. He drew in voters from beyond the usual constituencies. Young people defied precedent and predictions by turning out for Obama in droves. Independents, unaligned to either major party, did the same.

Before today, Obama was a media sensation and a clear danger to

Clinton's status as the Democratic front-runner. But some suspected his candidacy to be more about hype than substance, and that, like Howard Dean and others before him, he would fade away the closer voters got to making an actual choice. Indeed, nobody was more aware than Obama's team that if they lost in Iowa, the excitement that had sustained their campaign might suddenly evaporate. After today, nobody can deny that Obama may go on to win not only the nomination race, but the biggest prize of all.

His euphoric supporters certainly believe so. They chant, with absolute conviction now, the refrain that Obama has been using in his stump speech: 'Yes We Can.'

For Clinton and her team, this is a painful and disorienting blow. Some of her advisers had already been rueing the day they decided to compete in earnest in a state where she had no political roots. But the scale of the defeat – and Clinton's third place – is completely unexpected, and shattering. A campaign constructed around the notion of Clinton as the front-runner will have to reassess a transformed political landscape and recalibrate its message. There isn't much time in which to do it. New Hampshire votes in only five days.

Before supporters at the Hotel Fort Des Moines, Clinton congratulates Obama and Edwards, seeking gamely to frame the outcome as a collective expression of America's desire for 'a new beginning'. It is, she says, a 'great night for Democrats'. It's plainly not a great night for her. On television, Hillary is shown flanked by a group of uniformly white, middle-aged, grey-haired supporters, including a red-faced Bill Clinton and a selection of vaguely familiar officials from his administration. It is a tableau of times past, contrasting poorly with the pictures of young, multi-racial crowds surrounding Obama.

Senators Dodd and Biden announce they are quitting, having failed to make an impact on the top three. Governor Richardson says he will carry on despite a weak showing, hoping to do well in later primaries nearer his home state of New Mexico. Edwards pronounces himself delighted with second place, though some feel that Iowa was effectively an all-or-nothing bet for him. He says that in Iowa 'the status quo lost and change won', a transparent attempt to hitch his wagon to Obama's. Edwards believes that if he hangs in until Hillary Clinton gets knocked out, he might stand a fair chance in a one-to-one fight with Obama.

Clinton's campaign suddenly faces the vertiginous prospect of being shunted from the race in five days' time. A loss in New Hampshire and many will declare the contest over. Her funding will dwindle, and the media will start talking about Obama as the presumptive nominee. Four years of careful planning and meticulous preparation – not to mention thirty years of deferred ambition – are in imminent danger of coming to nothing. As Clinton flies from Iowa to New Hampshire tonight, she considers her options: should she go for an all-out negative assault on Obama? Or should she concentrate on her own agenda? Some of her advisers feel, without saying so, that neither strategy is going to work now.

Republicans vote for change too

Somewhat overshadowed by Barack Obama's win, but remarkable in its own right, is Mike Huckabee's victory in Iowa. Huckabee has beaten Mitt Romney by a similar margin to Obama's victory over Hillary Clinton and John Edwards. It is quite an achievement. Huckabee's rise was even quicker than Obama's: he only started to surge in the polls in November. But he has overcome Romney's well-financed, highly organised operation by riding a wave of fervour amongst Iowa's evangelical Christians, and by appealing to other voters who were simply attracted to Huckabee's freshness, candour and easy charm.

Fred Thompson and John McCain come in joint third, with Rudy Giuliani in a humiliating last place. McCain is happy with his decent showing in a state he never expected to win. He believes it sets him up well for the one he must win if he is to make his comeback real: New Hampshire.

Romney congratulates Huckabee, declaring himself happy with 'silver', an allusion to his role in the Winter Olympics. The only person who might truly understand how Romney feels right now is Hillary Clinton. Like her, after fighting a hugely expensive, long-planned campaign in Iowa, he now finds himself having to come to terms with the horrific fact that it was all in vain. Like her also, he was beaten by a candidate he would not have given even a minute's thought to when he first planned his run. The Republican primary in New Hampshire is on the same day as the Democratic one. Romney knows, as does Clinton, that unless he wins there in five days' time, his candidacy will be in mortal danger.

Some 120,000 turned out to vote in the Republican ballot in Iowa, also a record number. Iowans have sent a loud message to both parties, and all candidates, that – in case they weren't fully aware – the country is in the mood for the new and the different. You would be hard pressed to find two more capable, better-disciplined, better-resourced candidates than Romney and Clinton. Both are masters of the political game as it has been played over at least the last fifteen years. In any normal year – if there is such a thing – they would win. But both have been toppled, at least temporarily, by two candidates who play the game by different rules.

Huckabee is keen to align himself with Obama's triumph. In his victory speech he even borrows Obama's rhetoric: 'Tonight, what we have seen is a new day in American politics . . . the election is not about me. It's about "we".' It's a slightly limp imitation, but Huckabee is not one for soaring speeches. He is more of a conversationalist and a comedian. Few commentators believe he has the substance to go all the way in this race. But then, all of the Republican candidates have their problems – and Huckabee has already proven the pundits wrong once.

As Iowans revel in the final moments of national and international attention, the surviving candidates on both sides move on to New Hampshire (the exception is Giuliani, who, after a brief stop there, flies to warmer climes in Florida, the state that his hopes are pinned upon). There they will begin five days of concentrated campaigning. The national media go with them. The *Des Moines Register* redirects its attention to local politics and the story of a man arrested for drunk driving.

Five days in New Hampshire

New Hampshire is rich with memories for Hillary and Bill Clinton. In 1992, Bill had forced himself to the front of the Democratic field. But his campaign faced collapse after his affair with Gennifer Flowers exploded into the news. Hillary joined him in a public display of contrition on national television, and Bill turned up on Arsenio Hall's late-night chat show to play the saxophone, impressing the public with his determination not to be bowed by the scandal. But it was his vigorous showing in the New Hampshire primary – he came in second to Paul Tsongas – that earned him the soubriquet of the 'Comeback Kid'. The Clintons have retained strong links with the state ever since, visiting it frequently and maintaining close relationships with local Democratic leaders.

Inside the Clinton campaign, arguments rage about who is responsible for the predicament they find themselves in, and about what they should do next. Roughly speaking, there are two camps.

One of them, represented almost solely by the powerful figure of Clinton's chief strategist, Mark Penn, has argued throughout that the core message of the candidate's campaign should be 'experience'. He is blamed by the others for not realising that experience isn't enough in a year when everyone wants change. Penn now claims that the key to a recovery is to take on Barack Obama more aggressively and ruthlessly. Other senior advisers, such as communications chief Howard Wolfson and advertising consultant Mandy Grunwald, argue that Clinton must continue the effort to soften her public image.

The disagreements within the camp are personal: most of Clinton's staffers simply can't bear Penn, who is reputed to be arrogant, opinionated and routinely rude to his colleagues. Others are unhappy with the campaign manager, Patti Solis Doyle, a long-time friend and confidante of Clinton's who has no prior experience of running a national political campaign, but whose closeness to the boss means that she gets away with an often imperious and brusque attitude to more experienced colleagues. It is not, to say the least, a harmonious team.

On the morning after Clinton's Iowa defeat, her campaign's top aides hold a conference call from their Virginia headquarters with the candidate, who is on the trail in New Hampshire. After arriving on the line Clinton gives a brisk greeting and makes it clear there is no time to spend indulging in long analyses of what went wrong; they must look ahead. Her dazed advisers have nothing to add, hamstrung, perhaps, by their bitter disagreements. Clinton carries on, growing angry. She complains of being painted as the establishment candidate in Iowa. Pausing, she is once again met with silence. 'This has been very instructive, talking to myself,' she snaps, and hangs up.

Later that day Bill Clinton is asked by a reporter if his wife can be the Comeback Kid this time around. 'Absolutely,' he replies. But he doesn't sound optimistic. He implies that the shortened calendar means they just don't have enough time to turn things around: 'I wish we had ten days instead of five.'

That evening, at the New Hampshire Democratic Party's 100 Club dinner, the candidates address an audience of more than 3,000 people. Obama, who speaks last, nearly starts a riot just by standing up. The crowd surges towards the stage, chanting 'O-ba-ma' and one of the refrains from his stump speech: 'Fired up! Ready to go!' The announcer has to intervene, asking people to take their seats for safety reasons. Earlier on, Hillary Clinton had been greeted with boos when she said she was working for 'change for you', and again when she said that the question for voters in New Hampshire is 'Who is ready to lead from Day 1?'

John McCain has fond memories of this state. It was the scene of his earthshaking triumph over George W. Bush in the 2000 Republican primaries. Its individualistic ethos – reflected in the state motto, 'Live Free or Die' – chimes well with McCain's maverick political persona. He has spent most of his time here in recent months; this is where voters, many of whom remember him warmly from last time around, have been turning up in ever-increasing numbers to see his town hall shows. McCain's campaign knows that it must win here or die. A victory will propel him to the front of a confused and confusing field. A loss and people will be talking about the comeback that never came off.

It is Mike Huckabee's win in Iowa that, by wounding Mitt Romney, has opened up this opportunity for McCain. Huckabee and McCain get on well, and the two candidates now form a tacit alliance against the man still considered to be the front-runner. Huckabee is not expected to win here – unlike Iowa, New Hampshire doesn't have high numbers of evangelicals, and his campaign has virtually no organisation on the ground. Still, Ed Rollins, Huckabee's veteran campaign manager, hopes they can still take care of some business:

'We're going to see if we can't take Romney out. We like John. Nobody likes Romney.'

It is in Huckabee's interest to see Romney out of the race, but Rollins's remark makes explicit something that is already apparent to those following the Republican candidates: whilst McCain, Huckabee, Fred Thompson and Rudy Giuliani enjoy a mutual, if wary, respect, they are united in their loathing of Romney. This is partly because Romney spends much of his massive advertising budget attacking them (and doing so on issues, such as immigration and gun control, on which he has changed his mind). They are contemptuous of Romney's attempt to reinvent himself as the only true conservative in the race. They are also, perhaps, envious of his deep pockets, resentful of his wealthy start in life and irritated by his prissy demeanour.

Romney recognises that McCain is the biggest threat to him in New Hampshire, and perhaps for the nomination itself. His strategy, refocused in the wake of Iowa's stunning results, is a familiar one. He now presents himself as the face of 'change' and portrays McCain as the ultimate Washington insider. Like Huckabee, he adopts some of Obama's rhetoric, though he too lacks the Democrat's natural eloquence. 'What we're going to do to change Washington is bring someone in,' says Romney. 'I'm talking about me,' he continues, in case voters are in any doubt.

New Hampshire's electorate prides itself on its independence from party orthodoxies, and nearly half of its voters are registered as independents, rather than Republicans or Democrats. Indeed, many voters here say they are trying to decide between McCain and Obama, the two candidates who appear least in thrall to their own party. The high number of independents represents a wild card in an already unpredictable primary.

The New Hampshire debates

The extremely short period between Iowa and New Hampshire means that each party's televised debate is likely to be pivotal. Both take place on the Saturday night before Tuesday's vote.

As the four remaining Democratic candidates take to the stage in Manchester, the state's largest city, some are wondering if this might be the last debate that Hillary Clinton participates in. Although Bill Richardson is hanging in there, the focus of the evening is undoubtedly on Clinton and Barack Obama, and to a lesser extent John Edwards.

It isn't long before the dynamic of the evening is established. Obama and Edwards know that a fatally wounded Clinton will be good for both of them and act as a team. Clinton sits at one end of the table. Obama and Edwards sit together, touch arms solicitously, use each other's first names and murmur gentlemanly apologies for interrupting each other. Edwards's rhetoric chimes with Obama's. 'Yes, Barack,' he says at one point, 'I agree with you completely that we need to unite America.' The two of them take turns to attack Clinton's record and character.

At one point, Clinton seeks to draw Edwards to her side by suggesting that Obama had hypocritically tried to portray him as inconsistent. All eyes turn to Edwards. He sides with Obama. 'Any time you speak out powerfully for change, the forces of the status quo attack,' he says, waving a contemptuous hand in the direction of Clinton. Obama nods in agreement. Gesturing to the man on his left, Edwards continues: 'He believes deeply in change, and I believe deeply in change.' He calls for an 'unfiltered debate between the agents of change'.

This is too much for Clinton. She smiles tensely, sits forward into the microphone and tugs her jacket tighter, as if pulling on an imaginary flak jacket. When the moderator intervenes she puts out a hand to cut him off. 'Wait a minute now, wait a minute,' she says, her voice harsh with anger. 'I'm going to respond to this. Making change is not about what you believe,' she says, clearly infuriated by the glibness of her opponents' attacks. 'It's not about a speech you make. It's about working hard.' She recounts examples of legislation she has passed to improve people's lives, punching each one home with her right hand. 'I'm not just running on a *promise* of change; I'm running on *thirty-five years* of change.'

In the second half of the debate, the questions move on from hard policy issues to questions about the candidates' public images. Clinton is asked to explain why voters find her less likeable than some of her rivals. 'Well, that hurts my feelings,' she responds, smiling, drawing warm and sympathetic laughter from an audience who sense what an uncomfortable question it is to answer. 'But I'll try to go on,' she says, inclining her head in a playful parody of martyrdom. Glancing over at Obama, she says, in girlish tones: 'He's very likeable, I agree with that! But I don't think I'm that bad.'

Obama, who has been gazing down at his notes during this exchange, suddenly looks up and unsmilingly interjects: 'You're likeable enough, Hillary.'

'Thank you very much. I appreciate that,' replies Clinton.

After the debate, as always, there is a frenzy of analysis and commentary from reporters, pundits and bloggers. The most-discussed moment is Clinton's outburst of anger. Opinions are divided on how viewers will have received it. Did it make her look unhinged, or will voters warm to this display of raw emotion from a candidate usually so controlled in public? One or two wonder if Obama's 'likeable enough' comment will be seen as condescending. The general consensus is that Clinton didn't do enough to change the momentum of the race. A poll on Monday, the day before people go to vote, shows Obama ahead by thirteen points.

Elsewhere in Manchester, the six remaining Republican candidates take the stage: Mitt Romney, John McCain, Mike Huckabee, Rudy Giuliani, Fred Thompson and the libertarian outlier, Ron Paul. Despite the large number of candidates, a simple dynamic soon establishes itself: it's Romney versus the rest.

The personal dislike that the other candidates reserve for the former Massachusetts governor spills out into the open. On question after question Romney is attacked by every figure on the stage. The theme of the evening is Romney's inconsistency: his record of flip-flops on issues such as abortion rights and gun control. McCain, who is the leader of the pack tonight, sums it up in a line delivered with a smirk: 'We disagree on a lot of issues. But I agree, you are the candidate of change.' Romney replies, in his mildly priggish fashion, that 'the personal barbs are interesting but unnecessary'.

New Hampshire's Republican debate reflects something about the race, and also something of the classroom. McCain has always been the cool kid: the boy that other boys want to be like, and be liked by. At the Naval Academy, he was the cocky son of a famous admiral, who never flinched from sticking two fingers up to the authorities. He was a dashing fighter pilot who survived a fire on an aircraft-carrier and was back in the skies within weeks. His first wife was a model, his second a rich girl nearly twenty years his junior. His heroism in Vietnam put his toughness beyond reproach; his wit made him the guy other guys wanted to hang out with.

Romney, on the other hand, has always been a swot: the boy and then the man who worked harder than anyone else, at school and in business. Driven by a desire to live up to his father's expectations, Romney got where he is by following rules, deferring to authority and being utterly focused on achievement. He is hardened to the derision of his peers.

Afterwards, commentators agree that Romney survived a tough night and may even have been strengthened as a result.

Closing pitches

In the New Hampshire campaign's final days, two candidates are brimming with confidence.

The Obama camp believe they are heading for a win that will set the Illinois senator on course for the nomination. In an interview with ABC, Barack Obama sounds sure of his victory: 'I think we are going to do well in New Hampshire.' He speaks to massive crowds at rallies across the state. 'Something is stirring out there,' he says.

John McCain has adopted the slogan 'The Mac Is Back' and is returning, superstitiously, to the venues he visited in his 2000 campaign. He is still telling the same jokes. 'We have so little water in Arizona that the trees chase the dogs.' He draws large, enthusiastic crowds at every stop. In Salem McCain says: 'Frankly, we're winning this campaign.' His staff already talk of the coming contest with Obama.

Clinton's advisers hope that a second-place finish will enable them to argue that their candidate has at least made an advance on her Iowa result. They then hope to survive a grinding battle until Super Tuesday, where her strength as a national figure will come into play. Hillary Clinton's new slogan is 'Talk vs Action, Rhetoric vs Results'. Whilst it is less than pithy, it represents her new focus: action over experience. But many observers think that the injury Iowa inflicted on Clinton's candidacy is too severe to recover from. As one Democratic official puts it, charmingly: 'She has the stink of a loser on her.'

Neither Hillary nor Bill Clinton shows any sign of giving up, however. They are driven on as much by fury at the position they find themselves in as by belief that they can win. Bill, taking a question at a town hall in New Hampshire, allows his anger at the media to boil over. Asked about Obama's claim to superior judgement, as evidenced by his opposition to the Iraq War, the former president launches into a diatribe of gathering speed and intensity about what he argues is the media's failure to scrutinise Obama's record on Iraq. Clinton's big hands are expressive instruments, and his right index finger jabs and slashes the air as he seeks to puncture the idea that Obama has consistently opposed the war. 'Give me a break,' he concludes, with a final dismissive gesture. 'This whole thing is the biggest fairy tale I've ever seen.' Realising that he has lost his cool, Clinton walks away from the spot he was fixed to as he let loose on his wife's opponent. 'Otherwise,' he says, 'I do not have any strong feelings about that subject.' He takes the next question.

Hillary Clinton is, famously, less ready to express her emotions in public than her husband. But now she does so for the second time in four days. Unlike last time, however, the emotion isn't anger.

The day before New Hampshire's verdict is due, Clinton holds a round-table discussion with undecided female voters in a café. In these situations she is at her best. The stridency she can display in debates or on the stump is absent, replaced by a warmer, more empathetic manner. She takes questions on health care, social security and energy policy, answering them with her usual relish for discussing the detail of policies that affect voters' lives. A question from the back of the room brings an unexpected change of tone. 'My question is very personal,' says the woman. Complimenting Clinton on her appearance, she asks: 'How do you do it? How do you keep upbeat and so wonderful?'

Clinton begins by mentioning, jokingly, the help she gets with her hair. But, she says, 'it's not easy. I couldn't do it if I didn't passionately believe it was the right thing to do.' Drawing a deep breath, she continues, tiredness subverting her syntax: 'You know, I have so many opportunities from this country.' She pauses, rests her chin on her hand, and carries on as her voice begins to break and her eyes mist over. 'I just don't want to see us fall backwards.' There is a ripple of sympathetic applause. Perhaps sensing that the audience within and beyond the café is listening more intently than ever, she keeps talking, her voice soft and frayed. 'You know, this is very personal for me. It's not just political, it's not just public. I see what's happening, and we have to reverse it. Some people think elections are a game, lots of who's up or who's down, [but] it's about our country, it's about our kids' futures.' She segues into a familiar attack on her main rival:

> Some of us put ourselves out there and do this against
> some pretty difficult odds, and we do it, each one of us,
> because we care about our country, but some of us are
> right and some of us are wrong. Some of us are ready and
> some of us are not. Some of us know what we will do on
> Day 1 and some of us haven't thought that through
> enough.

That evening, the clip of Clinton welling up is played, replayed and endlessly discussed. Everyone is fascinated by this display of emotional vulnerability in a woman whose public appearances are so controlled she is routinely accused of being inhuman. Will this be seen as a glimpse of the real Hillary, ask pundits – or as a contrived and desperate attempt to win voters' sympathy? John Edwards, interviewed on ABC, is resolutely unmoved: 'I think what we need in a commander in chief is strength and resolve, and presidential campaigns are tough business, but being president of the United States is also tough business.'

As voters are about to have their say, every opinion poll puts Obama ahead by a big margin. He is confident that the same surge of young and independent voters is about to help him repeat his Iowa victory. Speaking to a crowd in the college town of Lebanon, New Hampshire, he says: 'You are the wave and I'm riding it.'

It is only the Clintons themselves who appear to think they might have any chance of eking out a win here. Encouraged by the coverage that her moment in the café is getting, Hillary senses an opportunity to draw on the sympathy of female voters. She does a round of TV interviews about it, and speaks about her struggle against what she describes as the 'buddy system' formed by Obama and Edwards.

Out on the campaign trail, Bill Clinton pretends to lament that he can't, for electoral purposes, make Hillary 'younger, taller, male'. His unmatchable political antennae are sensing something about the mood of female voters. Back at campaign offices, he tells Hillary: 'You know, I think we can do something here.' Nobody else agrees with him.

Back from the dead

Later that evening it becomes clear that, not for the first time, the former president's instincts were correct when just about everyone else's were wrong.

At 10.30 p.m. Terry McAuliffe, former party chairman and long-time friend of the Clintons, bounds into the press room at the local party headquarters, where reporters gathered a couple of hours earlier to write Hillary Clinton's political obituary. Grinning widely, McAuliffe tells them something they can scarcely believe: Clinton is tonight's victor. 'This is a big, big win for us,' he says, and for once he is not exaggerating.

Clinton not only wins, she wins decisively, against all predictions and polls. Stunned commentators try to work out what happened. One thing quickly becomes clear: women swung behind Clinton in massive numbers at the last minute.

For days, pundit after pundit, mostly male, has declared that Clinton couldn't win in New Hampshire and that she was doomed to lose the nomination race. Many have failed to conceal their glee at this prospect. Barack Obama himself has oozed confidence to the point of complacency, and John Edwards ganged up with him, unattractively, at the debate. The female voters of New Hampshire have decided to let everyone know that this is their election, and nobody else is going to decide it for them – just as the voters of Iowa did when the media said a Clinton victory was inevitable. This is a declaration of independence.

But it is Clinton's win; of that there can be no doubt. In New Hampshire she focused relentlessly on her 'Solutions for America', shifting her emphasis from her track record to the changes that her experience would enable her to accomplish, a shift that came too late in Iowa. Of course, that isn't the whole story. Clinton's new focus on change happened in parallel with an evolution in her political person-ality; an accidental one, perhaps, but a crucial one nonetheless. Her most powerful moments in the short and intense New Hampshire campaign came when she was under stress, angered by Edwards and Obama in the debate, or desperately tired and moved by a sympa-thetic question at the café. On both occasions she allowed her mask of utter professionalism to slip for a moment, revealing someone more human underneath. Half aware of what she was doing, Clinton leaned into these moments, learning to ride the surges of emotion she felt rather than suppress them, and in the process she made a more direct connection with voters. Under the intense pressure of a presidential campaign, she finally seems to be acquiring something of her husband's gift for self-expression.

In her victory speech, Clinton thanks the voters of New Hampshire, telling them: 'Over the last week, I listened to you. And in the process, I found my own voice.'

Obama's campaign team is in shock. The giddy sense of anticipation created by the Iowa result has been abruptly dispelled. From dreaming about having the nomination virtually wrapped up by the end of the week, they must now readjust to what looks like being a battle that won't end until Super Tuesday, 5 February, at the earliest. In a conference call that night, David Plouffe, Obama's softly spoken campaign manager, seeks to calm his stunned and disappointed team. He methodically lays out their candidate's path to the nomination now that a quick victory looks out of the question. Towards the end, he briefly raises his voice from its customary whisper to say: 'Now let's go fucking win this thing.'

John Edwards finished third, despite a barnstorming campaign up and down New Hampshire. He declares his determination to carry on, hoping for a stronger showing in South Carolina.

The Mac is back

John McCain has proved beyond doubt that there are second acts in American political careers, by repeating his 2000 New Hampshire victory. In doing so, he scores an important victory over Mitt Romney and catapults himself to the head of the Republican pack, barely six months after being counted out of the race.

Exit polls show that McCain made inroads with conservative Republicans. But it was independent voters, attracted by McCain's maverick brand of Republicanism, that delivered this victory. Indeed, McCain's popularity with this group may have contributed to Barack Obama's downfall. Many Democrat-leaning independents who might have voted for Obama voted for McCain instead. Obama seemed certain to win, so why not give the hero of 2000 a bit of help?

The question for McCain is: can he keep his momentum going, or will his triumph prove as short lived as it did in 2000? Or, to put it another way, what next? The immediate answer is that McCain will have to find a way of winning or doing well in the next two Republican primaries: Michigan and South Carolina, scene of his downfall in 2000.

Romney gets a gold

Michigan is sick. The decline of the car industry and the outsourcing of jobs overseas have hit this part of the country hard, and it now has one of the highest unemployment rates in the United States and endemic crime problems in its major towns. Detroit, the city that once throbbed with the rhythms of heavy machinery and Motown, has gone quiet.

Mitt Romney remembers Michigan when it was in its pomp. His father was chairman of American Motors Corporation, and governor of Michigan for the best part of the 1960s. George Romney was a popular man in Michigan and is still remembered there with fondness. His son hopes that he can capitalise on this good will and improve on a second 'silver' from New Hampshire. Unless he succeeds, he will be out of this race for good.

Michigan's economic decline allows Mitt Romney to play to his strength as a can-do problem-solver who understands capitalism from the inside: the *Turnaround* king. His expensively assembled team of advisers have been divided on whether this should have been his main pitch all along, or whether he was right to present himself instead as a conservative ideologue in the mould of Ronald Reagan. Continuing his post-Iowa theme, Romney presents himself as the candidate of 'change' on a mission to 'fix Washington'. He tells voters that he knows how to turn around Michigan's economy, that they can get their jobs back if only the deadlock in Washington can be broken. McCain, displaying his characteristic discomfort with telling people what they want to hear – not to mention his discomfort with economic issues generally – does not follow suit. He tells voters bluntly that their old jobs will never come back.

It is Romney's message that prevails. He wins a commanding victory and declares it a 'comeback'. McCain finishes a creditable second and now looks to South Carolina to make him front-runner. Mike Huckabee does respectably, though few still see him as a serious contender for the nomination. Rudy Giuliani finishes sixth, behind Fred Thompson and Ron Paul. 'Our strategy remains on track,' says his adviser. Florida's primary is in ten days.

The Republican race continues to feel chaotic. Three different candidates have won the first three primaries. There is no clear front-runner. At least one serious candidate – Giuliani – has yet to seriously contest a primary. The state of the race reflects the confusion within the party's own ranks, as different constituencies, representing different visions of the its past and future, battle it out. National security hawks vie with economic Reaganites and Christian evangelicals. The candidates have to decide which corner to choose or whether to try and cover all of them. With George W. Bush's brand of conservatism so unpopular in the country, there is no common theme to rally around.

Meanwhile, Clinton wins a largely uncontested Democratic

primary. The Democratic National Committee stripped Michigan of all its convention delegates because the state scheduled its primary at an earlier date than that sanctioned by the party. Barack Obama and John Edwards were not on the ballot. Clinton wins handily, although there is a large vote for 'Uncommitted', in part because of an effort by Obama supporters urging people to vote that way rather than for Clinton.

Race enters the Democratic race

The tone of the Democratic contest is taking on a distinctly bitter edge. Hillary Clinton is sharpening her attacks on Barack Obama, accusing him of being 'a talker, not a doer'. For his part, Obama repeatedly accuses Clinton of being 'relentlessly negative'.

Despite having its biggest trade union declare for Obama, Clinton wins Nevada comfortably on 19 January, although, as a few people note, Obama actually wins one more delegate than her from the contest, due to the arcane rules of Democratic caucuses. Nevertheless, having won two contests in a row, Clinton is now the candidate with momentum, and South Carolina becomes a must-win state for Obama. He needs the great majority of its large black population to vote for him if he is to succeed here. This seems likelier than it did before Iowa. In 2007 Obama trailed Clinton in polls of African-Americans across the country. Most black voters wanted a Democrat president first and foremost, and there was a sense of pessimism amongst many that a black man could ever reach the White House. Not only that, but the Clintons have been supporters of black rights, and have enjoyed the loyalty of the black community, throughout their political careers. When Bill Clinton was disgraced by the Monica Lewinsky scandal it was in black churches that he sought forgiveness, and black leaders who stood up for him in public. But since Obama's Iowa win, African-American voters have flocked to him, persuaded that the implausible prospect of a black president might just have become real.

Obama's blackness, and the question of racism, were not often discussed in public during the Iowa and New Hampshire contests. But as the campaign has moved south, to states with large African-American populations and high racial tensions, the subject of race has suddenly become fraught in a way it never was in the early states.

Hillary Clinton, seeking to define the difference between Obama's rhetoric and her ability to get things done, draws a rather unwise analogy. Referring to civil rights legislation, she points out that although Martin Luther King proposed it, 'it took a president [Lyndon Johnson] to get it done'. Bloggers and TV pundits pick up on this remark and portray it as an insult to the memory of King and an attempt to suggest that Obama, as a black man, is not fit to govern. This is unlikely: King was a childhood hero of Clinton's, and it was the civil rights movement that drew her away from the Republican Party. In response to criticism, Clinton accuses the Obama campaign of stoking the controversy in order to drive up its share of the African-American vote in South Carolina. The argument rattles on for days, threatening to obliterate all other issues.

In a little-noticed sideshow, Obama's former pastor in Chicago, and the man he describes as his spiritual mentor, makes the news with a ribald remark about Bill Clinton. From the pulpit of his church, Rev. Jeremiah Wright says that Clinton will do to black people what 'he did to Monica Lewinsky'. Obama repudiates the comment, describing Wright as akin to a 'cranky uncle' with whom he often disagreed.

Two for the price of one

Bill Clinton is angry again. At a campaign stop in Nevada he is passing through a room crowded with supporters, aides and journalists, shaking hands and having his picture taken, when he is addressed by a nervous-sounding reporter from the local TV station. Nevada, like Iowa, holds a caucus, and there has been controversy over who is being allowed to vote and when. The reporter wants to know why the Hillary Clinton campaign seems to be supporting a lawsuit that would change the voting rules at this late stage. Bill Clinton turns back from a conversation with a supporter to hear the questioner, and as he does so his smile fades. He runs his tongue around his mouth and makes the reporter repeat his question. Behind Clinton stands one of his media handlers, head bowed, his face the picture of a man who knows exactly what is coming but doesn't have the power to stop it. Within minutes, Clinton is in full flow, his face empurpled, his finger jabbing towards the reporter's chest as he checks off the reasons why the voting process is unfair. 'Don't be accusatory with me,' he says, inches from the reporter's face. The whole encounter is posted to the internet and becomes a YouTube hit within hours.

Bill Clinton's temper is proving to be an unstable agent in the already volatile compound of Hillary Clinton's campaign. On the stump, Bill has become the campaign's attack dog – though nobody is sure how long his leash is, if indeed there is one. Using stronger language than his wife, Clinton repeatedly criticises Barack Obama for his record on the Iraq War and his inexperience. During Q&A sessions with voters he will often wind himself up into a red-faced, finger-wagging rant at the unfair treatment his wife receives from the media.

For Clinton, this contest is deeply personal. For one thing, he feels that his presidential legacy is in danger of being besmirched. Obama remarks in an interview that 'Ronald Reagan changed the trajectory of

America in a way that Richard Nixon did not and Bill Clinton did not'. Nothing could be more guaranteed to enrage the former president. To be lumped with Nixon! That hurts. But perhaps the worst of it is that Obama is running, in some ways, a similar campaign to Clinton in 1992: the candidate of youth and hope who promises to bring change to his own party. This time it is Clinton and his wife who are portrayed as the baggage that the party needs to discard.

There are signs that Clinton's angry aggression is destabilising the usually unflappable Obama, who believes that Clinton is wilfully distorting his record on Iraq. At an event in Greenwood, South Carolina, a *New York Times* reporter shouts a question to Obama. 'Are you allowing President Clinton to get in your head?' Obama's response is revealing. He snaps at the reporter for trying a 'cheap stunt'. Then he says he will answer but only off the record. When the reporter refuses, Obama accuses the other side of 'saying false things about us' before striding away. Without meaning to, he seems to have answered the question.

Obama tells an interviewer on *Good Morning America* that he faces a 'formidable opponent – in fact, two formidable opponents, between Senator Clinton and President Clinton'. In a debate during the week of the South Carolina primary, Obama tells Hillary Clinton he's 'not sure who he's running against sometimes'. The debate, which features the three remaining candidates, is by far the worst tempered of the Democratic ones so far. Obama and Clinton throw fresh grenades at each other, mentioning facts about their opponent's past they haven't raised before. Obama reminds the public of Clinton's time on the board of Wal-Mart, and Clinton raises the name of Tony Rezko, a former associate of Obama's now on trial for fraud. Clinton accuses Obama of 'never giving a straight answer', and Obama calls Clinton's honesty into question. The political has become deeply personal.

John Edwards has to struggle to be heard, although he leaps in on Clinton's side in a debate over health insurance. Edwards knows that unless he does well in South Carolina, which neighbours his home state, he will struggle to carry on as a viable candidate. Since New Hampshire he has changed his calculations, figuring that if Obama fails in South Carolina, he will emerge as Clinton's strongest opponent. He throws Obama an irritated glance when the latter, talking about the pioneering status of the contest, calls it a race between 'an African-American, a woman . . . and John'.

The debate closes with a discussion of who will be the best candidate to take on John McCain, a reflection of how much McCain is now perceived as the Republican front-runner.

If Clinton wins in South Carolina, Obama's candidacy is over. But it's a steep hill to climb. Clinton's aides play down expectations to the press, and in private advise both Clintons not to waste time there. But Bill insists, citing his ability to connect to black voters as well as working-class whites. He works the Palmetto State hard, moving from small town to small town to make the case for his wife, a southerner talking to southerners, confident that the old magic will prevail. 'We can win anywhere!' he says to colleagues who claim it is a waste of time and money. But when voting day comes, it becomes clear that he is wrong. The polls show Obama ahead, and this time, unlike in New Hampshire, Clinton does not sniff an upset.

On voting day morning, he is asked a casual question by a reporter about whether it takes 'two Clintons' to beat Obama. Clinton replies, seemingly à propos not very much, that 'Jesse Jackson won South Carolina in '84 and '88. Jackson ran a good campaign. And Obama ran a good campaign here.' For those who have accused the former president of attempting to pigeonhole Obama as 'the black candidate', this is devastating evidence. The clip becomes another YouTube sensation and sets off a firestorm of criticism from blacks and whites alike.

Whether or not Clinton's comment has any effect on South Carolina's vote is unclear. But that night, Obama wins such a convincing victory that he recaptures the momentum he lost after New Hampshire. He gains roughly double the votes of Hillary Clinton. Blacks vote overwhelmingly for him, and he wins a large slice of the white vote too, bolstering his contention that he can put together a winning coalition in the general election. In his victory speech, Obama describes the vote as a clear message to those who thought his Iowa win was 'a fluke'. He then turns his scorn on 'the idea that it's acceptable to say anything or do anything to win an election'. His target – the Clintons, including and especially Bill – is unmistakable.

The fact that eight out of ten African-Americans voted for Obama seems to suggest that Bill Clinton has damaged his own credibility, and that of his wife's, by engaging in what many have interpreted as an attempt to marginalise the Illinois senator as a minority candidate. Clinton's dismissal of Obama's position on Iraq as a 'fairy tale', and his reference to Obama as 'a kid', have aroused anger in a community sensitive to being patronised by white politicians. Jim Clyburn, an African-American congressman from South Carolina, calls Clinton on the night of the primary, unhappy with his remarks. He advises the former president to cool his tone. Clinton responds furiously, insulting Clyburn.

Some commentators wonder if, messy as it seems, Clinton is doing his wife a favour. His credibility with the black community has taken a hit. But by starting these fires, Clinton is getting voters across the country to think of Obama as the black candidate, rather than as a candidate who happens to be black. It may be worth losing South Carolina if it means winning in California and New Jersey. Clyburn, for one, believes the former president knows exactly what he is doing. 'Nothing in this campaign has been by accident,' he says of Clinton's various remarks.

Wittingly or not, however, Clinton's attacks rebound as much as they hit home. Or, as one who has known Clinton since his Arkansas days puts it, 'that gun kicks as bad as it shoots'.

A torch is passed

Another Democrat who privately asks Bill Clinton to tone down his attacks on Barack Obama is Ted Kennedy, the grand old man of the Democratic Party and a hugely influential figure. Just as Jim Clyburn did, he receives a blistering response. From that moment, Kennedy – already an admirer of Obama and never a great friend of the Clintons – begins to seriously consider a public endorsement of the young challenger. His niece shows the way. The day after South Carolina, the *New York Times* publishes an editorial by Caroline Kennedy, JFK's daughter, announcing her support for Obama, comparing the excitement he is inspiring to that generated by her father.

The next weekend, Ted Kennedy follows suit. Flanked by Caroline and his son Patrick (a congressman and early Obama supporter), Kennedy announces his endorsement of Obama at a huge rally in Washington, D.C. Though his heavy frame is stooped by age he moves and talks with vigour. He offers a rousing declaration of his belief that Obama's moment has arrived: 'It is time for a new generation of leadership,' he says. 'It is time now for Barack Obama.'

The passing on of the Kennedy torch is a resonant moment, and it comes as a powerful boost for Obama as he prepares to face his toughest test yet. Next week, twenty-two states will have their say, on the day known as Super Tuesday. For Hillary Clinton, Super Tuesday is a chance to re-establish her primacy as the front-runner, and perhaps even to finish the job off.

John Edwards, however, will sit it out. After coming third in

South Carolina, he finally decides that his long campaign for the 2008 nomination is over. He announces the end of his candidacy in the place where he announced its beginning a year ago: the Ninth Ward of New Orleans, devastated by Hurricane Katrina. Edwards says that he has extracted a promise from both remaining candidates to make the cause of fighting poverty central to their presidential campaigns. Both Obama and Clinton, covetous of Edwards's strong support amongst the white working classes, would love his endorsement. But, at least for the time being, Edwards remains neutral.

The Republicans: finally, a front-runner

On the day that Hillary Clinton wins Nevada, John McCain wins South Carolina, the scene of his defeat to George W. Bush in 2000. It's an emotional moment for the candidate and his closest advisers. 'It took us a while,' says McCain to the crowds at his victory celebration. 'But what's eight years between friends?'

Though Mike Huckabee comes a close second, his failure to take a state with such a high proportion of evangelical voters means that his chances of winning the nomination are now negligible. Fred Thompson's poor showing in a southern state signals the end for his campaign, and a few days later he drops out, his much-anticipated candidacy having never got out of first gear. Mitt Romney didn't spend much time in South Carolina; like Rudy Giuliani, his hopes are pinned on Florida at the end of the month.

Giuliani knows that he will be following John Edwards out of the race unless he wins in Florida. It doesn't look likely. Speaking to supporters in Longboat Key, sweat beading on his lip, he tells everyone to ignore the polls that show him trailing the field, and to 'vote for positive things, because positive things can change society'. The vacuity of his rhetoric betrays a candidate uncertain of himself. Giuliani is no longer the supremely self-assured figure who captivated audiences with stories of crimebusting in New York and heroism on 9/11 – the man who dominated the Republican field in 2007. He is nervous, eager to please, keen to get away.

When Florida's result comes in, Giuliani finishes a distant third behind Romney and McCain. The man seen as the Republicans' saviour less than six months ago drops out, perhaps with a measure of relief, and endorses McCain.

In some ways, Giuliani's campaign strategy went to plan. Three different candidates won the first three primaries, leaving no clear front-runner by the time the contest moved down to Florida. But his advisers miscalculated the national impact of his losses in the early states. They also, perhaps, misjudged their candidate. Unlike the new favourite to win the nomination, Giuliani does not wear adversity well. When confident of prevailing, he impresses and intimidates. But when he is losing, he shrinks in stature faster than most. The fatal mistake of his advisers was to construct a strategy that ignored the effect of momentum, around a candidate acutely reliant on it.

The night's big winner is McCain, now firmly established as the favourite to win his party's nomination. Romney says he will fight on through Super Tuesday, as does Huckabee. But the Republican establishment is now beginning to adjust to the likelihood that the man who has often been their biggest critic is about to take effective leadership of the party. It's that kind of year.

February 2008

Super Tuesday: California dreaming

It is 3 February, a Sunday afternoon. Before a crowd of thousands at the University of California, Los Angeles, three women take turns to make the case for Barack Obama: Caroline Kennedy, Michelle Obama and Oprah Winfrey. After they have all spoken, Michelle Obama tells the audience that they have a surprise guest. It is someone, she says, who is here 'not because anybody told her to be here', but 'because of what she believes' – a hint that this is not a conventional political endorsement. 'It is my honour', says Obama, 'to introduce to you the first lady of the state.'

Amidst screams of excitement a woman in a long orange coat bounds onto the stage: Maria Shriver, journalist, niece of John Kennedy and wife of California's Republican governor, Arnold Schwarzenegger.

After two minutes the crowd allow her to speak. 'OK, sit down, girls,' says Shriver to the women onstage. She apologises for not having brushed her hair or done her make-up, and explains that that she has come straight from her daughter's equestrian show. Shriver decided only a few hours ago to endorse Barack Obama at today's rally, and wavered up until the last minute (after all, her husband is supporting John McCain). Obama's aides were uncertain she would make it until virtually the moment she turned up.

Now she is here, Shriver explains why she took her decision. 'If Barack Obama was a state, he'd be California,' she tells her ecstatic audience. A cheer greets each of the attributes she says candidate and state have in common: 'Diverse. Open. Smart. Independent. Bucks tradition. Innovative. Inspirational. Dreamer. Leader.'

In two days, voters across the country will get to have their say in the great Clinton–Obama battle; twenty-two states will choose the man or woman they wish to be the nominee. Much of the media's coverage of Super Tuesday is focused on California, where Obama appears to be closing in on Hillary Clinton, who has long been confident of victory here. If he can make inroads into Clinton's voters, particularly women, he might just pull off an upset that will swing the whole contest decisively in his favour. Today's starry parade of prominent female supporters is designed to help him do that.

There is little discussion of policy this evening. As befitting a rally held in the shadow of Hollywood, this is entertainment as much as a political event. Stevie Wonder is led onto the stage by Michelle Obama. Standing at the podium he plays a few notes on his harmonica before asking the crowd to join him in singing the candidate's name, ascending and descending a scale: '*Ba-a-rack O-ba-a-ma. . . Ba-a-rack O-ba-a-ma. . .*' Giant screens play a video featuring will.i.am of the Black Eyed Peas and a host of other celebrities singing a tribute to Obama. The video, already viewed by millions on YouTube, cuts together clips from Obama's speeches, transforming the cadences of his words into song, and Obama's famous refrain into a chorus: *Yes We Can*.

The rally and the video embody something unique about Obama's candidacy: the sense that it is a pop-cultural phenomenon as well as a political campaign. Presidential candidates, especially Democrats, often get a little help from their friends in the entertainment industry. But the Obama campaign has its own star power. The candidate is an undisputed, hotter-than-hot celebrity himself: his face shifts magazines and sells books, and millions wear his familiar logo on a badge or T-shirt or baseball cap. Many of his supporters are young people who have previously shown little interest in politics. Thousands of them produce homemade tributes in the form of web videos. Some, like a spoof of Apple's celebrated '1984' ad, with Clinton in the role of Big Brother, may have had a real impact on the race in the months before Iowa. Others, like the cheeky 'Obama Girl' series, in which a young woman sings about her crush on the candidate, have been entertaining diversions. All have contributed to the sense that Obama's is not a conventional political candidacy.

But not all voters are impressed by pop songs, YouTube videos and celebrity endorsements. Many are suspicious of Obama's pop-cultural acclaim. What, they ask, lies behind it? After all, this man is running for the presidency, not for the job of presenting a talk show.

The battle for delegates

On 1 February at Southern Illinois University, Bill Clinton speaks for an hour to a crowded auditorium, filled mostly by college students who have queued up in the cold to get in. He covers his wife's ideas on health care, the environment, college tuition and the Iraq War. On his best behaviour, the former president doesn't even mention Barack Obama.

The Clinton campaign knows it cannot win Illinois, which holds its primary on Super Tuesday. Obama is highly popular in his home state. That Hillary Clinton's chief surrogate is making a stop here illustrates how both campaigns are focusing on the fight for delegates, rather than just states.

To win the nomination, one candidate must be awarded a majority of the party's delegates, and on Super Tuesday, almost half the remaining delegates will be allocated in primaries and caucuses across the country. Historically, one candidate has usually established himself as the clear front-runner by the time Super Tuesday comes around – it is often little more than a coronation. The primary calendar is designed to propel one candidate to the forefront early in the year, so that the race can be wrapped up quickly and the winner can focus on the general election.

If either Clinton or Obama had won both Iowa and New Hampshire, that might have happened this year. But the stunning results in those early states, awarding a victory each to the two strongest candidates, have turned what might have been a lightning campaign into trench warfare. This race now looks likely to go on long beyond Tuesday, and advisers to both candidates are grappling with the complex mathematics of delegate allocation in the remaining contests.

In such a close race, every delegate counts. Under Democratic Party rules, a state's delegates are awarded according to each candidate's share of the vote in that primary, and more delegates are awarded in districts where turnouts are historically higher. That's why Bill Clinton is stumping on Obama's home turf. By narrowing Obama's margin of victory in southern Illinois the Clinton campaign team hope to pick up a few more delegates in a state they know they will lose. The Obama campaign is running ads in New York, Clinton's adopted home state, in the hope of doing the same thing.

Super Tuesday is the first point at which the race for votes, and delegates, goes national. Unlike in the early states, it's a battle that must be fought remotely for the most part, via advertising, media exposure and local party organisation. It therefore rewards the well known and the well connected. Hillary Clinton has the most famous name in politics and over the years has built up, with her husband, strong relationships with Democrat officials in every state. In other words, she has a head-start on Tuesday. Obama, however, has David Plouffe.

Along with David Axelrod, Obama's chief strategic adviser, Plouffe is one of the two most important people on Obama's team. Axelrod oversees the campaign's overall message, and often appears on television as a spokesperson for Obama. Plouffe is Obama's campaign manager. He makes few media appearances and is rarely profiled in the press. His work does not lend itself to the easy characterisation that has turned spin doctors like James Carville and Karl Rove into Washington celebrities. Plouffe is a details man, a logistics man, a metrics man. He is fascinated by data. He sweats over every variable in the election and tries to put a number to it. He trusts his numbers more than he trusts conventional wisdoms or the abundant advice of well-meaning outsiders: he is not afraid to do things differently if the data suggest he should. In eighteen months, he has overseen the creation of the most innovative and effective presidential campaign in Democratic history.

At forty-one, Plouffe was by no means a well-known name, even in Democratic circles, when Obama picked him to manage his team. He had worked on Richard Gephardt's 2004 presidential bid and before that for the Iowa senator Tom Harkin's, but never on a general election. He co-owns a consulting business in Chicago with Axelrod, who introduced him to Obama. The three men bonded when they worked together during Obama's successful 2004 run for the Senate. Temperamentally, Plouffe and Obama are a good match: like his boss, Plouffe is rarely flustered, avoids emotional highs and lows, but possesses a driving, implacable will to win.

Pale, lean and understated, Plouffe speaks so quietly that colleagues complain it is sometimes difficult to hear what he's saying. But he is the dominant presence in the campaign's Chicago headquarters, and in his low-key way he exudes confidence, even when things aren't going well. He impresses on all staff the importance of staying calm, being disciplined, and keeping disagreements in house. Brilliant at raising money for his candidate, he hates spending it on anything other than the essentials. Staffers get paid less than their Clinton counterparts, and are asked to double up in hotel rooms when on the road. It is said that the bathroom towel-dispenser at Obama HQ issues only one towel per visit – try it a second time and a note comes out: 'See Plouffe.'

When he started his planning for Super Tuesday, nearly a year ago, Plouffe knew that its sheer scale played to Clinton's strengths. But as he sized up the states in play and performed delegate calculations, he realised that it might be possible to neutralise Clinton's advantages on 5 February by targeting winnable primaries overlooked by her campaign, and by applying a meticulous, precinct-by-precinct approach to caucus states. He set up field offices in Idaho, Kansas and Colorado long before Clinton's people arrived. Volunteers were recruited, voters canvassed and local operatives engaged. In Iowa, Plouffe planned and executed an on-the-ground operation of such originality and sophistication that it reached thousands of new voters untapped by Clinton's more traditional effort. The conventional wisdom is that Super Tuesday is all about the media 'air war' rather than the ground game. Plouffe differs. He aims to turn the entire country into Iowa.

The Republicans hold their own Super Tuesday on the same date. But with John McCain firmly in the driving seat, their race is looking more predictable. The nation – and much of the world – is transfixed by the Democratic contest.

Clinton and Obama are nearly neck and neck in national polls, with Clinton hanging on to a small lead. But the UCLA rally, and Maria Shriver's endorsement, contribute to the sense that Obama is unstoppable: that a Californian tidal wave of enthusiasm is about to sweep him to victory here and across the country.

Clinton would find it almost impossible to recover from a loss in the Golden State. Not for the first time, the pundits foresee an imminent end to her campaign.

Super Tuesday: the verdict

On the evening of 5 February, in a ballroom high up above Manhattan, Hillary Clinton's supporters are sipping drinks and nervously watching a big screen for the early results. At 9.46 p.m. CNN flashes the result of the Massachusetts primary. It shows Clinton winning, 59 per cent to 38 per cent. The crowd in the room roars appreciation. 'Holy shit!' exclaims a Clinton aide with delight, and perhaps relief. Clinton was expected to win this state. But after Ted Kennedy – the state's popular senior senator – had endorsed Barack Obama, and the state's other senator, John Kerry, had campaigned vigorously for Clinton's opponent there, many had predicted an upset. They were wrong. Clinton has not only beaten Obama in Massachusetts, she has trounced him.

As more results come in, it is clear that, at the very least, Clinton has held her own and fought off an apparent surge in Obama's support. She wins New Jersey, which despite its proximity to her home state of New York had seemed to be in the balance. Most satisfyingly, she wins California decisively. Two groups of voters, long loyal to her and her husband, see her to victory there: Hispanics and women, who back Clinton despite the exhortations of Oprah Winfrey and Maria Shriver.

At 11 p.m. Clinton appears on stage in the ballroom. Her speech is triumphal. 'Tonight we are hearing the voices of people across

America,' she says. Clinton dances and claps to the music as red, white and blue confetti rains down on a happy crowd. Her campaign surrogates, including the film director Rob Reiner and New York's governor, Eliot Spitzer, are on the floor talking to reporters, spinning the result as a sure sign that the country is swinging behind their candidate. They emphasise that the states Clinton has taken are the biggest, the most populous and the richest in delegates.

By contrast, the Obama campaign's spin is muted. His team remind reporters that Clinton had always been expected to win most of the states she took today, and that although she has done well on the coasts, their candidate has won a string of victories in states across the heartland, including Georgia, Colorado and – when the result eventually comes in – the key Midwestern state of Missouri, albeit by a whisker.

Spin and the spreadsheet

The next day it is Hillary Clinton who wins the battle of momentum. Predictions that she would be swept away by the enthusiasm for Barack Obama have been confounded, and the resilience of her support is acclaimed. Her team enjoy a moment of vindication. 'We had to listen to two weeks of "Oh, you're not having rallies, you're not appearing with celebrities, you're having these boring discussions about issues",' says one Clintonite. Some in the media declare that Obama's surge has peaked, that Clinton has regained her mojo, and that a candidacy fuelled by hype has come up hard against unyielding electoral reality.

But this story is itself a kind of hype. Those who examine the details of the likely allocations of delegates awarded on Super Tuesday, and in the remaining contests, discern something more fundamental. These two candidates are still in a tight race for delegates, and Clinton is only slightly ahead. What's more, the next two weeks hold a series of primaries in states favourable to Obama. By emerging from Super Tuesday within striking distance of Clinton, Obama has given himself every chance of overtaking her.

This is just about where David Plouffe thought the Obama campaign would be on 6 February. Back in 2007, Plouffe – who obsesses over baseball statistics in his spare time – spent countless hours studying the complex maths of delegate allocation in every primary or caucus right up until Puerto Rico had its say in early June. Combining demographic data with his own hunches he constructed an elaborate, colour-coded spreadsheet predicting how each state would swing in terms of the popular vote and delegate allocation. It showed that if Obama could keep things close on Super Tuesday, he would have a better-than-evens shot at winning a majority of elected delegates.

Even that wouldn't guarantee Obama the nomination, however. Not all delegates that count towards the nomination are allocated by the popular vote. About a fifth – or 800 of them – can make up their own minds. These are the so-called 'superdelegates'. They consist of members of Congress, governors, party chairmen and other senior officials: essentially, the Democratic Party establishment. Their official role is to act as an independent counterweight to the will of the voters.

Plouffe's spreadsheet told him that though his candidate might well win a majority of elected (or 'pledged') delegates, neither candidate was likely to win this contest with those delegates alone. Obama and Clinton were just too closely matched. Either would need the support of a good proportion of superdelegates to win an outright delegate majority.

The Clintons' powerful position within the party means that they can call on the votes of many superdelegates with whom they have relationships or for whom they have done favours in the past. Indeed, although only a minority of superdelegates have endorsed either candidate, most of those that have done so have declared for Hillary. Plouffe aims to ensure that the remaining superdelegates realise that Obama is the favourite to win more pledged delegates – and to seed the idea that bucking the popular will, thus expressed, would be undemocratic.

Two days after 5 February, as the party and the media are sifting through the implications of Tuesday's results, Plouffe arranges for his spreadsheet to find its way into the press. It is an unusual move for a campaign that abhors leaks. But it helps to achieve his aims: the compelling statistical argument convinces many that Obama has a very realistic chance of winning, despite Clinton's solid performance on Super Tuesday. It also starts to establish a candidate's total of pledged delegates as *the* standard for a victory. The spreadsheet is just one part of Plouffe's meticulous plan. Obama and his aides have been calling superdelegates for months, in a persuasion operation that far exceeds anything the Clinton campaign has attempted.

Not coincidentally, in the days and weeks after Super Tuesday a consensus begins to emerge in the party and the media that whoever wins more pledged delegates should be the nominee – and that party superdelegates should simply follow the will of the voters. Of course, this negates their original purpose. But it serves the purposes of the Obama campaign very well.

Romney concedes gold

Unlike the Democrats, the Republicans have a clear winner coming out of Super Tuesday. John McCain does well enough to establish himself as the almost-certain Republican nominee, winning the big states of California, New York and Missouri. His main rival, Mitt Romney, wins only a few small states alongside those to which he has a strong personal connection.

But Tuesday didn't bring McCain quite the kind of all-conquering sweep he would have liked. Mike Huckabee did surprisingly well, winning five southern states: Alabama, Georgia, Tennessee, West Virginia and his home state of Arkansas. Nobody expects Huckabee to overtake McCain and win the nomination, least of all Huckabee, who is already thinking beyond this election to the next one, when he might launch a more substantial challenge. But his victories expose McCain's weaknesses in the Bible Belt. Exit polls confirm that McCain did poorly amongst conservative Republicans everywhere.

The hard right of the party distrusts and dislikes McCain, and has done so ever since his explosive battle against their champion in 2000, George W. Bush. In the run up to Super Tuesday, McCain is on the receiving end of diatribes from high-profile conservative figures such as the radio host Rush Limbaugh and the evangelical leader James Dobson. 'I will never vote for that man,' says Dobson.

Though they also distrust Romney, conservative hardliners had relied on him to defeat McCain. But on Thursday of that week, their last best hope stands down. Speaking before a group of right-wing activists, Romney announces that his expensive quest for the nomination has come to an end. His audience are surprised and dejected.

As he speaks, Romney may be reflecting that it was his attempt to convince the party's conservative faithful that he was one of them that cost him the nomination. In 1994, after his defeat to Ted Kennedy in a race for the Senate, Romney vowed to friends and family that he would never again enter a contest he wasn't confident of winning. He planned his presidential run with characteristic care, hiring some of the party's best advisers and constructing an efficient organisation in the early states. His team's carefully worked-out strategy was to position Romney as a true social conservative, in contrast to the front-runner, Rudy Giuliani, and McCain. But they hadn't counted on Huckabee. The emergence of an unquestionably authentic conservative highlighted Romney's tardy conversion to the cause. By the time Romney switched emphasis and focused on a message of can-do economic competence aimed at a broader audience, it was too late. Voters had decided that he would say anything to win the nomination. In other words, they concluded that he was a typical politician, in a year when nothing could be a surer guarantee of defeat.

McCain is the fortunate beneficiary of the Huckabee factor, and two hours after Romney's resignation from the race, he speaks to the same audience. At first he is received politely. But when he mentions one of the issues on which he has differed with the right – immigration – he is loudly booed. McCain can only stand and grin uncomfortably as he waits for the crowd to settle.

The booing is in vain. Although Huckabee will carry on out of a desire to increase his national profile and through sheer enjoyment, nobody expects him to make much further impact on the race. Whether they like it or not, McCain and the conservative wing of the Republican Party are stuck with each other.

Dark days for Hillary Clinton

On 15 February Congressman Jim Clyburn goes public with his concerns about Bill Clinton's tone. He suggests that the high black turnout in South Carolina and subsequent states was partially motivated by anger at the Clinton campaign – and at the former president's use of racially charged language in particular: 'Those of us who live in the south, we know the code words when we hear them, and we understand the tone.' Clyburn's reverberant comments are just one reason that Clinton campaign's satisfaction with its Super Tuesday performance has dissipated.

On the weekend after 5 February, Barack Obama wins victories in Louisiana, Nebraska, Washington state and Maine. These are caucus states, like Iowa, and the Obama campaign once again out-organises the Clintons. It outspends them too; David Plouffe has conserved the campaign's money for this stretch of the race. By contrast, the Clintons have blown their budget on Super Tuesday. It is revealed that Hillary Clinton has had to personally lend her campaign $5 million.

Clinton fires her campaign manager, Patti Solis Doyle, and replaces her a with a highly respected aide and old friend, Maggie Williams, who had already been brought in to steady the ship. It represents a belated recognition by Clinton that her campaign has been grossly mismanaged - and that she is in imminent danger of losing this contest.

Solis Doyle was a long-time colleague, confidante and fixer for Clinton. The two were very close – almost sisterly. Her appointment to such a senior role was a cause of concern for some Clintonites, including Bill Clinton's old team, who pointed out that she had no experience of running presidential campaigns. But Solis Doyle had the unquestioned trust and confidence of Hillary, and that was enough to get her the job.

It is now clear, however, that the huge amount of money raised by the campaign has been seriously misspent. After Iowa, Bill Clinton sat down with staff at campaign headquarters and pored over the books, and was horrified to discover how little cash was left. Hillary Clinton's New Hampshire triumph gave Solis Doyle a stay of execution. But when the financial situation gets so bad that the candidate has to fund her own campaign in order to get through Super Tuesday – leaving no money to keep the following weekend's contests even close – a stunned Clinton acknowledges that her old friend has to go. It is a brutal severance: Clinton feeling betrayed by her friend's incompetence, Solis Doyle that she is being scapegoated.

Williams faces a tough job. None of Clinton's key lieutenants likes each other, and a noxious atmosphere of mistrust pervades campaign headquarters. On the day she takes over, Williams speaks to the assembled staffers. 'You may not like the person next to you,' she says. 'But you're going to respect them. And we're going to work together.'

Meanwhile, the Obama campaign rolls on, winning heavy victories in three 'Potomac states': Virginia, Maryland and Washington, D.C. He emerges with a lead of about 150 pledged delegates. Given the way in which delegates are allocated, Clinton will find it very hard to overtake unless she is able to pull out landslide victories in future primaries, a highly unlikely prospect. The Obama campaign is the first to realise this, or at least to fully understand its implications.

Plouffe now does something else unusual: he makes a bold public statement. Concerned that the press haven't quite grasped the new reality, he points out to them that to all intents and purposes, the Obama campaign has the race for pledged delegates wrapped up. He hopes to dispel the idea that the two candidates are in a dead heat, and to persuade superdelegates to rally to Obama by establishing that the people – represented by pledged delegates – have already spoken.

Clinton and her team scornfully reject Plouffe's assertion. But they are forced to open up two new fronts in the daily arguments they make to the press. First, the Michigan and Florida votes should count. Both states moved their primaries earlier in the process against the wishes of party bosses, and have been told that as punishment their delegates will not be seated at the convention. Clinton argues that the decision should be reversed, and that to do otherwise is to disenfranchise millions of voters. She 'won' both states, although Obama campaigned in neither and took his name off the ballot in

Michigan. Second, the party's superdelegates should exercise their own judgement about who would be the better candidate, rather than simply follow the verdict of the voters (it does not go unnoticed that these two positions may not be entirely harmonious). The Clintons recognise that only the superdelegates can save them now. Hillary, Bill and their surrogates work the phones, cajoling, charming and bullying every one of the 800 party officials who hold the future of this race in their hands. But it is hard going. The Obama campaign has done a good job of establishing the pledged-delegate count as the will of the people in numeric form. And, this year in particular, nobody wants to be seen to be opposing the will of the people.

Clinton fights back

Even more urgently, Hillary Clinton knows that she must do well in two big upcoming primaries: Texas and Ohio on 4 March. Having spent $120 million to end up in second place, her campaign is in a desperate scramble to raise money to contest two states it never seriously envisaged having to compete in.

The Obama campaign is riding high. It announces that the number of its donors has passed the million mark. A few days after the Potomac primaries, Obama wins Wisconsin and his home state of Hawaii, making it ten straight victories in a row. Clinton, campaigning in Ohio, makes a speech that evening denigrating Obama's lack of experience. Rather than waiting to hear that she has finished, as is customary, Obama starts his victory speech while she is still talking, forcing the cable networks to cut her off mid-flow. It is a small sign of the bad feeling between the two camps – and of Obama's burgeoning confidence.

Meanwhile, a comment made by Michelle Obama on the stump

in Wisconsin the day before has started a fire in the conservative blog-osphere. Speaking about the excitement and participation inspired by her husband's campaign, she says: 'For the first time in my adult lifetime, I am really proud of my country.' Critics immediately accuse her of not being a true patriot, or at least for displaying a peculiarly self-centred view of patriotism. Right-wing bloggers are starting to put together a caricature of the Obamas as elitists whose values are fundamentally alien to those of America – and they have just been handed a gift.

Clinton doesn't address Michelle Obama's remarks, but seeks other ways to tarnish Barack Obama's image in the weeks before Texas and Ohio. She employs several lines of attack at once.

A video finds its way on to YouTube showing a section of Obama's stump speech intercut with a speech by the Massachusetts governor, Deval Patrick. Obama appears to have copied a riff about how 'words matter' from Patrick. Clinton accuses Obama of plagiarism and ques-tions his integrity. Obama, a friend of Patrick's, attempts to brush it off. Elsewhere, a photograph of Obama in Somali garb, taken during an official visit, appears on the influential website the Drudge Report. Although the Clinton campaign denies sending the picture to the site, the Obama campaign accuses it of 'shameful fear-mongering'. Clinton also tries sarcasm, satirising Obama's high-flown rhetoric: 'I could stand up here and say let's just get everybody together, let's get unified. The sky will open, the light will come down, celestial choirs will be singing, and everyone will know that we should do the right thing, and the world will be perfect.'

But the theme that Clinton zeroes in on, as Texas and Ohio approach, is her superior readiness to be commander in chief. 'We need a president who knows how to deploy both the olive branch and the arrows, who will be ready to act swiftly and decisively in a crisis.'

The Clinton campaign also mounts a parallel attack: on the

media. The Clintons' grizzled *consigliere*, Harold Ickes, and spokesman Phil Singer sit down with reporters for breakfast in a D.C. restaurant. They express their frustration with how the race has been covered, arguing that there has been a strong bias towards Obama. Singer refers to a much-viewed *Saturday Night Live* sketch from the week before in which debate moderators ask Obama a series of absurdly fawning questions. The reporters do not take kindly to the comparison, and suggest that Ickes and Singer wouldn't be complaining if their candidate were winning. Ickes expresses his confidence in Clinton's victory, stretching credulity by cheerfully pronouncing that 'we're on our way to locking this nomination down'. A reporter reminds him that Obama's delegate lead is now of a size that Ickes once said would be 'significant'. 'As we all know in this town,' Ickes replies, 'I have a very short memory.'

In a televised debate at the end of the month, Clinton unexpectedly mentions the *Saturday Night Live* skit herself, launching into a tirade right at the beginning of the session after what she perceives to be an unfair opening question. She and her husband believe passionately that the media have set out to destroy her candidacy – and they want voters to share their outrage.

As the month comes to an end, Clinton is throwing punches in all directions and hoping that at least one of them will land.

The *New York Times* helps McCain

John McCain, now the Republicans' presumptive nominee, has been somewhat overshadowed by the continuing Democratic contest. But his efforts to consolidate his party's conservative wing behind him receive a boost from an unexpected quarter: the *New York Times*.

The newspaper publishes a story detailing McCain's relationship with a female telecommunications lobbyist. The story, ostensibly about a conflict of interest, hints heavily that the senator conducted an affair with the woman, but it does it not say so explicitly. The McCain team fight back ferociously, accusing the paper of engaging in a 'hit and run smear campaign'. Suddenly, conservative talk show hosts and politicians who have been sharply critical of McCain rally to him, united by a common enemy: the *New York Times*, which they have long regarded as a bastion of establishment liberalism. McCain's team even make an online fundraising appeal based on the story.

Hillary Clinton is hoping that the seeming hostility of the media to her candidacy will have a similarly galvanising effect on her supporters. And she needs every vote she can find if her candidacy is to survive the first week of March.

March 2008

Fighter, doer, champion

The news shows, blogs and papers buzz and crackle with data on the Democratic race: polls, delegate counts, fundraising figures, advertising spends. Beneath the analysis, one thing everyone agrees is that when Texas and Ohio vote on Tuesday 4 March, Hillary Clinton faces the stark possibility of defeat in her bid for the presidency.

Even her chief strategist appears to think the end may be near. In an email to a reporter, Mark Penn plays down his role in Clinton's campaign. He has 'no direct authority', he says, and is merely 'an outside message adviser with no campaign staff reporting to me'. His senior colleagues are quick to demur.

At the beginning of the month, polls show Texas in a dead heat, and in Ohio Clinton's lead has shrunk to a few percentage points. If both Texas and Ohio go Barack Obama's way on Tuesday, the game will be up for Clinton. Indeed, if she loses just one of them she will face huge pressure to end her run. Some senior Democrats, such as Governor Bill Richardson, the former candidate who dropped out of the race after New Hampshire and has since remained officially neutral, and Senator John Kerry, the Democrat nominee in 2004, who has endorsed Obama this year, suggest that Clinton should bow out unless she wins significant victories in both states.

Bill Clinton makes it clear that the stakes are high. Speaking to his wife's supporters in Texas, he says: 'If she wins Texas and Ohio, I think she will be the nominee. If you don't deliver for her, then I don't think she can be. It's all on you.'

But in the final days before Tuesday, Hillary Clinton is not behaving like a woman who believes she is about to face humiliation. Though her voice is increasingly hoarse, she joshes and laughs with reporters on her campaign plane as never before, even joining them in a game of 'roll the orange down the aisle' during takeoff. She makes an appearance on *Saturday Night Live*. 'Do I really laugh like that?' she asks an *SNL* impersonator who parodies Clinton's sometimes forced and overenthusiastic public laugh. The impersonator nods. 'Yeah, well. . .' shrugs Clinton.

On the stump across Texas and Ohio, Clinton speaks with renewed fire and attack. Her language, which in the past has often been convoluted and vague, has become stripped down and direct. 'We need a president who *gets it*,' she says, in Akron, Ohio, a town hit hard by the outsourcing of jobs overseas. Clinton says she will be held accountable for her 'solutions', whilst Obama offers only 'speeches'. 'I want you to come to the White House and say: "I heard you in Akron; when are you going to produce those jobs?"' She sounds very different from the woman who called for 'a new politics of meaning'.

Clinton is revelling in her new role as the feisty champion of ordinary people, expressing anger at the shady powers that be, which include the media and what she implies are their co-conspirators in the Democratic Party. Obama will give you words, she says; I will give you action. In Youngtown, Ohio, another economically depressed town, Clinton sums up her new self-presentation: 'I'm a fighter, a doer and a champion.'

Clinton returns to the question of Obama's readiness to be commander in chief, this time with increased urgency. A new ad, entitled '3 a.m.', intercuts pictures of a sleeping family with a red phone ringing in the White House. A reassuringly bespectacled Clinton is pictured answering the phone at her desk as the voiceover asks voters who they would trust more to deal with a national emergency. This is considered rough stuff for a primary campaign, and Clinton's critics accuse her of scaremongering. But the ad focuses voters' minds on just how well they know and trust Obama.

Clinton is launching lacerating attacks on Obama over a report that his senior economic adviser, Austan Goolsbee, had suggested to the Canadian ambassador in a private meeting that Obama's tough-talking opposition to the North American Free Trade Agreement (NAFTA) – an agreement blamed in Ohio for the loss of many jobs – need not be taken too seriously. The Obama campaign, she says, 'has done the old wink-wink. "Don't pay any attention. This is just political rhetoric."'

Her campaign also keeps up a steady drumbeat of criticism over Obama's association with Tony Rezko, a Chicago property developer and a former friend and benefactor to Obama. Rezko is currently on trial for fraud. The overall aim, along with the NAFTA attacks, is to demonstrate to voters that Obama is no different from any other politician: that his fancy words about a 'new politics' conceal an old-fashioned, shifty and dishonest operator. In a calculated show of fury, Clinton denounces Obama at a press conference in Cincinnati for mailings from his campaign that she alleges paint a grossly misleading picture of her health insurance plan. 'Shame on you, Barack Obama,' she cries.

The media, perhaps feeling the pressure of Clinton's accusations of bias, are giving Obama the hardest time he has had in the campaign so far. They hammer away at the questions over Rezko and NAFTA. Obama, unused to such aggressive scrutiny, appears touchy and overly defensive at press conferences, as if offended that he should even have to address such questions.

Texas and Ohio declare

As the votes are counted on Tuesday night, it is still unclear which of Hillary Clinton's multiple lines of attack proved most damaging to her opponent – but it is clear that, cumulatively, they worked. Clinton not only wins both big states, she wins them decisively.

After a long string of defeats, these big wins come as a joyous relief to the Clinton campaign. As the TV networks call Ohio for Clinton, her cheerleader in chief, Terry McAuliffe, is once again excitedly declaring a victory against the odds, taunting reporters for their eagerness to write Clinton off. 'We came back in New Hampshire, Nevada, Super Tuesday,' he said. 'And we're doing it again tonight.'

That night, at a raucous victory rally in Columbus, Clinton exults in her new role as an underdog battling for society's underdogs: 'For everyone here in Ohio and across America who's been counted out and refused to be knocked out, and for everyone who has stumbled but stood right back up, and for everyone who works hard and never gives up, this one is for you.'

Warrior and priest

The exit polls reveal that Hillary Clinton did well amongst her most loyal constituencies: white blue-collar voters, women and Hispanics. Barack Obama did well amongst blacks and middle-class whites in metropolitan areas but his failure to reach beyond these groups of voters cost him victory in both states. These results confirm what has so far been the pattern of these candidates' previous contests. Put simply, the votes went according to the demographic make-up of voters, and in Texas and Ohio the demographics favoured Clinton.

The Democratic race seems to have settled into a deadlock, each candidate having formed a loyal coalition of supporters, neither making significant inroads into the other's base. The make-up of their support, and the respective images of the candidates, echo a historic dynamic.

To use terms first coined by the historian John Milton Cooper, Democratic contests often pit a Warrior against a Priest. Obama's cerebral, highly literate style places him in the tradition of candidates such as Adlai Stevenson, Bill Bradley and Gary Hart, who maintain ironic distance from the sound and fury of the political campaign, and articulate a yearning for a different, purer form of politics altogether. Clinton's emphasis on 'solutions' and the combative, scrappy style she has developed since Iowa place her in a tradition that runs from Harry Truman and Hubert Humphrey: candidates of the kitchen table, champions of the blue-collar worker, for whom the unholy business of political combat is something to be relished rather than disdained.

Historically, working-class voters have been more likely to vote for candidates who they believe will defend their interests, middle-class voters for candidates whose values affirm their own. So far, Clinton seems to be winning the votes of the so-called 'beer-drinkers' of the white working class, whilst Obama is consistently strong with 'wine-drinking', highly educated voters. An important complication is Obama's overwhelming strength with blacks of all classes. But after his defeats in Texas and Ohio, observers suggest that he needs to find a way to reach the beer-drinkers if he is to knock Clinton out.

The last person to successfully combine both archetypes – to present himself as a transformative visionary and a gritty advocate of working-class interests – has kept a low profile in recent weeks. Bill Clinton has lately retreated from the spotlight, and didn't appear on stage with his wife at her victory rally. But he is busy behind the scenes, calling superdelegates and persuading them to back his wife, not always with great subtlety. The afternoon before Texas and Ohio, he calls superdelegate Jason Altmire of Pennsylvania, expressing his confidence that Hillary is about to win Ohio and probably Texas. Altmire, a first-term congressman, says he is doubtful about her ability to carry his state in the general election.

'How well did I do in your district?' asks Bill Clinton.

'You won it twice,' replies Altmire.

'Well, there you go,' says Clinton, as if his case has been proven.

'With respect,' Altmire points out, after a pause, 'you're not on the ballot this year.'

Meanwhile, Hillary Clinton's victories are dampened by new reports of vicious in-fighting amongst her staff. A *Washington Post* story details the campaign's internal divisions, particularly the widespread contempt for Mark Penn. The eminent attorney Robert Barnett, an old Clinton ally and adviser, can stand it no more. He sends an angry email to Clinton and her senior staff:

> STOP IT!!!! I have held my tongue for weeks. After this morning's *WP* story, no longer. This makes me sick. This circular firing squad that is occurring is unattractive, unprofessional, unconscionable, and unacceptable . . . It must stop.

Obama on the ropes

Both campaigns now move to Pennsylvania, where the next major primary will be held in six weeks' time. Barack Obama's team are bitterly disappointed by their campaign's failure to administer a *coup de grâce* on 4 March, and ponder on whether or not they should have concentrated on Texas, where they lost by only three points, instead of trying to win both. One of Obama's foreign policy advisers, Samantha Power, caught in an unguarded moment, admits that the campaign 'fucked up' in Ohio before going on to refer to Hillary Clinton as 'a monster'. Power is forced to resign after strenuous protests from the Clinton campaign.

Even after wins in Texas and Ohio, Clinton has not made up the delegate gap with her opponent. Indeed, it looks as though Obama will end up winning *more* delegates out of Texas than Clinton, due to the arcane local rules of delegate distribution. But the Clintons believe they are making headway with superdelegates on the vital issue of electability. In a competition to prove who is the most credible commander in chief, they argue, Hillary Clinton is the only Democratic candidate who can stand toe to toe with John McCain. If the superdelegates fail to slow the party's headstrong embrace of an untested candidate, insist the Clintons, the party will snatch defeat from the jaws of victory in November.

A confident Clinton starts to drop hints that she would consider making Obama her vice-presidential running mate, implying to wavering Democrats that they might get a dream ticket, with Obama succeeding her in eight years' time. Obama moves quickly to quell this suggestion, asking why Clinton would make him vice-president if she doesn't believe him to be a credible commander in chief. But he has been shaken by the events of the last week.

A convincing win in Wyoming steadies the Obama ship. But the victory is overshadowed when the issue of race is revived. It starts when Geraldine Ferraro, a former vice-presidential candidate for the Democrats and a Clinton supporter, makes comments that appear to suggest that Obama is where he is because, not in spite, of his colour. Then Obama wins Mississippi, but everyone notices that the vote is heavily polarised along racial lines. These events are mere rumblings, however. Two days after Mississippi, Obama's campaign is hit by a storm of such force and velocity that it threatens to engulf his candidacy and sweep him from the contest.

America meets Reverend Wright

On Thursday 13 February, ABC's morning show runs a report about the man Barack Obama characterised in January as a 'cranky uncle': his former pastor, Rev. Jeremiah Wright. Using DVDs purchased from Obama's church in Chicago's South Side, the programme has put together a montage of clips from Wright's sermons. The clips are intercut with footage of Obama praising his former pastor.

Over their morning coffee, viewers see a middle-aged black preacher in flamboyant, African-style robes addressing his lively, largely black congregation. Bobbing and swaying to the rhythm of his own words, he denounces America's treatment of its black citizens in a rasping, keening voice. 'The government gives them drugs, builds bigger prisons, passes a three-strike law, and then wants us to sing "God Bless America"?' says Wright. 'No, no, no. Not "God Bless America". "GOD *DAMN* AMERICA".' From the pews, his congregants applaud and call out affirmations. Next, in a sermon viewers are told was given in the week of September 11, Wright links the terrorist attacks to what he describes as America's 'state terrorism'. As his congregation cheers, Wright looks up and waves imaginary birds down from the sky. 'America's chickens . . . coming home . . . to *roost*'.

Had they been shown in full, Wright's sermons may have seemed more nuanced. But edited together into a series of explosive climaxes, the overall effect on the unsuspecting viewer is like a physical assault. Wright's delivery is loud and hoarse, his language garish, his movements possessed of a febrile energy. What's more, everything he says is amplified by the enthusiasm of his congregation. For millions of

Americans, it is a shocking glimpse of what seems to be an alien and hostile world. ABC's segment concludes with a few words from one of Wright's congregants, standing outside his church. 'I wouldn't call it radical,' she says calmly, referring to Wright's sermons. 'I call it being black in America.'

Within hours of ABC's report, the clips of Wright's sermon have been viewed by thousands on YouTube and, within days by millions. Every political blog posts the footage. Reporters, news editors and TV shows are bombarded with emails demanding that the story be covered in more detail. In the following days more clips emerge on Fox News, including ones that show Wright suggesting that the US government invented the AIDS virus to target the black population, and that 'the US of KKK' is 'a country run by and controlled by rich white people'. The videos are run on cable TV news channels almost non-stop. By the weekend the story dominates the news in all media.

The power of the story derives from Obama's genuine relationship with Wright. Obama has been a member of the Trinity United Church of Christ, where Wright was the pastor, for twenty years. Wright married the Obamas and baptised their children. Indeed, Obama describes Wright, in *Dreams from My Father*, as a spiritual mentor. Voters are alarmed. How could Obama have been so close to a man with such abhorrent, anti-American views? Does Obama share Wright's anger at white society? Even Obama's supporters wonder how on earth he could have associated with such a figure for so long.

The answer may be found in Obama's relationship with Chicago. When he first moved to Chicago, the young Kenyan-Kansan from Hawaii longed to put down roots. He wanted to feel African-American by culture as well as by birth, and Chicago was, as he later put it, 'the capital of the black experience in America'. Previously a religious sceptic, Obama began going to church towards the end of his time as a community organiser in the South Side. By doing so he

sought to satisfy a yearning for spiritual development that was inter-
twined with his desire to belong. He may also have had a more earthly
goal in mind: if he were ever to grow a base of political support in
Chicago, he would need the grounding of a church.

Jeremiah Wright, a former US marine and theologian, ran a lively
and growing church and was very much involved in improving the
lives of poor blacks. Obama was impressed by Wright's work in the
community as well as by his charismatic, passionate personality, and
experienced a kind of epiphany during a sermon given by Wright
entitled 'The Audacity to Hope' (years later Obama adapted the
phrase for his famous speech at the 2004 convention, and used it as
the title of his second book, *The Audacity of Hope*).

The two men were indeed close for a while. But over the years,
Wright became more influenced by the radicalism of black nationalist
ideology, and his rhetoric grew more fiery. Obama, whose natural
temperament is cool and conciliatory, did not follow him down that
path. Although Obama remained on friendly terms with Wright,
when his new campaign team planned his run at the presidency, they
were aware that Wright's taste for provocation might prove a liability.
At the last minute, Wright was disinvited from Obama's announcement of his candidacy in Springfield, Illinois. The reverend took this
as a slight, but did not publicly complain.

Obama speaks on race

The day after Rev. Wright's sermons erupt into the public domain,
Barack Obama releases a statement saying that Wright's words had
'pained and angered him', that he 'vehemently condemned' his
controversial statements, and that he had never been present in
church to hear any of them. He gives a press conference and repeats

these basic points. But as the storm continues to rage over the weekend, Obama calls his senior staff together for a meeting at the campaign's headquarters in Chicago. About half a dozen people are present, including David Axelrod, David Plouffe and Obama's long-time Chicago ally and adviser, Valerie Jarrett. He asks everyone present to share their opinion on how to proceed. Jarrett, an African-American herself, has a clear point of view that chimes with Obama's own instincts. You need to make this about more than Wright, she says. This is an opportunity to confront the wider issue of race in America – a topic she knows Obama has thought, written and spoken on at length over the years.

It is a high-risk approach. Up until now, Obama has presented himself as a presidential candidate who happens to be a black man, rather than as a black man running for president, and his instincts are always to play down the importance of social divisions, racial or otherwise. But the rage against white America embodied in the figure of his former pastor forces the uncomfortable subject of race relations to the fore, and makes Obama's race a contentious issue whether he likes it or not.

Obama agrees with Jarrett and decides to address his relationship with Wright in a set-piece speech that will range across the subject of race in America. He calculates that only by taking the issue head on does he stand a chance of defusing a controversy that threatens to end his hope of becoming president. He also senses what he later calls 'a teachable moment': an opportunity to go beyond the usual platitudes about race in political campaigns and to throw light on a relationship of much mutual incomprehension.

He has to work fast. Stealing time between campaign events, and staying up late into the night in Pennsylvania hotel rooms, Obama drafts the most important speech of his career, while his team search for an appropriately historic venue in which to deliver it. On 18 March, barely five days after the story broke, he stands before a small audience of local supporters and elected officials in the National Constitution Center in Philadelphia. His speech will be broadcast live on national television. Behind him, like sentries, are eight US flags.

Obama starts with words from the preamble to the US constitution, first drafted in a building across the street from where he is speaking: 'We the people, in order to form a more perfect union. . .'. He emphasises the sense, implicit in its founding document, of America as a work in progress, a constant striving towards an ideal. He says that the 'original sin' of slavery has never been expunged from American life, that it is 'a part of our union we have yet to perfect'. With his usual skill at weaving the story of his candidacy with a larger historic narrative, he says: 'I chose to run for the presidency at this moment in history because I believe deeply that we cannot solve the challenges of our time unless we solve them together.'

After a brief summary of his own biography, he admits: 'It's a story that hasn't made me the most conventional candidate. But it is a story that has seared into my genetic make-up the idea that this nation is more than the sum of its parts – that out of many, we are truly one.'

He goes on to address Wright's inflammatory words directly. He describes them as 'divisive' – the ultimate crime in Obama's worldview – and as offering a 'profoundly distorted' view of America. But he refuses to repudiate Wright himself. He reminds people of Wright's service in the marines and of his work for the poor. Wright is, says Obama, 'like family to me . . . he contains within him the contradictions – the good and the bad – of the community that he has served diligently for so many years. I can no more disown him than I can disown the black community. I can no more disown him than I can my white grandmother', a grandmother who he says raised him lovingly but who can still occasionally make racially charged comments that make him 'cringe'.

In a daring attempt to explain the anger of Wright – and his congregation – to white viewers, Obama describes how the legacy of racial injustice in America lives on:

> For the men and women of Rev. Wright's generation, the memories of humiliation and doubt and fear have not gone away; nor has the anger and the bitterness of those years. That anger may not get expressed in public, in front of white co-workers or white friends. But it does find voice in the barbershop or around the kitchen table. At times, that anger is exploited by politicians, to gin up votes along racial lines, or to make up for a politician's own failings. And occasionally it finds voice in the church on Sunday morning, in the pulpit and in the pews.

Obama compares this anger to white resentment at affirmative action, and argues that neither should prevent Americans of different races from coming together to solve the economic and social problems faced by the nation. The problem with Wright's views, he argues, is that they fail to admit the possibility that America might yet move closer to its ideal:

> The profound mistake of Rev. Wright's sermons is not that he spoke about racism in our society. It's that he spoke as if our society was static, as if no progress has been made, as if this country – a country that has made it possible for one of his own members to run for the highest office in the land and build a coalition of white and black, Latino and Asian, rich and poor, young and old – is still

irrevocably bound to a tragic past. But what we know –
what we have seen – is that America can change. That is
the true genius of this nation.

The speech draws on Obama's core beliefs. He learned about the importance of being rooted in a community by observing the wanderings of his own family. His maternal grandfather left the small town he was born in and travelled restlessly from place to place throughout his life, never quite finding fulfilment in his freedom. His mother journeyed even further, to Indonesia, and ended up with two children from two failed marriages. When Obama travelled to Kenya as a young man to meet his extended family he learnt of how his father had attempted to break free of the ties of tribalism only to find himself an unhappy outcast. The aunt that Obama met there said something to him that he took to heart: 'If everyone is family, no one is family.' You can't just conjure an identity, or a world, out of nothing, the young man concluded; history counts (later, this conviction informed his critique of the US government's belief that it could install a democracy in Iraq). By moving to Chicago, and by marrying Michelle, he sought and found the bonding of shared culture and tradition. He made the black community his family – and, as he argues in this speech, family by his definition includes elements that one won't necessarily like but shouldn't lightly disown.

The speech also exemplifies Obama's deep-rooted attraction to compromise. As a boy he was raised by a white family, but out in the world he was seen as black. Over the years he learnt how to shape this contradiction into a coherent whole, and now as a politician his instinct is always to search for areas of convergence between opposing points of view rather than to take one side or the other. His critics accuse him of naïveté, and even of cowardice – sometimes, they point out, conflict simply can't be talked away. But for better or worse,

Obama has staked his political identity on the promise that he can bring different American communities – liberal and conservative, black and white – together, if only around a few shared understandings.

Obama closes his speech with an anecdote from the campaign trail, first related to him by Valerie Jarrett. It concerns a young white woman named Ashley who was organising for his campaign in Florence, South Carolina. One day she asked her fellow volunteers to talk about what brought them to the campaign. To start them off she told of how, when she was nine years old, her mother had been diagnosed with cancer. Forced to take time off work, her mother lost her job and with it her health insurance, and filed for bankruptcy. Knowing that food was one of the family's biggest costs, young Ashley lied to convince her mother that she loved nothing more than mustard and relish sandwiches. She ate them for a year until her mother got better. Ashley said she was volunteering on behalf of all the children who now found themselves in the same position as her younger self. Everyone else in the room took their turn, giving different stories and reasons. The last person to speak was an elderly black man who'd been sitting there quietly the whole time. 'I'm here for Ashley,' he said.

Backstage after the speech, Obama embraces Michelle, who is sobbing with the strain and emotion of the moment. After a few words with her, he is all business. 'What next?' he asks his team. The question is already on their minds. Nobody is sure what the effect of the speech will be.

It certainly doesn't satisfy everyone. Critics ask why Obama didn't disown Wright, rather than just some of his comments. Wasn't the implied equivalence of Wright's incendiary rhetoric to his grandmother's admission that she sometimes felt intimidated by black people in the street grossly unfair to her and others like her? In the days and weeks that follow, however, it becomes clear that the speech has achieved its immediate objective of tamping down the controversy. Obama's polls numbers do not collapse. Other stories start to head the nightly news.

Some commentators argue that the speech's significance will transcend its political moment, and the immediate question of Obama's relationship with Wright. Which major politician of modern times, they ask, has addressed the topic of race in America with such candour and subtlety – let alone one in the middle of a close presidential race?

Hillary Clinton, other than making a few anodyne comments, has stayed out of the debate over Wright. But Republicans are licking their lips. Barack Obama's pastor problem, together with Michelle Obama's comment about being proud of her country for the first time, are suggestive of a larger narrative about their likely opponent in the general election, as somebody not quite in tune with American values.

One Republican, though, steps into the conversation about Wright, not to attack Barack Obama but to defend him. Mike Huckabee, in a little-noticed intervention, tells a TV interviewer that 'you can't hold the candidate responsible for everything that people around him may say or do'. Going further, he defends Wright himself:

> As easy as it is for those of us who are white to look back and say 'That's a terrible statement', I grew up in a very segregated south, and I think that you have to cut some slack. And I'm going to be probably the only conservative in America who's going to say something like this, but I'm just telling you: we've got to cut some slack to people who grew up being called names, being told: 'You have to sit in the balcony when you go to the movie; you have to go to the back door to go into the restaurant; there's a separate

waiting room in the doctor's office; here's where you sit on the bus.' And you know what? Sometimes people do have a chip on their shoulder. And you have to just say, I probably would too. I probably would too. In fact, I may have had more of a chip on my shoulder had it been me.

Clinton under fire

On 21 March, Bill Richardson, the Hispanic governor of New Mexico and former presidential candidate, announces his endorsement of Barack Obama. It comes at a welcome time for his chosen candidate, but it has the Clintons and their supporters spluttering with anger.

Richardson was handed his first big jobs in politics by President Clinton, and both the Clintons had gained the impression from their conversations with him that he was to endorse Hillary or nobody at all. Although Hillary Clinton makes no comment, long-time Clinton associate James Carville describes Richardson as a 'Judas'. Whatever Richardson's motivation, it is a sign that, even in the wake of the Wright affair, superdelegates have not lost their confidence in Obama.

But there is worse to come for Clinton. In the last week of the month, the media begin to pick up on an apparent discrepancy between an account Clinton is giving on the stump of a visit to Bosnia in 1996 and the recollections of people who were on the same trip. In her speeches, Clinton tells a dramatic anecdote about having to disembark from the aeroplane under sniper fire: 'There was supposed to be some kind of a greeting ceremony at the airport, but instead we just ran with our heads down to get into the vehicles to get to our base.' The first lady travelled in a party that included some American entertainers and now one of them – a comedian named Sinbad – contradicts Clinton's story, quipping that the most dangerous part of the visit was working out where to eat. Questioned about it at a press conference, Clinton sticks by her story.

But then a video emerges of Clinton's landing at Tuzla airport in Bosnia twelve years before. It does not, to put it mildly, support her version of events. She is pictured strolling across the tarmac from the plane, smiling and waving to people in the welcoming party, her teenage daughter Chelsea in tow. An eight-year-old girl is introduced to Clinton, and the first lady takes time to squeeze her hand and talk to her. No shots are heard.

Confronted with this evidence, Clinton backtracks, acknowledging that she 'misspoke'. It's too late. Now it has pictures, the story is up and running. The relevant section of Clinton's speech, juxtaposed with the footage of her Bosnia landing, becomes a staple of every cable news channel and nightly news show. It is irresistible fodder for late-night comedians and bloggers. The controversy is particularly damaging to Clinton because it appears to confirm people's worst suspicions of her: that she will say anything to get elected, even to the point of making up stories about her bravery.

Clinton's opponents in the media and within the party renew their calls for her to quit the race. They point out that it is close to impossible for her to catch Obama in terms of elected delegates. Many Democrats are worried that the continuing battle between the two is damaging the eventual nominee and will give John McCain a head start. The prospect of the contest going all the way to the convention in August fills party leaders with horror. But in public and private, Clinton shows an unflinching determination to carry on.

Over the years, she and her husband have made an art out of survival against the odds. When the Gennifer Flowers scandal blew up in the weeks before the Iowa caucus in 1992, Bill Clinton's presidential candidacy was written off. But, with the staunch support of his wife, he fought on to win the nomination. In 1994, after a series of missteps in the White House, the Clintons watched as Republicans swept through both houses of Congress; most commentators then deemed a second Clinton term highly unlikely. They were wrong. The Lewinsky affair threatened to end in impeachment, and certainly seemed likely to destroy the Clinton name in American politics forever. But by the end of his time in the Oval Office, Bill Clinton was as popular as ever, paving the way for his wife to win election to the Senate in 2002. Then, of course, there was New Hampshire, 2008.

The Clintons are used to hearing a chorus of voices, in the media and in the party and even amongst their own circle, telling them that the game is up. They have learned to trust their own political judgement above everyone else's. They may even have come to believe that they are indestructible. Bill Clinton once told Newt Gingrich, who had just led the GOP to victory in 1994's congressional elections: 'I'm the big rubber clown doll you had as a kid. And every time you hit it, it bounces back. That's me – the harder you hit me, the faster I come back up.' Hillary Clinton shares her husband's rock-like self-belief. She *knows* that she is supremely well qualified to do the job of president, and that her opponent is not. This drives her on, along with her privately expressed conviction that Obama will lose to McCain in a general election.

Clinton and her closest advisers see a path to victory, albeit a very narrow one. It involves winning Pennsylvania in April, and then Indiana and North Carolina in early May. At the same time, they will fight to seat the disputed delegations from Michigan and Florida. If all these bets come good, they trust that the party's superdelegates, spooked by the possibility that Obama is a losing electoral proposition, will find the courage to overturn what might by then be a very small lead in elected delegates.

As the month ends, another superdelegate – Senator Bob Casey of Pennsylvania – announces his endorsement of Obama. A prominent Obama supporter, Senator Patrick Leahy, calls on Clinton to leave the race for the good of the party. Clinton pushes back, seeking to rally her supporters. In one of her periodic invocations of sympathy as a woman in a male-dominated party, she says that she refuses to be bullied out of the race by the 'big boys'. She even uses the attacks as the basis of a new fundraising appeal to her donors.

Hillary Clinton and her husband may be the only people in America who believe that she can still win the nomination. But then, based on their joint history, that's good enough for them.

April 2008

McCain shadow-boxes

John McCain is in Mississippi, his family's ancestral home. He is speaking not far from McCain Field, a navy airfield named after his grandfather, a pilot. McCain's father was a submariner. Both elder McCains were admirals.

'They were my first heroes,' says McCain. 'They gave their lives to their country and taught me lessons about honour, courage, duty, perseverance and leadership.' These weighty nouns form the core of McCain's political identity, anchored as they are in the moment when, given a choice between release from his terrible suffering in Hanoi and a code of honour, he chose the code.

Over the next week, McCain is visiting parts of the country that have mattered to him in his life: his high school in Alexandria, Virginia; the naval academy he attended in Annapolis, Maryland; Florida, where he was posted and received flight training; and Arizona, where he got his start in politics. He is seeking to 'reintroduce' himself to Americans: to embed firmly in the popular mind the narrative of a life lived in service to country. McCain's first campaign ad as the Republican nominee shows images of him as a prisoner of war. 'Where has he been?' asks the voiceover. 'Has he walked the walk?'

McCain finally secured the nomination after winning Texas and Ohio, on the same day that Hillary Clinton did. Mike Huckabee, the only other candidate left in the Republican race, conceded, warmly endorsing the man to whom, by deposing Romney in Iowa, he helped deliver the nomination.

On that day, McCain began a stretch of weeks, quite possibly months, in which he faces no Democratic opponent. This is a rare luxury. It gives the Republican candidate the time and space to define himself to the public, raise money and build an election-winning campaign operation, without having to worry about reacting to a barrage of attacks and negative advertising from his opponent.

But there are a couple of drawbacks to this situation. First, it's proving difficult for McCain to get anyone to take notice. The media, and the voters, are still transfixed by the battle between Hillary Clinton and Barack Obama. McCain is learning that there is a fine line between looking serenely confident and being irrelevant. Second, not having an opponent means it's hard for McCain to know how to pitch his message. Certain things about his candidacy – his life story, his devotion to patriotic service – are givens. But much of his strategy will depend on who his opponent turns out to be. McCain's team think they will be facing Obama. But until they're sure they are campaigning in a vacuum.

Pennsylvania: the blue-collar show

Nobody wants that vacuum filled more quickly than Barack Obama. Having failed once to kill his opponent off in New Hampshire and again in Texas, Obama is now campaigning hard and spending millions of dollars on advertising in Pennsylvania, in the hope that if he beats or even comes close to beating Hillary Clinton here on 22 April, he can finally snuff out her candidacy. It's an uphill struggle: Pennsylvania, outside of cosmopolitan Philadelphia, is full of the kind of white, older, socially conservative working-class voters that have formed the bedrock of Clinton's support. She leads by a significant margin in all polls.

Obama spends most of his time in rural or semi-rural areas, speaking at low-key town hall-style meetings, paying visits to local dignitaries, or making stops at diners in the company of the cameras. He cuts down on the massive, flag-waving rallies that his campaign has become known for (when some of his advisers suggest stopping them altogether, the staff responsible for organising voters complain that such events are a vital source of names and email addresses. A compromise is reached: rallies will only be held at night, after the main news bulletins so that they can't be featured as the day's main story). Out here, voters need to be convinced that Obama is not just a celebrity but a man who has their interests at heart. On the stump, he focuses on jobs, taxes and the price of gasoline.

Obama also knows that if he's to get anywhere in this state, he can't afford to be seen as a creature of the dandified metropolitan elite. So he is performing, somewhat gingerly, in a familiar pantomime of politicians on the campaign trail: the blue-collar show.

Left to his own devices, Obama favours a healthy diet on the trail. His 'body man', Reggie Love – the aide whose job it is to ensure that the candidate's day-to-day life is as bearable as possible – keeps him supplied with mineral water, fruit and vegetables. But in Pennsylvania, Obama is munching on hot dogs, french fries and homemade chocolates in the diners and cafés he visits to meet with voters. Never a big drinker, he's also knocking back a few beers.

In Altoona he tries his hand at bowling – a staple sport of Pennsylvanians – at the Pleasant Valley Bowling Alley. It is a brave attempt to look the part of a regular guy, but it doesn't go well. Ball after ball veers into the gutter, and his final score is a disastrous 37 out of 300. Obama's poor performance becomes a YouTube hit and instant material for the talk show hosts. 'Afterwards,' says Conan O'Brien, 'Obama told reporters: "That's it, no more white guy sports for me. That's it." He cancelled his weekend at Hockey Camp.'

Clinton, on the other hand, is in her element. She revels in the pantomime, swigging beers and knocking back shots of whiskey for the cameras. Hoarse voiced but as energised as anyone has ever seen her, she is rousing crowds across the state with a populist paean to the ordinary American. At every stop she connects their own plight with hers: scrappy underdogs who won't give up. Clinton has taken to comparing herself with Rocky Balboa, the boxer who just doesn't know when to quit: at campaign events she walks onstage to the accompaniment of his theme tune, 'Eye of The Tiger'. 'I know what it's like to stumble. I know what it means to get knocked down. But I've never stayed down!' she yells out to appreciative crowds. Vigorously pumping hands at the ropeline afterwards, she laughs heartily with supporters and returns their hugs. Clinton is no longer the awkward and mechanical campaigner of Iowa. Passionate, fiery, even charismatic, she has undergone a remarkable transformation that started somewhere in the bitter cold of New Hampshire in January.

Surrogate trouble

But Hillary Clinton has to deal with a couple of unwelcome distractions, caused by her two chief advisers – Mark Penn and Bill Clinton.

Reports appear that Penn, in his private capacity as head of a lobbying firm, held a meeting with officials from Colombia to advise them on how best to secure passage of a bilateral free-trade agreement with the United States. The problem is that Hillary Clinton has been campaigning vigorously against the treaty. Penn's meeting brings her integrity into question once again. Having blasted Barack Obama over the Goolsbee affair the month before, it's particularly embarrassing for her. Furious, she asks a contrite Penn to resign. Her team rejoices.

Having dealt with the Penn affair, Clinton hopes that she can get the focus away from questions about her character and back on to Obama. But then her husband inadvertently brings the sniper fire story back into the headlines.

Although he has retreated from the front line of the campaign, Bill Clinton is working harder than ever on his wife's behalf. He believes he can help her in areas of the country that candidates or surrogates don't usually get to, working under the radar of the national media. He tells campaign staff to double the number of his daily appearances. 'Look at this schedule – you've got me down for four events,' he says. 'Give me six, eight a day. Get me to the suburbs where I can make a difference.'

But these days, it is all but impossible to campaign under the radar, especially if you're Bill Clinton. At a small event in Indiana, Clinton extemporises on the recent fuss about his wife's visit to Bosnia, blaming the media for making too much of it. In retelling the story, he manages to make half a dozen factual errors in the space of little over a minute. He says the Bosnia trip was in 1995, when the country was still at war, rather than 1996, when it was largely at peace. He says that Hillary made the mistake 'late at night' when she was tired, and 'immediately apologised for it'. In fact, she first told the story in a speech given in the morning, and retold a similar version on other occasions. Also, her campaign at first denied any error, only backing off after further evidence emerged.

A video of Bill Clinton's talk is posted on the web and within hours it is generating headlines as commentators pour scorn on his near-fictional version of events. The incident returns the sniper fire story to

prominence just as the media were losing interest in it, and gives them
another excuse to play the Tuzla tape. Questioned by reporters the next
day, a clearly chastened Bill says he won't talk about the trip any more:
'Hillary called me and said: "You don't remember this, you weren't
there. Let me handle it." And I said: "Yes ma'am."'

The former president's factual errors, such as his suggestion that
he and George Bush Sr were to launch a diplomatic mission together,
or that he was against the Iraq War from the start, or that he once
spoke to a crowd of a million people in Africa (when it was in fact
200,000) are a recurring problem for his wife's campaign, as are his
unpredictable outbursts of anger.

Clinton is the acknowledged master of the modern political
campaign. But he learnt and practised his trade in a different media
environment. In previous elections, reporters from established media
organisations dominated coverage. They had protocols about what
should and shouldn't be reported. Clinton, a brilliant improviser, had
more opportunities to hone his riffs off camera or off the record
without worrying too much about getting his facts straight. But this
is the first YouTube election. Reporters and even voters carry hand-
held cameras enabling them to record everything anyone says. They
upload their snippets online, there to be passed on, blogged about
and played on cable news shows. All protocols are abolished. The
scrutiny is intense, pervasive and unrelenting. The master is visibly
struggling to adjust.

'Bitter'

Bill Clinton is soon saved from the worst of his wife's displeasure by
their opponent. This time, it is Barack Obama who is tripped up by
the new rules of campaigning.

A report of an Obama fundraising dinner in San Francisco appears on the popular political website The Huffington Post ('HuffPo'). The event is closed to reporters, but one of the attendees is a blogger for HuffPo and posts on the site an audio tape of Obama's speech to his donors. On the tape Obama can be heard musing on the voting habits of working-class Americans for the benefit of his well-fed and expensively bejewelled audience:

> You go into some of these small towns in Pennsylvania, and like a lot of small towns in the Midwest, the jobs have been gone now for twenty-five years and nothing's replaced them. And they fell through the Clinton administration, and the Bush administration, and each successive administration has said that somehow these communities are gonna regenerate and they have not. And it's not surprising then they get bitter, they cling to guns or religion or antipathy to people who aren't like them or anti-immigrant sentiment or anti-trade sentiment as a way to explain their frustrations.

HuffPo's report, and this passage in particular, is immediately picked up by other bloggers and reporters. Coming at a relatively quiet moment in the campaign, the story moves with incredible velocity: within twenty-four hours it dominates the news across all media. Attention is focused on Obama's use of the word 'bitter' to describe the attitudes of small-town Americans, and on his suggestion that they 'cling' to religion and guns out of economic frustration.

Obama's words sound condescending to the very voters he is trying to court in Pennsylvania. The fact that he made the comments in San Francisco, before an audience drawn from the moneyed west-coast elite, makes things even worse. Critics point out that people own guns because they enjoy shooting, not because they are 'bitter' about their economic circumstance. Many also find Obama's conflation of religion with racism offensive.

The remarks are especially damaging because they play right into one of the familiar archetypes of losing Democrat candidates, the liberal elitist. From Adlai Stevenson (who described his failed presidential campaign as a test the American people had flunked) to the windsurfing John Kerry, Democrats have produced candidates easily caricatured as condescending characters who, whilst they don't really like or understand their fellow countrymen, are quite happy to tell them what's good for them.

With the Pennsylvania primary just over a week away, the Clinton campaign team are as excited as they have been since New Hampshire. Obama's remarks bolster the argument they have been making to superdelegates about his candidacy: that he cannot extend his appeal amongst white voters beyond the wine-drinking professional classes, and that he will be acutely vulnerable to Republican attacks on his character. For the first time since the Rev. Wright story, the Clintons sense that the long-hoped-for collapse of Obama's candidacy is about to take place.

But it doesn't, quite. Obama's poll numbers do not plummet and there is no flood of superdelegates to the Clinton camp, despite a bad night for Obama at the last debate before the Pennsylvania primary. That evening, Obama is peppered with questions by the moderators about his character. They quiz him on his 'bitter' remarks, on Wright, and on the reservations he has expressed about wearing a flagpin. Under more pressure than he has been in previous debates, Obama does not respond well. He comes across as flat, tired and tetchy – and piqued that he should be asked such questions. After the debate Clinton's spin doctors argue that Obama cannot handle the pressure of a punishing contest: another reason for superdelegates to think twice.

Although Obama's candidacy does not disintegrate, he no longer has much momentum. In the last days before the Pennsylvania primary, Hillary Clinton settles on a line of attack: that Obama wilts under the spotlight of a tough campaign. She runs an ad containing a montage of threatening images, from Osama bin Laden to the Pearl Harbor attacks. It suggests that Obama won't be able to 'stand the heat' of the presidency. In response, Obama's campaign is getting more aggressive itself, running ads that accuse Clinton of being a compromised Washington insider. It all feels a long way from the optimism of Iowa.

Deadlock

On the day of the Pennsylvania primary the Clinton camp is confident, despite the Obama campaign's bigger ad spend and massive organisational effort. That night, in the Clintons' hotel suite, Bill playfully compares his effectiveness as a campaigner with his wife's. He pores over county-by-county returns, pointing out to Hillary where he has done better than her at turning out votes.

Their optimism is justified. Hillary Clinton wins by a substantial margin. Despite all those beers, Barack Obama fails, once again, to steal her loyal voters: Clinton runs up big margins amongst white voters on low incomes. At a noisy victory rally, she reprises her new role as fighter for the underdog: 'You know, tonight, all across Pennsylvania and America, waitresses are pouring coffee, and police officers are standing guard, and small businesses are working to meet that payroll. And you deserve a champion who stands with you.' She declares that, unlike her opponent, she can soak up pressure: 'Some people counted me out and said to drop out. But the American people don't quit, and they deserve a president who doesn't quit either.'

The Obama camp is disappointed, but there is relief too.

Notwithstanding her strength in Pennsylvania, Clinton didn't run up the kind of massive victory that might have scared superdelegates into backing her. Obama's campaign argues that given Clinton's inherent predominance in this state, the result is unsurprising. The battle now turns to Indiana and North Carolina, the next big states to vote.

As the month comes to a close, Obama's turbulent former pastor causes him yet more trouble. Rev. Wright, who has made no public appearances since his abrupt rise to national prominence, goes on a media tour, including an interview on TV and an appearance at the National Press Club in Washington, D.C. He displays no willingness to soften his image. Quite the opposite: he is cocky, defiant and provocative. He repeats his belief that the September 11 attacks were payback for America's own 'terrorism', and his claims that HIV was invented by the government to kill black people.

After a long day's campaigning in Indiana, Obama is shown the tapes of Wright's appearances, and is made angry in a way that his advisers rarely see. In particular, Wright's suggestion that Obama's speech on race was just political manoeuvring infuriates him. He orders his aides to arrange a press conference.

Forced to appear before the cameras to talk about Wright once again, Obama retains his customary cool. But his stiff posture and terse delivery betray his strong feelings. He uses harsher language than ever before to condemn Wright's words. Indeed, he repudiates him, saying: 'The person I saw yesterday was not the person that I met twenty years ago.' Some commentators wonder how Obama can wash his hands of Wright only weeks after saying that he could 'no more disown him than I can my white grandmother'. It is a sign of Obama's personal disappointment with Wright – and of his ruthlessness – that he does so.

The Democratic race is in a strange state of limbo. By all the usual factors – electoral victories, momentum, positive coverage – Clinton is beating Obama. She is the one winning big states; she is the one hitting her stride on the campaign trail. Obama is getting rattled by the closest examination he's yet had to face, and is further shaken by Wright's return. But for Clinton, it's all three months too late. The delegate mathematics won't budge. Obama still sits on a significant lead, and it's highly unlikely he'll lose it in the remaining contests. Clinton can hardly concede defeat, though. Not while she's winning.

May 2008

Obama refocuses, Clinton charges on

Two days after losing Pennsylvania, Barack Obama sits down with Michelle, David Plouffe, David Axelrod and a few other senior campaign staff around the dining table of his Chicago home.

After the roughest patch of the year so far, Obama wants to reassess the direction of his campaign. He tells the table that he feels that his campaign has become stuck in a rut, that he has been drawn into a battle of negative attacks, and that the optimism of his message is getting lost. He wants to get back to the spirit of Iowa, embodied by that seminal Jefferson-Jackson dinner speech.

It is decided that Obama should get back his core theme of change and avoid tit-for-tat battles. The team also agree to make the campaign 'more intimate and less iconic'. Obama will focus on small gatherings, town hall meetings, house visits and churches, accompanied by his wife and daughters where possible. His campaign team know that they must win North Carolina and at least run Hillary Clinton close in Indiana to stand a chance of forcing her out of the race. To do that, they need to get their groove back.

Clinton is firmly in hers. Every one of her stump speeches now contains the sentence 'My campaign is about jobs, jobs, jobs.' On the trail in Indiana, Clinton is recounting memories of her father's fabric-printing business, describing in rich, painterly detail the cloth, silk screen and sponge he used to make curtains for hotels and offices in Chicago. At a union-hall in the depressed town of Gary, she evokes romance from the unpromising materials of industrial production. Her eyes widen and her hands – as tiny as her husband's are large – dance as she talks of magnets and wheelbases.

Just as Obama is playing down his reputation for soaring speeches, Clinton is enjoying a new-found taste for rhetorical flamboyance. Indeed, she can get carried away. Talking about outsourcing, she intones: 'They came for the steel companies and nobody said anything. They came for the auto companies and nobody said anything. They came for the office companies and nobody said anything. So this is not just about steel.' The passage is an allusion to a famous poem by the German pastor Martin Niemoller about the victims of Nazism ('First they came for the communists, and I didn't speak up because I wasn't a communist. Then they came for the Jews and I didn't speak up because I wasn't a Jew').

Large crowds turn out to see Clinton at every stop. The more her chances of winning are written off by the press, the more fervent her supporters become. Clinton finds a resonant rallying cry in her call for the tax on gasoline to be suspended over the summer, in order to give voters some relief from their current financial difficulties. Every economist agrees that the gas tax holiday would be pointless and probably counter-productive. No president would be able to get such a bill through Congress anyway. In other words, Clinton's gas tax holiday is the epitome of an irresponsible promise.

But Clinton, at this point, doesn't care about such niceties. For most of her career she has been the voice of responsibility in the Clinton partnership, the one who brings her husband back down to earth. Now she seems liberated, exhilarated by the awareness that she must do anything she can to win every vote, or else face defeat.

Standing on the back of a pick-up truck in Gastonia, North Carolina, Clinton is well into her stump speech when she spots a group of Obama supporters holding up a large yellow placard that reads 'GAS TAX HOLIDAY IS BLATANT PANDERING'. The earlier version of Clinton would have pretended not to see it. Today, however, she confronts the sign-holders directly. 'Why shouldn't the oil companies pay the tax instead of people who hold their breath every time they show up at the gas pump?' she asks, to cheers from the crowd. 'Don't they deserve a break every once in a while? I'm tired of being a patsy!' It's quite a sight to see this millionaire power-player transplant herself into the shoes of people who, as she puts it, 'count their pennies as they walk down the supermarket aisle'. But Clinton convinces through sheer exuberance. She is having fun – and so are her audiences.

Clinton is taking a significant political risk by even spending time in North Carolina. Obama has a big lead here, due to the state's high proportion of African-American voters. The cautious political campaigner of old would have stayed away from a state she is expected to lose and instead concentrated entirely on Indiana, where she leads in the polls. But at this late stage, Clinton decides that her only option is to gamble on an upset in North Carolina. If she wins or even runs Obama close she might set off the kind of earthquake she desperately needs to upset the equilibrium of the race. As Clinton herself tells an audience in North Carolina, winning there could be a 'game-changer'. She dips into her personal fortune again to fight as hard as possible in both states, lending her campaign another $1.4 million.

Of course, if she loses badly after raising expectations, her campaign will take a blow even more significant than the one it suffered after South Carolina, perhaps even a terminal one. Whatever happens in North Carolina will have a dramatic impact on the contest.

Her husband knows that they are in a desperate fight for survival.

During daily conference calls with Hillary's advisers, Bill Clinton implores them to be tougher on Obama: 'We've got to take him on every time.' He even reviews the campaign's TV spots, telling the ad people to make them harder, faster and harsher. Out on the trail, he is working the small towns of Indiana and North Carolina at a furious pace. Between Saturday morning and the following Monday night he makes twenty-one stops. Often speaking from front porches, Clinton is greeted with warmth and wonderment in every town he visits. Most of the places he goes have never seen a president before.

After a campaign in which he has too often made headlines for the wrong reasons, Clinton is once again demonstrating his intuitive genius for face-to-face campaigning and his unrivalled ability to connect with ordinary voters in places that few Democrats dare venture to. In North Carolina he mentions that his wife will reverse George W. Bush's unpopular education bill, and remarks on his audience's warm reaction. 'Every time I say this it's a guaranteed applause line. You can drop me in the middle of Idaho, where there's not a Democrat in 200 miles, and an elk would applaud me on that.' The crowd of 300 or so voters are enthralled. They hoist children on their shoulders and bring their pets. 'People say Bill Clinton's been banished to the backwater, but that's not how it is,' says the former president, who was raised poor in rural Arkansas. 'I'm from the backwater. I like it here.'

Meanwhile, Obama is taking up the theme of the gas tax holiday, but from the opposite direction to his rival. He dismisses it as a gimmick, a political trick straight from Hillary Clinton's Washington playbook. It is a risky position. Obama knows that Clinton's proposal, however incoherent, will have a powerful appeal to all voters struggling to pay their bills. But he gambles that most will see through her promise and respect him for not stooping to the same level. It proves a galvanising argument for him and his campaign, reminding his supporters of why they chose Obama over Clinton in the first place.

On 6 May, election night in Indiana and North Carolina, the Clintons are optimistic. They think that they might have just done enough to cause an upset. But as the results roll in, they contain little but bad news for Hillary Clinton's campaign.

Clinton loses her bet

The North Carolina result comes first. Barack Obama wins – and by a landslide, bigger than Hillary Clinton's margin of victory in Pennsylvania. Black voters, who some thought might have been put off Obama by his handling of the Wright affair, stayed overwhelmingly loyal, and younger voters once again came out in strength for the senator from Illinois.

If that wasn't bad enough for Clinton, the Indiana vote appears too close to call until late into the night. Returns from some counties are very slow to come in. Even if she wins, it looks as though Clinton will be robbed of an opportunity to make a victory speech in prime time. At campaign headquarters, the Clintons are in a foul mood. Bill in particular is furious at the delay in counting. A campaign aide is ordered to track down the mayor of one of the cities whose returns are late. 'I've got an angry president here and a candidate who wants to know whether or not she won,' says the aide. On the other end of the line, the mayor can hear Bill Clinton yelling at him to get the numbers out.

But the fury is for nothing. Although Clinton ends up being declared the victor in Indiana, it is only by a handful of votes. The closeness of the result, and North Carolina's landslide, mean that Obama increases his already significant lead in pledged delegates. It will do nothing to staunch the drift of superdelegates to Obama, who has won five times as many superdelegate endorsements as Clinton since Super Tuesday. What's more, tonight's results give the media the excuse they need to call an end to the race. The new consensus is crystallised by NBC's influential anchor Tim Russert, who declares, with a glint of excitement in his eyes: 'We now know who the Democratic nominee is going to be.'

Obama looks to the general election

The Obama camp is exultant and relieved after a tough few weeks. Barack Obama can justifiably claim to have answered Hillary Clinton's question about his mettle under pressure. In the face of Rev. Wright's return and questions over his patriotism, judgement and stamina, Obama has come through, in part by returning to his central message of changing the political culture.

In North Carolina that night, he delivers one of the strongest victory speeches of his campaign. He tells a version of his life story that is infused with patriotism, referring to his grandfather's service in General George Patton's army, and the journey that has taken him here. Explaining his purpose in running for the presidency, he says: 'I love this country too much to see it divided and distracted at this moment in history. I believe in our ability to perfect this union because it's the only reason I'm standing here today. And I know the promise of America because I have lived it.' The new emphasis on country is a reaction to the questions raised by the Wright affair, and it displays one of Obama's most impressive attributes: his ability to adapt and evolve as a candidate.

Obama also spends time in his speech attacking John McCain. He is clearly ready for the general election battle to begin. Unfortunately for Clinton, so are the media. Political commentators publish obituaries of the Clinton campaign, giving their analyses of 'what went wrong'.

They ask what Clinton will want to negotiate from the Obama camp as a reward for a gracious exit.

Clinton herself doesn't seem quite ready to give up. In an interview with *USA Today*, she argues once again that she is more electable than Obama. Veering into territory not usually explored by presidential candidates, she notes her relative strength amongst white voters. Her remarks set off a minor storm of controversy which does her no favours. It's not just that the remarks are seen as divisive and inflammatory after a campaign in which race has figured so prominently and often painfully. It's that discussing the finer details of exit polls is somehow unpresidential. Clinton's remarks revive a potent criticism of the Clinton administration: that it was too fascinated by the minutiae of political tactics to set a clear course for the country.

Even electoral success doesn't help Clinton now. She wins West Virginia – a rural state with a large population of white working-class voters – with room to spare. The win is embarrassing for the presumptive nominee: Obama loses the white vote by a massive margin, and more than half of West Virginia's voters indicate that they would be unlikely to back him in the general election. Clinton supporters suggest that this result should give superdelegates pause for thought.

But Obama is helped out of this uncomfortable moment by his former rival for the nomination. The day after West Virginia, John Edwards steps forward to announce that he is endorsing Obama's candidacy.

As soon as Edwards ended his presidential campaign after coming a distant third in South Carolina, there was much speculation over who he would endorse. Both candidates made pilgrimages out to the Edwardses' home in North Carolina to ask for his backing. At first it was assumed he'd back Obama as a fellow candidate of 'change'. He certainly expended more effort during the campaign attacking

Clinton than Obama. But as the weeks went by the rumours were that Clinton had done a more assiduous and persuasive job of courting both John and Elizabeth Edwards, and that Elizabeth in particular – a great influence on her husband and a political force in her own right – believed that Clinton's health care plan was superior to Obama's.

It now appears that Clinton's lobbying succeeded only in stopping John Edwards from endorsing Obama earlier in the race, when the outcome was less clear than it is now. Whilst Edwards's endorsement counts for less than it would have done had it come, for example, right after Pennsylvania, it still matters, particularly as a way of deflecting news coverage and commentary from Obama's poor showing in West Virginia.

Edwards makes his endorsement at a rally in Michigan in front of 12,000 people, and is joined on stage by Obama. 'The Democratic voters in America have made their choice, and so have I,' says Edwards. Referring to his lament during the campaign that the nation is divided into 'two Americas', he says: 'There is one man who knows in his heart that it is time to create one America – not two – and that man is Barack Obama.' Mrs Edwards is nowhere to be seen.

On the same day, NARAL Pro-Choice America, the leading abortion rights group, also endorses Obama. Although this story doesn't make as many evening bulletins, it is an even harsher blow to Clinton. A staunch pro-choice advocate throughout her career, she receives news of its decision as a stinging betrayal. When NARAL's president calls Howard Wolfson, Clinton's loyal spokesperson, to inform him, Wolfson loses his temper and shouts down the phone.

But once again Clinton runs into trouble of her own making when, in an attempt to remind people of how long Democratic races have continued in the past, she points out that Bobby Kennedy was still running for the nomination in June 1968, when he was assassinated.

Her words are misinterpreted as a suggestion that Obama may suffer a similar fate. Given the concerns surrounding the high-profile candidacy of an African-American, Clinton's reference is certainly ill judged.

She is infuriated at the barrage of criticism that hits her, however, seeing it as yet another example of unfair treatment by the media. Some in her own campaign wonder if by staying in the race she is simply allowing herself to become a punching bag for the press, at the expense of her long-term reputation. But Clinton tells supporters she will stay in until the last primary, in Puerto Rico at the beginning of June.

On 20 May, the two candidates split victories in Oregon and Kentucky. Obama wins Oregon easily, and Clinton trounces Obama in Kentucky. It might have been seen as a reminder of Clinton's strength amongst blue-collar voters. But the headlines in the newspapers the next day all focus on Obama's passing of an electoral milestone: he now has an absolute majority of pledged delegates. He needs fewer than 100 superdelegate votes to put him over the top. Few doubt that he will get them.

An unexpected intervention by President Bush into the race highlights the new reality. In a speech to the Israeli parliament, Bush likens those who would negotiate with 'terrorists and radicals' to the appeasers of the Nazis. His comments are widely interpreted as an oblique attack on Obama's controversial suggestion that he would engage, as president, with rogue states such as Iran without preconditions. John McCain hurriedly issues a statement agreeing with the president and backs it up in a speech.

Obama hits back, seizing the opportunity to tie McCain to a massively unpopular president:

> If George Bush and John McCain want to have a debate
> about protecting the United States of America, that is a
> debate that I'm happy to have any time, any place, and

that is a debate I will win because George Bush and John
McCain have a lot to answer for.

The exchange appears to mark the opening of the general election
campaign and to anticipate the lines of attack: McCain accusing
Obama of being weak on national security, and Obama aiming to
create the impression that a vote for McCain is a vote for a third Bush
term. It has the side-effect of making Clinton look like a bystander as
the two viable contenders for the presidency square up to each other.

Clinton's last path to victory is cut off

On the last weekend of the month, the Democratic National
Committee (DNC) holds a special meeting to decide what to do
about Michigan and Florida. In theory, when they moved the dates
of their primaries up the calendar without permission from party
leaders, those states forfeited the right to have their delegates counted
at the convention. But in reality, the Democrats can ill afford to be
seen ignoring the millions of votes cast in two states important for
victory in November. Calls for revotes have come to nothing after
nobody could agree on how to go about it. So now the DNC has to
make a decision on how to distribute the delegates between the two
remaining candidates, and find a settlement acceptable to all sides.
This is all in the interest of what party leaders repeatedly and somewhat
nervously declare to be paramount: party unity. But the meeting
exposes the bitter divisions that have opened up within the party over
the course of this long and often acrimonious contest.

Hundreds of Hillary Clinton's supporters show up to rally on
her behalf outside the hotel in Washington where the meeting is
convened. Many hold out the hope that their candidate can still win

the nomination if the party decides in favour of seating all of the delegates Clinton 'won' in these states. The mood is mutinous. Reporters find it all too easy to elicit angry denunciations of Barack Obama and his campaign from the crowd.

Inside the atmosphere is more subdued as the thirty members of the party's Rules and Bylaws Committee hear competing arguments for how to deal with the delegations. The audience of party members hear nine hours of legalistic discussion unlikely to stoke any strong feeling other than exhaustion. The committee then holds a three-hour closed-door session to agree a solution. When the doors open, Alice Germond, secretary of the DNC and officially neutral in the race, rises to speak. She begins by reminding everyone of the importance of playing by the rules. . . at which point Clinton's supporters sense that things haven't gone their way. Over a rising noise of protests, Germond says: 'I'm feeling very badly that we can't seat Michigan and Florida in full.' As she continues she has to yell in order to be heard over boos and cries of 'Shame on you!'.

The committee has voted for a compromise solution that turns out to be very close to that proposed by the Obama campaign: seat both states' delegations, but as a penalty grant each only half a vote per delegate.

Harold Ickes, the Clinton loyalist and veteran party man who sits on the committee, smoulders with rage, particularly about the allocation of four disputed Michigan delegates to Obama. Speaking from the platform, he issues a dramatic *j'accuse* to his fellow committee members, warning them, in darkly sardonic tones, that they are sowing the seeds of division. 'There's been a lot of talk about party unity . . . "Let's all come together and put our arms around each other" . . . I submit to you, ladies and gentlemen, that hijacking four delegates . . . is not a good way to start down the path of party unity.'

As the meeting comes to an end, committee members are assailed by further jeers and boos from the floor. A chant of 'McCain '08' goes up. Clinton supporters sit, inconsolable, on the floor, many in tears. A retired teacher from Pennsylvania tells the cameras: 'If it's not Hillary, I'm voting for McCain. Seventeen million people voted for Hillary and I'm telling you many of them are going to defect.'

The DNC's decision is significant not just because it closes down Clinton's last hope of changing the delegate equation, but for what it demonstrates about the abrupt shift in power within the party. For more than fifteen years, the Clintons have between them exerted a tighter grip on the party's governing structures than any other politician or faction. They were the party's unofficial king and queen, and their courtiers – including Ickes – dominated its affairs. The committee's decision to back the Obama campaign's solution shows how swiftly the party's establishment is consolidating behind a new leader.

Thousands of miles to the south, Clinton is swigging from a bottle of Presidente beer and dancing to salsa music in Puerto Rico, which holds its primary on the first day of June. Hispanic voters have historically been loyal to Clinton and her husband, and Clinton is expected to win easily here. She has been in telephone contact with Ickes throughout the day, but hearing that her last hope of winning the nomination is disappearing only seems to renew her determination to enjoy her last days of campaigning. She travels through Puerto Rico's poor neighbourhoods, speaking from the back of a flatbed truck on sweltering afternoons, and is met everywhere by cheering supporters imploring her to carry on.

Back at campaign headquarters, Bill Clinton is still working the phones, calling superdelegates, making the case for his wife, and frequently raising his voice in anger as one by one they politely refuse to submit to his once-irresistible powers of persuasion. It is becoming apparent to everyone, except, perhaps, the former president, that the sun has set on the Clintons' reign over the Democratic Party.

June 2008

Puerto Rico, as expected, delivers an overwhelming victory to Hillary Clinton. The result shows her enduring strength with Hispanic voters, one of the key constituencies in November's election, even as she faces up to the probability that she must concede the race within days.

Clinton and her supporters can't quite believe that despite winning more states and votes in these final weeks, party insiders show no sign of coming over to her camp. Ed Rendell, the Pennsylvania governor and a loyal Clintonite, expresses her campaign's frustration: 'Most Clinton supporters are filled with bewilderment that this is happening. We are willing to go on, and we understand the inevitability of this, but we are filled with disappointment and amazement. Why haven't these results caused the superdelegates to come around?'

On the phone from San Juan, Clinton tells a reporter that she is still considering an appeal against the DNC's decision on Michigan and Florida. Diehard supporters urge her to take her fight for more delegates from these states all the way to the party convention in August. But to do so would be to risk destroying her reputation as a loyal Democrat.

There are two days between Puerto Rico and the final primaries, in Montana and South Dakota, on 3 June. The Clintons spend the final day of the primary campaign on the trail in South Dakota. Hillary is suffering from coughing fits; Bill is suffering from fits of fury. When asked about a piece in *Vanity Fair* detailing rumours about his private life, he tells a voter that the journalist who wrote the article is 'a scumbag'. Hours later he issues an apology for his intemperate language. An exasperated Clinton aide remarks to a reporter: 'It's the last day of his wife's campaign, and he couldn't keep a lid on his emotions. How much more narcissistic can you get?'

The Obama campaign is engaged in an intense final stage of its highly organised effort to secure superdelegate endorsements. The team want to be able to claim an unambiguous victory on Tuesday night. The effort pays off. More than forty superdelegates declare for the Illinois senator on the final day of the primary campaign.

That night, Obama wins Montana, as expected. Adding his pledged delegates from that state to the new superdelegates pushes him over the threshold of 2,118 total delegates.

Obama's campaign has travelled on a wildly unpredictable journey to reach that number. But as David Plouffe looks at a copy of the spreadsheet he put together in 2007, containing his best guesses as to which states his candidate would win and by what margins, he might permit himself a moment of self-congratulation. Out of twenty-seven projections, he got just three wrong: he predicted wins in Indiana and South Dakota, which Obama lost, and a loss in Maine, which Obama won narrowly. His delegate projections look even more impressive: he predicted that Obama would end up with 1,683 pledged delegates and that Clinton would accumulate 1,551. The final tallies are 1,704 for Obama and 1,553 for Clinton.

Finally: a Democratic nominee

The most extraordinary nomination race in living memory is over. After sixteen months of speeches, debates and advertising; after record turnouts and unprecedented organisational efforts in states across the country; after a thrilling switchback ride that raised new hopes and smashed expectations; after a national debate that brought out the best and worst of America: Barack Obama is the Democratic nominee for president.

The Obama campaign team have booked a venue in St Paul, Minnesota to hold their victory rally. The venue is significant for two reasons. First, it is in a state that will be closely contested in November. Second, it is the venue in which John McCain will be accepting the Republican nomination in September; the Obama team like the aggressive symbolism of their man getting there first.

But his speech is preceded by that of the rival he has vanquished – and Hillary Clinton is not in the mood to get out of his way and applaud.

Obama doesn't win both of the final states. Clinton gains South Dakota, despite the Obama campaign making a significant effort there. For Clinton, it is yet further maddening evidence that her campaign is being brought to a premature end. She isn't ready to give up the fight quite yet, and neither are her supporters.

Clinton holds a rally in the gymnasium of Baruch College in New York City. With accidental symbolism, the gym is in a concrete bunker two floors beneath street level. There is no mobile phone or BlackBerry coverage, and no TV screens in the main hall, so supporters don't have to watch the Obama celebrations in St Paul. The loud-speakers play Tom Petty's song 'I Won't Back Down'.

Barack and Michelle Obama watch Clinton's speech on television before he goes on stage in St Paul, unsure what to expect. They see Clinton being introduced to an enthusiastic crowd by her loyal aide Terry McAuliffe as 'the next president of the United States'. They observe the absence of cheering when Clinton pays polite tribute to Obama. They note, as everyone else does, that Clinton does not concede the race, or even acknowledge that she cannot win it. Indeed, the senator from New York sounds defiant, arguing once again that she is the strongest candidate and asserting that she has won the popular vote – a notion that the Obamas might shake their heads at, counting as it does the full votes in Michigan and Florida.

Speaking in the third person, Clinton repeats the question that many in the media have been asking with regard to her immediate and longer-term ambitions: 'What does Hillary want?' She gives an ambiguous answer. 'I want the nearly eighteen million Americans who voted for me to be respected.' Her supporters respond with raucous chants of 'Denver, Denver' (referring to the forthcoming Democratic convention in Colorado's capital city) and 'Yes She Will!'. Clinton declares that she will ask her supporters, via her website, to decide 'where we go from here'.

Obama's aides, watching the speech from St Paul, are furious. Their candidate has won, and they want the focus of tomorrow's coverage to be on Obama's victory, not on Clinton's refusal to back down. But like her husband, Clinton – perhaps remembering the moment after Wisconsin when Obama interrupted coverage of her speech to start his own – does not yield the spotlight easily.

Perhaps as a result of the scenes he has just witnessed, Obama seems unusually hesitant in the opening minutes of his speech. He doesn't project the sunny demeanour of a victor. But after a while he finds his rhythm, and delivers a memorable address. As in Iowa, Obama alludes to the historic nature of his victory without explicitly referring to his race: 'Tonight, we mark the end of one historic journey with the beginning of another – a journey that will bring a new and better day to America,' he says. 'Because of you, tonight I can stand here and say that I will be the Democratic nominee for president of the United States of America.'

Back in the Baruch gym, Bill and Hillary Clinton are still working the 200 or so supporters left in the hall, shaking hands and exchanging hugs. Hillary is cheered and embraced by supporters telling her she mustn't give up, just as she has been everywhere she has visited in the past few weeks, long after the media declared the race over. The PA system blares out a song by John Cougar Mellencamp that has the refrain 'This is our country, this is our country'.

What does Hillary want? Nobody is quite sure, perhaps not even Clinton herself. Some of her supporters hint that she would like to be offered the vice-presidential slot on Obama's ticket – it's rumoured her husband is convinced she should go for it. Others suggest she would prefer to wait for another turn to run. If, as she seems to believe, Obama will lose in November, that could be in four years' time.

Obama and Clinton speak briefly on the telephone in the early hours of Wednesday 4 June. Clinton congratulates Obama. Obama offers to meet Clinton at a time and place of her choosing for a longer conversation.

The reconciliation begins

The next day, the Democratic candidates cross paths at a pre-scheduled event they are both speaking at: the annual conference of the influential Jewish lobbying group AIPAC. The choreography of their accidental meeting reveals something of the new reality. Backstage at the Washington Convention Center, Hillary Clinton spots Barack Obama in a crowded hallway and presses herself against the wall in order to let him and his entourage past. Obama, who is on his way out after giving his speech, sees Clinton and instigates a chat. After a few words the nominee strides away to the elevator as his Secret Service agents bark out 'Make way for Senator Obama!', scattering Clinton's aides.

Later that day Clinton addresses her staff at headquarters in Arlington, Virginia. Many are in tears. She doesn't explicitly announce the end of her campaign, but neither does she attempt to rally her troops. On a conference call with key supporters on Capitol Hill, she is gently advised to arrange a graceful exit from the race.

Clinton really has no option. If she carries on, many of her powerful supporters in the party will desert her. The Democratic leadership will strong-arm her to the margins, just as she found herself pressed up against the side of the hallway at the convention centre. One Democratic observer puts it colourfully, with reference to the Democratic leader in the House of Representatives: 'There's a new sheriff in town, Nancy Pelosi. She is driving the bus, and she will drive it right over the Clintons and if they miss the fact they got run over, she will back up and run over them again.'

One evening later in the week, Clinton and Obama meet face to face at the home of Senator Dianne Feinstein, a Clinton supporter. It is the first lengthy conversation the two have had since the race began. The meeting is held in secret, with Obama's press corps getting on his plane to another event only to discover – much to their annoyance – that he is not on board.

At Feinstein's house, the two former candidates for the nomination sit facing each other in plush armchairs, armed only with a glass of water each. There are no aides present. After ushering them in, Feinstein disappears upstairs, telling them to shout when they're ready. At 10 p.m., after about an hour, Feinstein is called down and thanked for her hospitality. The two seem in good humour as she sees them out.

On Saturday, Clinton gives the speech many in the party had been hoping for first time around. Standing on a podium surrounded my thousands of supporters, as sunlight pours down through the 100-foot high atrium of the National Building Museum in

Washington, Clinton concedes the nomination, and unequivocally endorses Obama's bid to be president.

Clinton manages to speak warmly of her former rival, saying that after taking a 'front-row seat' to his candidacy she has come to admire his 'strength and determination, his grace and his grit'. When Clinton exhorts the crowd to 'do all we can to help elect Barack Obama the next president of the United States' the applause is mixed with boos, which accompany each of the half-dozen occasions she returns to a variation on that theme. It's clear that many of her supporters, especially the female ones, are not reconciled to Obama's victory.

Clinton speaks proudly about the historic nature of her candidacy, fusing her political messages with the more personal tone she acquired after New Hampshire. Most strikingly, she addresses the matter of her gender more directly than she ever did during the campaign:

> When I was asked what it means to be a woman running
> for president, I always gave the same answer, that I was
> proud to be running as a woman, but I was running
> because I thought I'd be the best president. But I am a
> woman and, like millions of women, I know there are still
> barriers and biases out there, often unconscious, and I
> want to build an America that respects and embraces the
> potential of every last one of us.

The highest glass ceiling of all may not be shattered, but, says Clinton in the most memorable phrase of her campaign, there are now 'about eighteen million cracks in it'.

In a dramatic parting tableau, Clinton raises the hands of her daughter Chelsea and mother Dorothy. Her husband does not take the stage.

Obama prepares for Stage 2

The weeks that follow are quiet. The nation turns its attention to other matters. Hillary Clinton and Barack Obama finally have some time to recuperate from the toll that this intense sixteen-month race has taken on their bodies and minds.

Meanwhile the Obama campaign sets about preparing for the general election with the confidence and efficiency that characterised its nomination-winning effort. Large parts of the Democratic Party's staff in Washington are moved to Obama HQ in Chicago in order to better integrate the party's efforts with the candidate's. The move is another indication of the extent to which Obama has seized power within the party.

In a video message emailed to supporters, Obama announces that his campaign will opt out of the system of public financing, and be financed with contributions from private donations only. The announcement provokes controversy. The public financing system was instituted after Watergate in an attempt to lessen the influence of private money on elections. Usually, both candidates are allocated a certain amount of money by the government to spend in the two months before the election. In theory this creates a level playing field, although extra spending by the parties and lobby groups behind either candidate means this isn't necessarily the case in practice.

But the public financing system, imperfect as it is, has generally been seen as a good thing, and along with John McCain, Obama has given every indication that he will opt into it. He said he would pursue it 'aggressively' and he committed himself to it in a written questionnaire. He even said, repeatedly, that he wished to meet McCain to discuss an agreement on it.

Obama offers an unconvincing explanation for his change of mind. He complains that the McCain campaign may profit unfairly from attack ads made by outside pressure groups (though the only attack ads from lobby groups to have run so far go in the opposite direction). He also says that his campaign, financed as it is in large part by small contributions from ordinary supporters, is consonant with the goals of public financing.

The real reason for Obama's *volte-face*, as everyone is aware, is that he believes his campaign will raise far more money from private donations than it would be allowed to spend under public financing rules. By opting out of the system, he hopes to be able to outspend McCain's campaign by a massive amount.

McCain angrily accuses Obama of breaking his word, arguing that it shows he cannot be trusted. Even some of Obama's supporters express their disappointment at his reversal. The Obama campaign team clearly expect the move to be controversial but have decided that any short-term hits taken by the candidate on this issue will be outweighed by the longer-term benefit of a financial advantage. Although that does depend, of course, on their campaign raising money at the rate they project.

Few are betting against that. The Obama campaign's fundraising has been prolific, ever since he announced his run for the presidency. Clinton, with her grip on the party machine, and her deep and wide relationships with rich donors, never expected for a moment that she might be outspent by any rival, least of all a relative newcomer to the political scene.

But the internet team assembled by David Plouffe – which included the co-founder of Facebook – quickly built a sophisticated web-based platform designed to make it easy for supporters to organise their own mini-fundraising drives amongst friends and neighbours on behalf of the candidate. The resulting army of small donors, most of whom make small and repeated donations, provide a bigger cash flow to the campaign than Plouffe and Obama had dared hope for when they began. In addition, the campaign courted wealthy donors in California, many of them young and rich on the proceeds of dotcom money, who leaned Democratic but had never been part of the Clinton circle.

The campaign hopes to use this lucrative model to stretch the McCain campaign to breaking point. With money to spare, they can afford to buy advertising and organise supporters in states that they have only an outside chance of winning. In Plouffe's terms, they can 'expand the map'. He wants to target states that are usually considered solidly Republican. Many old hands in the party advise him against wasting his money. But Plouffe trusts his numbers, and his instincts, and believes that Obama can win in places that haven't voted Democrat in a generation by drawing new voters to the polls.

Of course, even with a financial advantage Obama can't win unless Democratic voters are united behind him, and to a large extent that now depends on the person he has beaten to the nomination. Clinton's whole-hearted public support of his candidacy is seen as key to win over some of those supporters – especially women – who are deeply disappointed that they can't vote for her in November.

Hillary reflects

Bill Clinton is still angry. Angry with the media, and angry with an Obama campaign he thinks 'slimed' him with the taint of racism. His office issues a terse statement of support for Barack Obama, but the man himself says nothing publicly. His wife, however, is beginning to reconcile herself to the fact that, if she is to preserve her reputation as a loyal Democrat, she must now support her former rival's bid to be president.

Hillary Clinton has been reflecting on how she lost a race that

everyone thought was hers for the taking. She admits to an interviewer that she made a 'fundamental miscalculation' is choosing to
focus, in the lead-up to Iowa, on her readiness to be commander in
chief, at the expense of a more forward-looking message.

Separately, David Axelrod agrees. He confesses that his biggest
worry in the months before Iowa was that Clinton would adopt the
populist, elite-bashing stance she took up later in the race, after
Obama had amassed an unassailable lead in pledged delegates. He
was relieved when she chose to focus on her qualifications: it facilitated
Obama's strategy of running against the political establishment.
Clinton's mistake was understandable: it was born of her instinct
that, as a woman, she would have to work extra hard to cross the
threshold of trust invested in the leader of America's armed forces,
especially in a time of war.

But it wasn't the only reason she lost. Clinton might have made
better strategic decisions if she'd had better advice. As she prepared
for 2008, Clinton put together a talented team of advisers. But they
were chosen on the basis of personal loyalty rather than experience in
presidential primaries. One anecdote, revealed whilst Clinton was
still running, conveys an idea of the problem.

In a 2007 planning meeting Mark Penn predicted confidently
that by winning California and thereby amassing all of its delegates
Clinton would win the race. But in Democratic races delegates are
awarded according to a candidate's share of the vote. Sitting nearby,
Harold Ickes, a veteran party insider, looked at Penn in horror. 'How
can it be', he asked, 'that the much vaunted chief strategist doesn't
understand proportional allocation?'

But the campaign's focus on big states remained. It failed to put
together proper organisations in smaller states, including the caucus
states that followed Super Tuesday, allowing Obama to rack up
massive wins that built him an insurmountable advantage in pledged

delegates. It ran out of money just when it needed it most. It neglected to organise a concerted effort to win over superdelegates until late in the game.

This story illustrates the other big problem with Clinton's team: it was crippled by rancorous rivalries. Colleagues constantly briefed against each other and fought for influence over the message and the candidate. They were too easily influenced by the latest Washington wisdoms: by setting up headquarters near the capital, Clinton exposed her campaign to the winds of gossip and head-turning advice from well-meaning outsiders (Obama's decision to set up headquarters in Chicago was a deliberate attempt to keep his distance from Washington's siren voices). Unsurprisingly, the result was often confusion: new strategic directions were regularly announced and different slogans rolled out every month. Clinton seemed unable, or unwilling, to impose discipline and direction on her warring team.

Then there was the candidate's so-called 'character problem'. Penn displayed impressive foresight early in 2007 when he identified the coalition of voters that would form Clinton's base in the primaries: female and working-class voters (he called them 'Invisible Americans'). But by convincing her that voters cared about little else except her ability to be 'ready to lead from Day 1', Penn's advice over-rode the concerns of others who worried that voters needed to like as well as respect Clinton if they were going to back her. By the time Clinton started to address the question of her personal manner it was in such a ham-fisted way (laughing loudly at unexpected moments, going on a 'likeability tour') that she exacerbated the problem. It wasn't until Pennsylvania that she truly found the voice she had begun to discover in New Hampshire: a happy warrior, always ready with a hug and a quip, battling bravely on behalf of America's hard-working families. But by then it was too late.

Of course, the person most responsible for Clinton's defeat wasn't the candidate, or any member of her staff.

If, before the primary campaign began, a group of crack political strategists with creative imaginations had been asked to design the perfect candidate to beat Hillary Clinton, they might have come up with someone resembling Barack Obama. In a year when Democratic voters were ready to be inspired, the charismatic and eloquent Obama made a candidate who had always been more comfortable talking policy than vision look flat footed and small minded. In a year when voters were angry about the Iraq War, Obama was able to say he had been against it from the start – unlike Clinton. In a year when loyalties were tested, African-Americans, the constituency that Clinton and her husband had always relied upon to see them to victory in difficult times, deserted them for one of their own.

Above all, in a year when voters were crying out for change, Obama's youth and newness to the scene offered a stark contrast to Clinton – and the colour of his skin amplified the sense that he, more than she, represented a new direction for the country.

One more thing: beneath all the sound and fury of message and personality, the Clinton campaign was simply out-organised. From Iowa, where the Obama team proved far more effective at getting new voters to caucus, to a fundraising model that took full advantage of the new technologies, to the methodical targeting of delegates and super-delegates, to the foresight to open offices in later states earlier on, to the prudent allocation of budgets, the relentlessly intelligent Obama campaign was more efficient, creative and prescient at every stage. It is one of the ironies of the contest that Clinton, master of policy detail, should have allowed her campaign to be so comprehensively outplanned by a candidate she frequently accused of being all talk and no substance.

Clinton has emerged from the nomination race a loser, but a bigger figure in the political landscape than she was before. She appears both more iconic, and – partly as a result of losing – more human. For the first time, she is a more consequential politician than her husband. She now commands something he had always managed to elicit from the millions who voted for him, but she had never enjoyed to the same extent: love.

In North Carolina, a few weeks before the end, Bill Clinton sat in the back of a car with Tom Vilsack, the former governor of Iowa and a firm Hillary supporter. The sun was setting on a long day of campaigning. As Vilsack later told reporter Roger Simon, Clinton was in a reflective mood. He ruminated on whether, if the campaign was lost, it had all been worthwhile.

'Even if she doesn't win, they will know Hillary better and like her better,' Clinton finally said. 'She's a complex person. They just didn't know her. If you know her, you just love her.'

A place called Unity

As the two leading Democratic candidates take to the same stage for the first time since the end of the nomination battle, it is Hillary Clinton who must implore the crowd to bring about the election of President Obama.

Party bosses, desperate to consolidate the candidates' support, have chosen to stage this event in Unity, New Hampshire. It is the perfect venue: Obama and Clinton won 107 votes each in this tiny town when New Hampshire held its primary in January.

Today, in front of an audience of 6,000, Clinton spells out her message of loyalty in somewhat formal terms: 'To anyone who voted for me and is now considering not voting, or voting for Senator McCain, I strongly urge you to reconsider.' When Obama speaks he showers both Clinton and her husband (not present) in praise. 'We need them. We need them badly,' he says. 'That's how we're going to bring about unity in the Democratic Party. And that's how we're going to bring about unity in America.' The message of harmony is signalled by their sartorial choices: she wears a powder-blue suit, he wears a light-blue tie. But the sense of an uncomfortable rapprochement is there in other details, at least for those who wish to find it. The chair provided for each candidate to sit on whilst the other makes their speech is perfectly designed for Obama's long body, but too tall for Clinton to sit on with dignity. She makes do with standing when it's his turn at the podium.

Meanwhile, in airless Washington offices, lawyers for the Obama and Clinton campaigns are working through the details of the peace. A thicket of thorny issues, large and small, need to be settled: what to do about Clinton's debt from the campaign; what role she might play at the convention and during the general election campaign; whether Obama's campaign will provide her with a plane and staff.

As the candidate believed by most, right up until March, to be the most likely next president of the United States negotiates her exit from the race, the final round of this titanic contest takes shape.

McCain vs Obama

The two candidates left standing are a study in contrasts.

One descends from a storied family of American military heroes; the other is the son of a Kenyan and a wandering Kansan. One is a twenty-year veteran of the Senate on his second presidential run; the other is a newcomer to national politics. One is defined by his experience of military combat and is a believer in the old-fashioned virtues of honour and duty; the other formed his worldview on the streets of Chicago's South Side and at Harvard, and is at home in a world of cultural differences, iPods and email. One is impulsive, sometimes fiery by temperament; the other is cooler, more calculating. One is a natural improviser, at home in the cut and thrust of a town hall debate; the other is the master of the set-piece speech, and prefers to prepare his public statements with meticulous care.

The key political contrast, of course, is that one is a Republican and the other a Democrat, a fact that this year bestows a big advantage to Barack Obama. But the Republicans have chosen the only candidate who might be able to escape the taint of his own party; John McCain is a political brand in his own right.

In a meeting in the last week of June, however, McCain's advisers are still having trouble answering the central question of any candidacy: why elect this person? Some argue that McCain should run on his record of bipartisan legislative achievement; others deem this too dry. After a long, inconclusive discussion, Mark Salter, McCain's closest friend and adviser, speaks up. There's a reason why McCain bucks his party, he says with feeling. It's because he puts his country before political interest. 'We're talking about someone who was willing to *die* before losing his honour! He would *die*!' Having said his piece, Salter leaves the room to smoke a cigarette. His colleagues, impressed by his passion, agree with Salter in his absence. They settle on the slogan 'Country First'.

Obama's answer to the question is the same as it has been since he announced his candidacy: he is the candidate of change. After two terms of any president, Americans usually turn to the other party. The exceptions, as in 1988 when George Bush Sr succeeded Ronald Reagan, come when the incumbent is still popular at the end of his term, or when the opposing candidate is weak. But this year, with Bush Jr's ratings plumbing the depths, Obama knows that if he can tie McCain to Bush and the Republicans, he will have won half the battle. The other half will be persuading Americans that he is an acceptable alternative.

July 2008

Obama and 'the world as it is'

When Barack Obama was twenty-four, he left New York City, where he had studied and worked for four years, to take a job in Chicago. The job didn't pay the salary that a political science graduate from Columbia University could command. But Obama had an itch he needed to scratch and he thought this job would help him do that.

Without being entirely clear on what a 'community organiser' did, Obama had known he wanted to be one whilst he was still a student. As an idealistic and politically interested young man, he was inspired by the stories of the civil rights movement. In *Dreams from My Father* Obama recalls pronouncing to his classmates on the need for change in the country, telling them that 'change won't come from the top . . . change will come from a mobilised grassroots'. Having missed the civil rights struggle by twenty years, Obama was travelling to Chicago to see if he could turn this talk into action.

Obama joined an organisation called the Development Community Project (DCP). The DCP worked in largely African-American communities in the South Side that had been ravaged by the decline of the steel industry. It agitated citizens to demand better services from the city authorities, from job banks to safer streets to asbestos removal from public housing. Obama's new bosses were white Jews in need of a black colleague to give them more credibility with local people. They were professionals who worked where there were problems, and they practised the teachings of Saul Alinsky, the founding father of modern community organising. Alinsky had been dead for thirteen years by the time Obama arrived in Chicago but his legend lived on, and much of his thinking was absorbed and internalised by Obama over his three years of work as an organiser.

Saul Alinsky was a captivating character, profane and profound, with a line in brutal epigrams. He attended the University of Chicago, where he studied Al Capone's gang, gaining insight into the subject that fascinated him more than any other: power. He aspired to be a modern Machiavelli, on the side of the people rather than the princes. Leaving university, he set up a neighbourhood council in Chicago's Meatpacking District. It organised a series of sit-ins and protests in poor areas of Chicago, with the aim of forcing landlords and employers to meet the demands of the community for better services. It worked. Conditions improved, crime fell and cooperation between various ethnic groups increased, as blacks, Irish and Jews united around a common self-interest. Alinsky gained funding to start similar organisations in the slums of several American cities.

One of the Alinskian maxims that Obama was introduced to as an organiser was 'power is good, powerlessness is evil'. The end of achieving power, in Alinsky's view, justified a wide range of means. He would intimidate city officials and sometimes resort to dramatic stunts such as the ceremonious dumping of ghetto rats on the steps of City Hall. Alinsky had no time for idealistic do-gooders who didn't want to dirty their hands with the realities of power. 'A liberal', he sneered, 'is the kind of guy who walks out of a room when an argument turns into a fight.' Neither did he have much time for extremists, who often returned to their comfortable lives the moment things didn't go their way: 'He who lives by the sword shall die by the champagne cocktail.' Both types commit the ultimate crime in Alinsky's book: they refuse to begin with '*the world as it is* rather than as we would like it to be'.

Obama is a very different character from Alinsky. His conciliatory instincts oppose Alinsky's overtly confrontational style (a 1970 profile of Alinsky in *Time* magazine says he had 'possibly antagonised more people – regardless of race, colour and creed – than any other living American'). He also came to regard Alinsky-style organising as insufficiently rooted in the communities it seeks to change. But the principles and methods that Obama learned during these years in Chicago still inform his political outlook.

First, Obama adopted Alinsky's core insight: that the way to get things done is to organise ordinary people, and the way to organise people is to appeal to their common self-interest. Obama's 'One America' rhetoric is based on the Alinskian idea that different groups of people with conflicting beliefs can be bound together by issues they have in common. In a video posted on his campaign website Obama says: 'Ordinary people can have an enormous influence in Washington. The problem is they're just not organised right now. The main thing is to get people to understand that their self-interest is wrapped up with what happens in Washington.' The prodigious success of Obama's campaign in raising money and creating effective get-the-vote-out operations – and all in record time – has been down to its expert marshalling of a millions-strong army of donors and volunteers. Never before in a political campaign have so many been organised so effectively.

The second principle Obama has inherited from Alinsky and his disciples is a relentless focus on the only game in town: power. As Alinsky demonstrated, that focus requires a certain ruthlessness of method. Now, less than five months before the 2008 election,

Republicans are quickly learning that the man they had down as another naïve, unworldly liberal (before Iowa, Karl Rove described Obama as a 'vitamin-starved Adlai Stevenson') is in fact a fierce competitor, unusually clear eyed about how to gain power in 'the world as it is'.

Obama's decision to opt out of public financing is a case in point. The sheer chutzpah of it has Republican jaws hitting the ground. Obama declared his decision in a video message to supporters, explaining that the current system had become corrupt. He sounded for all the world as if he hadn't for a moment considered the effect on his ability to win the election.

Obama is also adept at mixing high-minded rhetoric with low tactics in campaigning. For a candidate who conveys the impression of being above negative campaigning, his team are adept at responding to and initiating attacks, as Clinton discovered and McCain is finding out. The speed and ferocity with which Obama's campaign coordinates such attacks has not been seen from a Democratic candidate for a long time.

But as the first full month of the general election campaign gets underway it isn't just Obama's opponents who are shocked by his hard-nosed pragmatism. In a series of policy announcements, Obama appears to be making a sharp tack towards the political centre, to the dismay of some on his own side. He holds a press conference to explain a 'refinement' in his policy of withdrawing from Iraq within sixteen months. Such a timetable, he explains, is premised on the assumption that the troops are safe and Iraq is stable, and is thus subject to events. Although the substance of his statement is not inconsistent with his message during the primaries, the language he uses is more restrained, and some of the Democrats who voted for him fear that it signals a softening of his opposition to the war.

Obama also announces that he will coopt one of George W. Bush's signature policies, the investment in religious-based initiatives intended to fight poverty and perform community aid work. By embracing the 'faith-based programme' Obama hopes to attract evangelical voters away from the Republicans, but he risks upsetting those on the left who abhor any blurring of the separation between church and state.

In a flurry of other moves Obama indicates his determination not to be painted as a traditional liberal. He votes for a bill that allows the Bush administration to pursue its policy of wiretapping without a warrant. In response to two controversial Supreme Court decisions he states his support for the death penalty in cases of child rape, and his belief in the right of Americans to carry handguns. In an interview with a Christian magazine he separates himself from most pro-choice advocates by arguing that 'mental distress' is not sufficient reason to allow a late-term abortion. He suggests that his campaign pledge to dismantle NAFTA (a free-trade agreement despised by the unions) was a case of 'overheated rhetoric'.

Presidential candidates often pivot to the middle ground when the general election begins. But the speed and comprehensiveness of Obama's manoeuvre takes everyone by surprise. A petition signed by 22,000 supporters goes up on Obama's own website asking him not to vote for the wiretapping bill. Prominent liberal commentators express their anger and disappointment with his statements on abortion, guns and capital punishment. We thought we were voting for the candidate of change, they say; are we now getting more of the same?

Obama does not seem concerned by these complaints. He has his sights set firmly on winning an election in 'the world as it is', and is certain that he needs to be positioned in the political centre in order to do so.

McCain reboots

John McCain seeks to capitalise on the questions being raised by Barack Obama's manoeuvrings by denouncing him as a fake: a man who presents himself as a candidate of change but who is in fact a 'typical politician'. But McCain is also experiencing some problems with his own party.

Republicans are worried that despite McCain's three-month head-start over his rival, he has not put together an operation capable of fighting a successful general election campaign. He still relies on the small number of advisers who stuck by him after the near-implosion of his candidacy last year. As with Hillary Clinton's team, McCain's staff frequently offer clashing points of view on how to proceed. The result is a campaign that seems confused about whether to present its candidate as a reform-minded maverick or as a committed conservative – and about whether to portray Obama as an extreme liberal or a cynical flip-flopper.

The campaign is also making too many basic errors of political stagecraft and presentation. McCain's speech on the night of Obama's victory over Clinton is a prime example. That evening, McCain's team are determined not to let their presumptive opponent completely dominate the evening news. They arrange for their candidate to make a speech to supporters in Louisiana, comparing his record of achievement with Obama's. But Republicans who watch the evening's events unfold on television are horrified by a different contrast from the one they envisaged.

Obama speaks to 17,000 cheering supporters in a massive hall, looking fully in command of his surroundings. In shot behind him are rows of fresh-faced supporters. He looks like a powerful orator in his element. McCain, on the other hand, speaks to a room of 600 supporters, who applaud politely and raise the occasional, somewhat half-hearted, cheer. His backdrop is a screen of sickly green hue.

McCain's delivery is appalling. He sounds stilted and nervous. His eyes too obviously follow the autocue, and his smile, when it comes, is like a nervous twitch. He displays a wayward grasp of cadence, his voice rising and falling in unexpected places. He frequently seems bored by his own words. His refrain – 'That's not change we can believe in' – is an attempt to turn Obama's slogan against him, but comes across as a desultory sneer. Worst of all, McCain looks and sounds tired and old.

Everything about the speech is a resonant mistake and visible evidence of McCain's erratic campaign operation. After his organisation was reduced to a skeleton in the summer of 2007 McCain was slow to rebuild it, and the lines of command in his team remain unclear. Other mistakes follow. McCain launches a campaign ad boasting that he 'stood up' to President Bush on global warming, but on the same day he travels to Houston to tell oil executives of his support for a new proposal on offshore drilling, one that Bush himself endorses the next day. The ad's message about the political distance between McCain and Bush was wasted. His campaign never sticks to a theme for more than twenty-four hours at a time. New speeches are scheduled too late to make the evening newscasts.

Responding to increasing concern within his own party, McCain announces a reorganisation of his campaign staff. The key change is his appointment of adviser Steve Schmidt to be in charge of day-to-day campaign operations.

Schmidt is a tall, heavily built 38-year-old with a shiny bald head who resembles a sumo wrestler stuffed into a suit. Intense and driven, he was a key player in Bush's much-admired 2004 campaign team; two years later he helped re-elect Arnold Schwarzenegger as governor of California. He speaks in the short, spare rhythms of his native New

Jersey. His blunt manner and physical appearance instil nerves in those who work for him (he is well aware that he can be an intimidating presence: during the Schwarzenegger campaign he stopped attending planning meetings because people were afraid to speak up when he was in the room). Although often spoken of as a Rove protégé, Schmidt rejects the description. Like McCain, he is no ideologue, and he is uneasy with Rove's ultra-partisan approach to politics (Schmidt is close to his gay sister and was appalled by the White House's Rove-inspired push for a constitutional ban on gay marriage). But he shares his former boss's focus on constant tactical aggression.

Schmidt has been working for McCain for only eighteen months but has quickly gained his respect and trust. He was one of the few staffers to stick around, working for no pay, after McCain's campaign collapsed in the summer of 2007. From then on he wielded more influence, forming something of a father–son bond with McCain. After the embarrassment of McCain's speech on the night of Obama's nomination victory, Schmidt tells his boss that unless he allows him to take control of the faltering campaign, he will face defeat. McCain consents, hoping Schmidt will introduce the focus and discipline of Bush's operation to his own bid for the presidency.

In the weeks that follow, a more consistent line of attack on Obama starts to develop: that he is out of his depth on foreign policy. McCain repeatedly returns to Obama's promise to withdraw troops from Iraq within sixteen months, pointing out that such a policy risks undermining the success that the recent 'surge' of troops to that country – a McCain-sponsored initiative – has brought. He accuses Obama of not knowing what's going on in Iraq, and asks why he hasn't visited the country in over two years.

Obama's planned trip to the Middle East and Europe assumes even more importance.

Obama's grand tour

Presidential candidates do not usually spend more than a few days, if any, out of the country during a campaign. But Barack Obama knows that unless he can persuade voters that he will be a strong and capable commander in chief, he will lose the election. With this in mind he decides to spend a week meeting US troops and foreign leaders in Europe, Iraq and Afghanistan.

The pictures, language and livery of the trip are carefully designed to suggest a presidential aura. Credentials issued to the travelling press say 'The visit of Senator Obama to the Middle East and Europe', echoing the language of a White House trip. Back home, Americans see pictures and watch video of Obama shaking hands with presidents and prime ministers, and meeting the troops in the Middle East, and never looking or sounding less than fully at ease. Indeed, Obama's trip illustrates one of his most prominent characteristics: uncommon self-assurance.

Almost everyone who knows or has encountered Obama emphasises how comfortable he seems with himself. One of his professors at Harvard remembers him as being 'almost freakishly self-possessed and centred'. In person Obama conveys warmth without the suggestion of intimacy, and is relaxed without being chummy. Although far from humourless, he has an acute sense of his own seriousness. 'Gore and Bush both have this jokey quality,' the academic Robert Putnam, who has met all three, told the *New Yorker*. 'They can be goofy. Obama is not goofy.'

Obama's confidence has a self-reflexive quality. He has a remarkable ability to make cool assessments of his impact on others, almost as if he is always standing off to one side, observing himself. Obama's best friend, Marty Nesbitt, remembers walking alongside him in Boston in 2004, on the day he was due to give the keynote address to the

Democratic convention (the speech that was to make him famous in America and across the world). On the most important day of his political career to date, Obama was supremely calm. A small crowd began to follow them, as there was already a buzz in town about the young black Democrat from Illinois.

'Barack, man, you're like a rock star,' said Nesbitt.

'Yeah, if you think it's bad today, wait until tomorrow,' replied Obama.

'What do you mean?'

'My speech is pretty good.'

So it proved. Now, answering an interviewer's question about the purpose of his trip, Obama says: 'To have substantive discussions with people like Prime Minister Maliki or President Sarkozy or others who I expect to be dealing with over the next eight to ten years.' This kind of casually confident aside, from a politician only four years out of the Illinois state senate, is no longer surprising.

Obama's luck is also on display. His strategic aim during the trip is to shift the focus of the national-security debate away from Iraq and towards Afghanistan in order to neutralise the issue that John McCain – after the success of the surge – considers to be his greatest strength. He is now given significant help in this endeavour from an unexpected quarter: Nouri al-Maliki, the Iraqi prime minister. In an interview with the German magazine *Der Spiegel*, Maliki endorses Obama's sixteen-month withdrawal plan as 'the right timetable'. After a blistering phone call from the White House, Maliki's office backtracks, claiming, unconvincingly, that the prime minister has been misinterpreted. Nobody believes it. Maliki made a calculated intervention designed to boost his own standing at home, and in doing so he has handed Obama a gift. Maliki's intervention makes it far more difficult for McCain to accuse Obama of proposing a reckless and irresponsible withdrawal. McCain has acknowledged that US troops should stay in Iraq only as long as the Iraqis want them to stay. If the Iraqi government wants them out within sixteen months, he can hardly argue.

Flying from the Middle East to Europe in a plane that has 'Change We Can Believe In' emblazoned on its fuselage, Obama arrives in Germany on 24 July to meet Chancellor Angela Merkel and to make a speech. In Berlin, beneath a blue sky, he addresses a crowd of around 200,000 – the largest of the campaign so far. Declaring himself a 'proud citizen of the United States and a fellow citizen of the world', Obama aims to bring a global resonance to his theme of unity across divides: 'People of the world – look at Berlin, where a wall came down, a continent came together, and history proved that there is no challenge too great for a world that stands as one.'

The speech receives much positive coverage in the US media. But two recurrent criticisms are also heard. First, that the speech contained nothing but a collection of grand-sounding but empty phrases: Obama said almost nothing that anyone could disagree with in his speech, other than a very mild suggestion that Germany might send troops to help out in Afghanistan. Second, that the speech, indeed the whole trip, was an indulgent exercise in self-glorification at a time when Americans are suffering from an economic downturn back at home. Obama's magical self-assurance strikes some as hubris.

The McCain campaign, now under Steve Schmidt's more single-minded and aggressive management, senses an opening.

August 2008

McCain finds his groove

John McCain's new ad opens with pictures of the crowds gathered in Berlin to hear Barack Obama's speech. The soundtrack plays a slightly distorted recording of the crowd's chant: *Obama, Obama, Obama*. 'He's the biggest celebrity in the world,' says a female voiceover. Pictures of Britney Spears and Paris Hilton are intercut with pictures of Obama accepting the adulation of the crowd. 'But is he ready to lead?'

The McCain campaign is aiming squarely at the Obama 'cult of personality'. Striking opportunistically after Obama's speech in Berlin, they portray him as a shallow egotist, the weightless creation of an excitable media elite. In a year that favours the Democratic candidate, the McCain camp believe they can win this election by turning it into a referendum on the character of this unknown, untested newcomer.

The ad's use of Hilton and Spears generates enormous amounts of headlines and commentary. McCain is accused by some of trivialising the campaign and of eroding his image as a serious statesman. Others are simply amused and entertained. The ad doesn't have a heavy media budget behind it, but it doesn't need one: it is posted and played everywhere, generating spontaneous spoofs, and even elicits a video response from Paris Hilton herself, who parodies her airhead image by discussing the finer points of energy policy while reclining by the pool. For the first time in this election, it is the McCain campaign making headlines and generating 'buzz'.

Up until now, McCain has seemed passive and helpless in the face of Obama's star power, reacting with bad-tempered grumbles to his opponent's popularity. But by taking on the Obama cultural phenomenon with wit and cheek he has found a way of galvanising his candidacy whilst knocking his opponent off balance. Obama isn't quite sure how to respond: should he be outraged or dismiss it all with a shrug and a joke? He does both, neither to great effect. Meanwhile McCain releases further ads on the same theme. The gap between the two candidates starts to close in the polls. With only weeks until the party conventions – and the traditional kick-off of the campaign proper – McCain finds himself only a few points behind Obama. Given the underlying advantages enjoyed by the Democratic candidate in this race, McCain and the Republicans are pleased with their progress.

Then, as they are apt to do in presidential elections, events intervene. News comes that Russia has sent troops into Georgia. McCain's standing is given a further boost by his quick and authoritative response. He angrily denounces Russia and says that the United States must do everything in its power to stand up for Georgia. Obama, who is visiting his grandmother in Hawaii, issues a statement to the press and convenes an impromptu press conference, at which he takes a cautious and even-handed approach. He sounds uncertain where McCain was sure, vague where McCain was clear. The public and the media judge McCain's response to have been more impressive. McCain's team see this as a turning point: the moment when their candidate proved his superior presidential mettle in the heat of an international incident.

McCain's run of form continues when the two candidates appear on stage together for the first time during the campaign.

Rick Warren is a large, tubby man with thin red hair and a goatee. He is also one of the most powerful people in the world. Warren is the pastor of Saddleback Church in Lake Forest, California, one of the new breed of 'megachurches': massive, multi-purpose centres of worship that have sprung up to service the spiritual needs of people in the suburbs and exurbs of America. His congregation numbers some 22,000. He is the most prominent of a new generation of Evangelist pastors and the unofficial heir to Billy Graham in his position as the nation's Christian leader. His book *The Purpose-Driven Life* has sold twenty-five million copies. He is courted by presidents and senators, and the work his affluent church does on behalf of the poor in Africa means that he has the ear of leaders around the world.

Warren is a social conservative: passionately anti-abortion and opposed to homosexual marriage. But he is very different from older, more controversial figures like Pat Robertson and James Dobson. He rejects the explicit identification they make with the Republican Party. He is not, he says, a member of 'the religious right' or a 'fundamentalist'. His tone is emollient, affable and conciliatory. He stresses the importance of not demonising those who disagree with him and his followers.

It is evidence of Warren's influence that both candidates accept an invitation to appear at Saddleback on 16 August to answer his questions, in a televised event. It's also a sign of Obama's eagerness to discuss his faith. It was an appearance at Warren's church in 2006 that helped convince Obama that he should run for the presidency. What other Democrat, he mused to a friend afterwards, could emerge from a meeting of evangelical Christians unscathed? Obama is making a significant effort to court the evangelical vote this year, despite the knowledge that his stance on abortion means most of them will vote for McCain. He hopes that if he can convince at least some of them that he is not a godless (or worse, Muslim) heretic bent on laying waste to American's Christian values, then some of those who are unenthusiastic about the Republican candidate might be persuaded to vote for him come November.

Warren invites the two candidates on stage to begin the event. They shake hands before Obama pulls McCain into a slightly awkward embrace. Warren interviews them, one at a time, reading from the same list of questions. He asks about each candidate's personal convictions and biographies, largely staying away from direct questions about policy. The contrast in styles is vivid.

McCain's answers are crisp and to the point. He uses powerful anecdotes that are familiar to those who have watched him on the stump but new to most voters. He is emotionally direct: as he relates stories about his time in captivity he appears moved anew in the telling. When asked about his greatest moral failing, he answers, without hesitation and with a convincing sense of regret: 'The failure of my first marriage.' He is fiery with indignation when discussing Russia's behaviour towards Georgia, and unequivocal in his denunciation of Islamic terrorism as an 'evil' that must be defeated.

By contrast, Obama is, as usual, even-toned and measured in his answers. He seems keen to impress Warren, and seeks to address his questions on their own terms rather than revert to riffs from the campaign trail. But his long, meandering answers can sound like waffle, or even evasiveness, to viewers on TV. He is also a little too casual at times: he twice uses the incongruous phrase 'screw up', and says that the question of when a baby gains human rights is 'above my pay grade', a response he later deems too flip.

McCain wins better reviews for his performance. Republicans are reminded of what a compelling candidate he can be. Some Democrats start to worry about how Obama will fare at the upcoming presidential debates, and more generally about McCain's recent run of good news. They hope that a popular choice of running mate and a successful Democratic convention will set Obama back on course for victory.

Obama picks his partner

The media's speculation about who Barack Obama will pick as his vice-presidential candidate has been building for months and now reaches a screeching pitch of intensity. The main contenders, as the deadline grows near, appear to be Evan Bayh, a senator from Indiana, Tim Kaine, the governor of Virginia, and Joe Biden, the veteran senator from Delaware and former presidential candidate (he dropped out after placing poorly in Iowa).

Bayh has been discussed as a possible VP pick before. A popular Democratic governor and then senator in a traditionally Republican state, he has a proven ability to appeal to voters in the heartland. A firm Clinton supporter in the primaries, his presence on the ticket might send a positive signal to her disaffected supporters. But Bayh is a little bland. He won't create much excitement around the country, and his laid-back style doesn't lend itself to the kinds of aggressive attack on the other side that presidential candidates usually like to leave to their running mates.

Kaine, like Obama, is a charismatic speaker, and hails from another red state that Obama would dearly love to turn blue in November. He was an early supporter of Obama's run against Clinton and the two are personally close. But Kaine has been governor of Virginia for only three years and hasn't achieved much in office. An Obama–Kaine ticket might look very thin on experience.

As the conflict in Georgia dominates the headlines, Senator

Biden's stock rises. He is acknowledged as one of the country's foremost foreign policy authorities. As Russian tanks roll into Georgia, its president, Mikheil Saakashvili, personally invites Biden to visit his country. Biden's high-profile trip and his effortless grasp of the situation remind Democrats, including those within Obama's campaign, of how impressive he is on the international stage.

In the days before the convention, some commentators wonder if Obama is going to spring a surprise and name Clinton as his running mate. She seems to have dropped out of consideration in recent weeks, and it has always seemed doubtful that Obama regarded her as a serious option. (Apart from anything, she would come with her husband, and Obama would be forgiven for thinking that one Clinton in his White House would be difficult enough, but two. . .) Now that McCain is gaining ground, however, some Democrats believe she is the only running partner that can help Obama win. They mention John Kennedy's choice of his vanquished rival Lyndon Johnson in 1960 as a precedent (although few point out that Kennedy offered the position to Johnson under the firm impression that he would reject it, and was horrified when he accepted).

The third of Obama's major opponents in the primaries, John Edwards, was touted by some as a potential vice-president for a while. But no longer. A story that was first floated last year by the tabloid *National Enquirer* – that Edwards had had an affair and fathered a child with an aide named Rielle Hunter – is given credence when in July the paper catches Edwards visiting Hunter's hotel in Los Angeles at 2 a.m. That night Edwards is reduced to locking himself in the toilets to avoid the paper's photographers. In the second week of August, he stages a brief television interview in which he admits to the affair but denies paternity of the child. His version of events leaves more questions than it answers. For a man who placed his marriage to Elizabeth (now suffering from cancer) at the centre of his candidacy, this is a devastating revelation. Edwards will play no further role in the campaign.

Obama has promised his supporters that they will be the first to hear who his running mate will be: everyone who has registered via his website will receive a text message and email notifying them of his choice. At 3 a.m. on the Saturday before the first day of the convention (in what is interpreted as a playful reference to Clinton's infamous '3 a.m.' ad) the message goes out: it's Biden.

Joe Biden is a familiar name to millions of Americans. He has been a senator for thirty years, and has made two failed runs for the presidency, the second of which ended earlier in the year. In his first run, in 1988, he brought international ignominy upon himself by plagiarising a speech by Neil Kinnock. In the original, Kinnock said he was the first in a thousand generations of Kinnocks to attend university (itself a case of severe rhetorical overkill). Biden lifted the entire passage, complete with references to his forefathers being miners – true in Kinnock's case, but not in his own. Neither was Biden the first person in his family history to attend college. A member of his rival Michael Dukakis's campaign team spotted the lift, hastily put together a tape of the two speeches and leaked it to the press. Biden's campaign was over before Iowa. A few months afterwards he went to see his doctor about pains in his head. He was diagnosed with a brain aneurysm and immediately taken to hospital for surgery. He later credited the Kinnock controversy with saving his life: if he'd still been in the race he wouldn't have found time to see the doctor.

Biden's forefathers may not have been miners, but he does share certain characteristics with Kinnock: Celtic roots and a love of words. Biden was raised a Catholic by his Irish mother and English father. He spent the first years of his life in Scranton, Pennsylvania (the home town of Hillary Clinton's parents) along with the rest of Catherine Biden's (née Finnegan) extended family. But Biden's father, also Joseph, a car salesman, fell on hard times, and the family moved to a poor part of Delaware when Joe Jr was ten. At school Biden was bullied for his stutter and developed an enduring sense of social insecurity.

Having attended law school and entered state politics, Biden made a successful run for the Senate in 1972 at the age of twenty-nine, overturning Delaware's Republican incumbent. The month after his euphoric victory, his wife Neilia was out shopping for a Christmas tree with their three children when her car was broadsided by a drunk driver at the wheel of an articulated lorry. She was killed instantly, along with their only daughter. Their two sons were seriously injured. Biden was sworn into the Senate by their hospital bedside. For the next five years, Biden raised them as a single parent. Unlike most senators, he did not move to Washington, but made the ninety-minute journey back and forth to his home in the Delaware suburbs every day (a practice he continues). In 1977 he met his second wife, Jill, to whom he is still blissfully married. More than most of his colleagues, Biden can claim to live a life similar to that of many middle-class Americans. He is one of the minority of senators not to be a millionaire.

Biden recovered from the embarrassment of 1988, and his subsequent illness, by steadily building a reputation as one of Washington's foremost experts on world affairs. As chairman of the Senate Foreign Relations Committee he came to wield considerable influence over the country's foreign policy, and was respected by Democrats and Republicans alike. Biden didn't just learn about the world from his advisers or from reading journals; he travelled the globe meeting foreign leaders, getting to know them and their political peers and rivals at first hand. The former US ambassador to Romania recalls sitting with Biden in a car from the airport to the embassy in Bucharest. Biden peppered him with informed questions about everyone of note on the Romanian political scene. The ambassador, unused to displays of such detailed knowledge from visiting US senators, reflected that eastern Europe wasn't even Biden's particular area of expertise; he could have done the same in dozens of countries around the world.

Biden's 2008 run for the presidency got off to a farcically bad start when, in his opening press conference, he described Obama as 'the first mainstream African-American who is articulate and bright and clean and a nice-looking guy'. His campaign staggered on despite the contumely heaped upon for him this slip. Biden, as Obama unhesitatingly acknowledged, is no racist. But the gaffe reminded everyone of his biggest liability: his mouth.

Biden loves to talk. He very much enjoys the sound of his own voice. When speaking off the cuff, he piles on adjectives and builds elaborate labyrinths of clauses and subclauses to the point where he often finds it exceedingly difficult to return to where he started. He likes to talk about himself, too. He is renowned, in Washington, for referring to his many qualifications and accomplishments, and needs little encouragement to slip into the third person in order to do so. Many people have found him to be insufferably pompous and self-regarding. But most in Washington, even those whom he annoys from time to time, retain a regard and affection for Biden. His flaws are in plain sight, his insecurities endearingly close to the surface.

Biden is more at ease with himself than he used to be. In 1988, he wanted to prove himself with such an unhealthy level of intensity that it brought out the worst in him. But in 2007, at the age of sixty-four, and knowing that his chances against the leading contenders would always be minimal, he seemed far more relaxed – to be enjoying himself. He was impressive in the early debates before Iowa, employing a newfound crispness of expression. At one, asked by the moderator if he had the discipline to control his verbosity, Biden answered 'Yes' and left it there. After a second's beat, the audience burst into laughter.

Now, as he jogs onto the stage in Springfield, Illinois on 24 August to join his new running mate, Barack Obama, Biden looks as if he's entirely ready to embark on one more shot at the White House. From Obama's point of view, Biden brings strengths to the ticket that he cannot himself supply: an ability to connect with working-class whites, particularly Catholics, who are suspicious of or unconvinced by Obama, together with enough credentials on national security for the two of them. Obama is thinking ahead to the White House: Biden's long experience on Capitol Hill will make him a trusty ally as the new president sets about trying to get things done.

The appointment is warmly received by Democrats and by the media, although it doesn't generate much excitement. Some question whether the choice of a thirty-year Senate veteran undermines Obama's claim to be bringing change to Washington. But the generally positive response forms a welcome wind behind Obama's back as he enters the most important week of his candidacy so far.

The Democratic convention opens

Party conventions are not what they used to be. In the past, they were where presidential and vice-presidential candidates were chosen, after a series of ballots, compromises and back-room deals. They were also where arguments – sometimes riotous ones – about the party's platform and future took place. These days, the nominee is still formally chosen at the convention, but as delegates are pledged to back whoever 'won' them in the primaries the process is a formality. Party managers have largely succeeded in ironing out unpredictability from the event and turning each convention into a four-day advertisement for the candidate. Nevertheless, nobody can know in advance if a convention will really come alive, if the viewers across the country will tune in, or if they will be impressed or repulsed by what they see and hear when they do. Officials can check all the speeches but they can't control how well each speaker performs: reputations can still be made and broken during conventions.

This year's Democratic convention is in Denver, the capital of Colorado, a state that has voted for a Republican president in every election in the last sixty years except 1992. The Democrats believe they could win this state in November, and holding their convention here is a way of signalling their commitment to doing so.

Barack Obama has three major goals to achieve from the week. First, to introduce himself to the millions of Americans that have been paying scant attention to politics over the last year – in particular, he needs to convince people that he is not the fly-by-night celebrity depicted by John McCain, but someone who is serious about fixing the problems of the country. Second, to unite the party; specifically, to forge a bond with the millions of Democrats who voted for Hillary Clinton in the primaries – and he won't be able to do that without Clinton's assistance. Third, to define McCain ever more sharply as the heir to George W. Bush.

On the opening night, Monday 25 August, Ted Kennedy provides an early emotional highlight. He has recently been diagnosed with brain cancer. After surgery and chemotherapy, he had not been expected to make an appearance at this year's convention. But he shows up and makes a brief speech, as his nieces Caroline Kennedy and Maria Shriver, along with most of the Democrats in the hall, wipe away their tears. He urges them to get Obama elected, promising that 'I will be there on the floor of the US Senate in January'. Harking back to the inauguration of his brother in 1961, he says: 'The torch will be passed to a new generation of Americans.'

Later that evening Michelle Obama speaks to the convention in a speech shown on prime-time TV. Her appearance is the climax of a carefully orchestrated presentation. It is preceded by a soft-focus biographical video – a privilege normally extended only to candidates – and before that by weeks of appearances on popular daytime shows such as *The View* and photographic spreads in weekly magazines with her beautiful daughters. Ever since she made her now infamous remark about being proud of her country 'for the first time', she has been under attack by elements on the right determined to portray her as an angry radical. The Obama campaign has put a great deal of effort into dispelling this idea. Given that Barack Obama is a relative newcomer, that he does not come from a home town or state that most Americans are familiar with, and that he doesn't have close relatives to speak on his behalf, it is even more important than usual that voters get to know and like his wife.

Michelle Obama is an accomplished public speaker, having stumped for her husband many times before. This evening, she shies away from the harder-edged political themes she has addressed in the past and sticks to safe territory: the story of her working-class upbringing in the South Side of Chicago and, of course, how she met, fell in love with and raised a family with her husband. The speech is warmly received in the hall and goes down well amongst those who watch it on television. It is followed by a contrived but still touching 'meeting' between Barack Obama, appearing on a huge screen by satellite connection from Missouri, and his daughters, on stage in the hall.

Hillary's moment

The next day, before the hall fills up or the speeches begin, two young men walk onto the stage with four different women's suit jackets – red, orange, light blue and teal – and test how they look under the lights. Hillary Clinton is to speak this evening.

In the weeks leading up the convention, there has been renewed chatter about Clinton's mood and intentions. Many express scepticism that she will be able to bring herself to offer a convincing, whole-hearted endorsement of her former rival. Some of her supporters and major donors still grumble to the press about their treatment by the Obama campaign. Barack Obama, in a symbolic concession to Clinton and her supporters, agrees to place her name 'in nomination' at the convention as an acknowledgement of the historic nature of her candidacy.

But it is up to Clinton to persuade those who backed her during the primaries to unite behind Obama in the general election. There is much speculation that she is still sore from her defeat and reluctant to encourage her supporters to get behind Obama in anything other than the most formulaic terms. In response to these rumours, she protests that by campaigning for Obama around the country, and encouraging her donors and staff to work for him, she has exceeded historical precedent. She has a point. During the era in which primaries have determined the nominees there have been three marathon, down-to-the-wire battles, including this one. In the previous examples – Reagan and Ford in 1976, Carter and Kennedy in 1980 – the losing candidate did his level best to undermine the winner and nearly split his party apart in the process.

When Clinton emerges that evening, she is in vibrant orange. She doesn't waste time in addressing doubts about her loyalty. 'I am honoured to be here tonight,' she begins. 'A proud mother. A proud

Democrat. A proud American. And a proud supporter of Barack Obama.' She continues: 'I haven't spent the past thirty-five years in the trenches advocating for children, campaigning for universal health care . . . and fighting for women's rights, to see another Republican in the White House squander the promise of our country . . . No way. No how. No McCain.' The crowd erupts, many of them waving banners with Hillary's name and website address on. 'Barack Obama is my candidate,' says Clinton. 'And he must be our president.' The possessive pronoun is significant: it personalises Clinton's endorsement, signalling that this time she really means it.

Clinton looks fondly back on her campaign and its 'sisterhood of the travelling pantsuits', and remembers some of the voters who placed their faith in her along the way. Then, just as she seems to be engaging in self-glorification, she pivots, challenging her followers directly:

> I want you to ask yourselves: Were you in this campaign
> just for me? Or were you in it for that young marine and
> others like him? Were you in it for that mom struggling
> with cancer while raising her kids? Were you in it for that
> boy and his mom surviving on the minimum wage? Were
> you in it for all the people in this country who feel invisible?

It is a convincing and powerful appeal to the consciences of her supporters.

The speech showcases Clinton's newfound presence. It doesn't contain much poetry or many moments of high drama. But she moves a convention that, until tonight, had been in danger of feeling flat. The emotional charge of Ted Kennedy's speech aside, there has been a dearth of excitement; few of the speakers have had the crowd on their feet. Cable commentators started to wonder if the

Democrats were blowing their chance to fire up their supporters. Clinton's speech raises the temperature of the event several notches.

Obama's supporters are cheering as hard as anyone, if only out of relief. Clinton has come through, for Obama and for the party. TV viewers see Bill Clinton, sitting up high in the audience, wipe a tear away, sigh and mouth the words 'great speech'.

The nomination

The next day, Wednesday 27 August, sees the roll-call of states. Hillary Clinton's name has been placed in nomination as a symbolic gesture, though every state will vote for Barack Obama as the presumptive nominee. One by one, each state declares, from the floor, the award of its delegates to Obama. The roll-call is choreographed so that Clinton's home state of New York follows Obama's home state of Illinois. As New York's moment approaches, excitement surges through the hall as a small figure in a light-blue suit makes her way through the crowd on the convention floor to the spot where her state's delegation stands.

'New York,' says the convention secretary. 'New York, you have 282 votes. How do you pass them?'

Clinton is flanked by her fellow senator, Chuck Schumer, and New York's governor, David Paterson, who replaced Eliot Spitzer when Spitzer was forced to resign over a sex scandal. From the floor she speaks into the microphone. In a moment of pre-planned procedural theatre, she moves to end the roll-call.

'Madam Secretary,' she says, 'with eyes firmly fixed on the future, in the spirit of unity, with the goal of victory, let's declare in one voice, right here, right now, that Barack Obama is our candidate and he will be our president.' A cheer goes up. 'Madam Secretary,' she continues, 'I move that Senator Barack Obama of Illinois be selected by this convention, by acclamation, as the nominee of the Democratic Party for president of the United States.'

From the podium, Nancy Pelosi asks if the convention will second Clinton's motion. The crowd replies as one, with a joyous 'Aye'. The cheering is long and ecstatic. The nomination battle is officially ended. Barack Obama is the first African-American to head a major party's bid for the presidency.

Bill's turn

That evening, Bill Clinton is due to speak. Dark rumours have been swirling around the former president. It is suggested that he and the Obama campaign team have been arguing over the scope and subject matter of his speech, and that he, far more than Hillary, is still bitter about his treatment during the primaries. Certainly in the few public appearances he has made since the end of that contest he has seemed surly. When asked recently in an interview if Barack Obama is qualified to be president, he said that the senator is certainly 'consti-tutionally' qualified: praise as faint as it's possible to muster.

People who know Clinton well advise Obama, via the press, that there is a very simple way to keep Clinton happy: 'Just call him,' says one former associate to a reporter. 'Call him any time of day or night. Talk to him about anything. Talk to him about the Olympics or what he thinks about a certain congressional district or even about the *New York Times* Sunday crossword puzzle. Obama could even put the phone in a drawer and just let President Clinton talk away. It wouldn't take much. It could be so easy.'

Clinton's reputation has suffered more than anyone else's during this campaign. Having managed to establish himself as a relatively non-partisan figure, pursuing good works around the globe, he is now a politician again. This was inevitable once he decided to get so closely involved with his wife's campaign. What he might not have foreseen was the bitter rows that have ruptured old friendships – such as that with his former ally Ted Kennedy, to whom he hasn't spoken since Kennedy came out for Obama – and tainted his name with racism. Voters have been reminded of Clinton's less attractive attributes: a certain looseness with the facts, a willingness to play dirty and a tendency to lose his temper. It is in his own interest, as well as Obama's, for him to be reconciled with the party's new leader.

If he has been remotely nervous about the reception he will receive at the convention, he knows from the moment he strides out on stage to make his speech that, as far as the delegates in the hall are concerned, all is forgiven. He receives a giant, almost overwhelming dose of affection from the floor. The crowd leap to their feet, to cheer, clap and yell out their love for the only two-term Democratic president of the modern era. They won't stop. After soaking it up for a couple of minutes, Clinton tries to get them to sit down, jokingly at first, but then with increasing urgency. 'Please stop. Sit down. Please sit.' But the applause and the cheers keep pouring out of them. Finally, he manages to make himself heard. 'I love this,' he says, 'but we have important work to do tonight.'

Just as his wife did, he gets straight to the point. 'I am here, first, to support Barack Obama.' He makes a nod to the hard feelings created by the primary battle: 'That campaign generated so much heat it increased global warming.' But then, after noting that the job of the next president is to 'rebuild the American dream and restore American leadership in the world', he says what the Obama campaign team have been longing to hear him say: 'Everything I learned in my eight years as president, and in the work I have done since in America and across the globe, has convinced me that Barack Obama is the man for this job.' Each word of the last phrase is sent on its way with a swish of Clinton's index finger. He goes on to offer an elegant and convincing encomium to Obama, lauding his intelligence, curiosity and insight into the country's challenges. He declares that he '*loves* Joe Biden', giving the impression that Obama's choice of running partner has helped him come round to his former opponent.

Next comes the case against the Republicans. Clinton skewers what he suggests is the reckless foreign policy of his successor, George W. Bush: 'People the world over have always been more impressed by the power of our example than by the example of our power.' He cites a litany of Republican failures at home, before concluding that 'America can do better than that'. The crowd cheer as they are reminded of Clinton's unparalleled ability to draw the dividing lines between his party and its opponents with clarity, intelligence and power. 'And Barack Obama *will* do better than that,' he adds. This sets off a chant of 'Yes We Can, Yes We Can' in the hall. Clinton, momentarily knocked off his rhythm, steps back from the podium, but then returns with the ad lib 'Yes he can. But first we have to elect him.' The crowd laughs and applauds. Clinton is fully in control of the hall now, deploying his extensive repertoire of gestures: throwing his arms wide to invite the audience to agree with his assessment of Republican mistakes, rolling his tongue thoughtfully around his mouth before making a particularly sharp point, narrowing his eyes to convey strong feeling. In the concluding section of his speech, he places a massive hand over his heart and recalls: 'Sixteen years ago, you gave me the profound honour to lead our party to victory.' He recalls that he prevailed despite Republicans claiming that he was too young and inexperienced to be commander in chief. With raised eyebrows and open arms, he asks: 'Sound familiar?' The crowd roar back 'Yes!' and break into ecstatic applause.

Clinton closes by echoing the phrase he became known for after

the 1992 convention – 'America is a place called Hope'. He says that
Obama will 'lead us away from the division and fear of the last eight
years back to unity and hope. So if, like me, you believe America
must always be a place called Hope, then join Hillary and Chelsea
and me in making Barack Obama the next president of the United
States.' By comparing Obama with his 1992 self, Clinton anoints the
party's nominee as a worthy successor in the most personal terms. It
is a moment of profound political generosity.

Clinton's speech is acclaimed as the best of the convention; and
one of the best of his long career. How does he do it, some wonder.
How does Clinton turn bitter acrimony into dazzling praise? Simple
self-interest is involved: Clinton must be seen to be loyal to the
party's nominee if he is to retain his position as the Democrats' most
respected elder. But the conviction with which he delivers tonight's
address indicates that he has made something of an internal shift too.
He has convinced himself intellectually that Obama would be a better
president than any Republican; even if his heart isn't with the man
who defeated his wife. His deep-rooted competitiveness may also be
in play. If this convention is to be remembered for a Clinton speech
– or any speech – he surely wants it to be his.

Clinton decides not to stay for Obama's appearance the following
evening. As he leaves Denver tonight, it is easy to imagine the old
master muttering to himself: 'Beat that, kid.'

Obama at Invesco

In early July, the Obama campaign announced that its candidate
would deliver his nomination address outside the convention hall, in
a nearby sports stadium named Invesco Field. It was acclaimed at the
time as an inspired move that would demonstrate Barack Obama's

ability to draw massive crowds and rekindle memories of John
Kennedy, who in 1960 gave his acceptance speech in the Los Angeles
Memorial Coliseum.

But as the climax of the convention approaches on Thursday
night, Obama supporters, including some of his own staff, are getting
jumpy. John McCain has been making progress by characterising
Obama as an arrogant celebrity, pumped full of adulation, out of
touch with the everyday concerns of most Americans. Pictures of
Obama delivering his speech in a grand stadium seem likely to
reinforce this image. When a plan of the set on which Obama will
make his speech is leaked to the press, it shows something resembling
a faux-Greek temple. The McCain team is delighted at this further
evidence of their rival's pretensions. Obama will have to work hard in
his speech to convince voters that he understands their concerns. It
is, as former Clinton aide Dee Dee Myers notes, 'a long way from the
stadium to the diner'.

Obama has drafted tonight's speech himself, during late nights
and bleary-eyed mornings and snatched moments in between campaign
stops. He scribbled down thoughts on yellow legal pads, before
logging the best ones onto his laptop and shaping them into a long,
meandering first draft that was then circulated to his chief speechwriter, Jon Favreau, and other colleagues, who sent it back with their
thoughts attached. In the walkthrough at Invesco yesterday, Obama
was still making changes to the final text.

This afternoon, attendees from the convention are joined in
Invesco Field by thousands of Obama supporters from Colorado and
elsewhere. They are entertained by a series of speakers, including Al
Gore. Sheryl Crow and Stevie Wonder perform a few of their greatest
hits to get everyone in the mood for the main event.

By the time Obama takes the stage, night has fallen. Walking out,
he is faced with an awesome panorama. The stadium is packed with

people of all ages and colours. Placards, flags and banners are waved amidst a glitter of flashlights. A tsunami of noise crashes over him: 80,000 bodies shaking with the effort to be heard. After acknowledging the crowd's happy, deafening clamour from the front of the stage, Obama takes his place behind the lectern, clasps his hands, raises his head and waits patiently for it to subside. On the most important night of his political career, in the midst of this maelstrom, he appears completely calm.

'To all my fellow citizens of this great nation, with profound gratitude and great humility,' – he pauses for a beat, and, addressing the camera directly in his sightline, stares straight at the millions of viewers at home – 'I accept your nomination for presidency of the United States.' The stadium explodes in recognition of a historic moment.

Obama turns immediately to the problems facing the country. 'Tonight, more Americans are out of work and more are working harder for less. More of you have lost your homes and even more are watching your home values plummet. More of you have cars you can't afford to drive . . . bills you can't afford to pay.' He lists a series of Republican failures and proclaims: 'America, we are a better country than this.' His face stern, he continues: 'Tonight, I say to the people of America, to Democrats and Republicans across this great land: *enough*!' The crowd interrupts him with a roar. That single word, bellowed into the microphone, carries an electric charge for his supporters, after eight years of Republican rule.

Next, Obama addresses the subject of his opponent. After paying tribute to McCain's service to the nation, he seeks to bind him tightly to the current president. 'The record's clear: John McCain's voted with George Bush 90 per cent of the time. I don't know about you, but I'm not willing to take a 10 per cent chance on change.' It is not, he says, that McCain doesn't care about the plight of Americans in tough times, it's just that he doesn't 'get it'. In a skilfully written passage, Obama seeks to persuade Americans that he does. He braids together episodes from his own life, such as his time as a community organiser, with the stories of voters he has met during the campaign: 'When I listen to another worker tell me that his factory has shut down, I remember all those men and women on the South Side of Chicago who I stood by and fought for after the local steel plant was closed.' He concludes this section with a tribute to the hard work and determination of the grandmother that raised him: 'I don't know what kinds of lives John McCain thinks that celebrities lead. But this has been mine.'

This is not the only moment at which Obama squares up to his adversary. After a section on America's role in the world, Obama looks at the camera, as if staring his opponent in the eye: 'If John McCain wishes to have a debate about who has the temperament and judgement to serve as the next commander in chief, that's a debate I'm willing to have.' Obama pays tribute to America's soldiers before addressing his opponent directly once more, referencing his rival's slogan: 'I've got news for you, John McCain. We all put our country first.'

He closes by returning to the theme of his campaign. 'Change happens', he says, 'because the American people rise up and insist on a new politics for a new time.' Forty-five years ago to the day, Martin Luther King Jr made his "I have a dream" speech in Washington. Now, without directly naming him, Obama invokes his memory.

> It is America's promise that forty-five years ago brought
> Americans from every corner of this land to stand together
> before Lincoln's memorial, to hear a young preacher from
> Georgia speak of his dream. 'We cannot walk alone,' the
> preacher cried. 'And as we walk, we must always march

ahead. We cannot turn back.' America, we cannot turn
back.

It is a lyrical passage in a speech that does not, for the most part,
attempt rhetorical flight. Obama's performance has a sense of gravity
and a more severe tone than any of its predecessors. Unlike his 2004
convention speech or the Jefferson-Jackson address, Obama does not
set out to induce swoons this evening. His purpose is more pragmatic:
to convince people of his readiness to be president, and to define
himself as the only choice of those who want real change. Above all,
tonight Obama seeks to root his candidacy firmly in the soil of
ordinary Americans' hopes and fears, to dispel the idea that it is an
airy confection of the media elites.

Few of his supporters feel that the fears about the setting were
realised. On television, viewers see Obama framed against a neutral
background. The Grecian columns are not too much in evidence. It
is Obama's delivery, though, that makes tonight's address work. His
grasp of stagecraft, his control of pitch and pacing, are superb: from
the controlled fury with which he delivers the cry of 'enough', to the
way in which – softening his tone as he refers to his daughters – he
makes a stadium of 80,000 feel like a living room.

The Democrats have had the convention they wished for. After a
quiet start the Clintons, with their respective appearances, brought
the week to life and helped give the party the catharsis it badly needed
after a long and emotional nomination battle. Other speakers,
including John Kerry – who surprised everyone with a speech better
than anything he gave during his own presidential run four years ago
– and Joe Biden, delivered powerful addresses. But, as he had to do,
Obama has ensured that it is the speech of the party's candidate that
will be remembered as the highlight of the week.

McCain interrupts

With less than a week to go before the Republican convention, John McCain still hasn't announced his vice-presidential pick. In part, the uncertainty has been advantageous: it has kept the Democrats guessing and has ensured a steady stream of media coverage as reporters vie to work out who it will be. But this is not a purely tactical ploy. McCain hasn't decided.

As time runs out, there are two main contenders in the frame: Mitt Romney and Joe Lieberman. The former, who McCain defeated in the primaries, is reconciled with his victor and has been campaigning with vigour on his behalf. Romney's economic knowledge, his links with the key battleground state of Michigan and the sheer energy he puts into campaigning make him an appealing pick for many in the party's establishment, who urge McCain to choose him. But McCain, formal reconciliation notwithstanding, is not Romney's biggest fan. A conservative activist acting as a go-between for the two camps calls Romney and tells him not to wait for McCain's call, because 'he doesn't like you'. He adds: 'With John McCain, all politics is personal.'

The man McCain does like and wants to pick is Senator Lieberman, the Democrat turned independent and staunch supporter of the war in Iraq who has been campaigning hard for the Republican. McCain knows and trusts Lieberman, and enjoys the prospect of a ticket that goes beyond party lines, highlighting the conventionality of Obama's choice. But Lieberman is a supporter of abortion rights. When McCain's camp floats his name in the press, it provokes a furious response from the party's conservative wing, who are adamant that the entire ticket should be pro-life; some say they would rather lose the election than have a pro-choice vice-presidential candidate. McCain's advisers tell him that to pick Lieberman would risk provoking an ugly floor fight at the convention. He resigns himself to not having his first choice, and prepares to take the biggest gamble of his campaign.

The name of Sarah Palin, governor of Alaska, has been floating around the edges of vice-presidential discussions in McCain's camp for a few months. Although her profile is far from high, a group of prominent conservative writers and party insiders have raised it to the point where she is considered a (very) long-odds bet for the Republican ticket. The year before, this group stopped off in Juneau, the Alaskan state capital, during a cruise organised by the conservative journal the *Weekly Standard*, and was entertained by the governor at her official residence. Over a luncheon of halibut cheeks, the all-male group were dazzled by her good looks, charm and confidence, and impressed by her conservative views – as well as the length of time she took to say grace. Like voyagers returning from the New World, they brought back word to Washington of an exciting political talent at the edge of the map. When McCain began his search for a running mate they eulogised about Palin's potential in public, and – to McCain's advisers – in private.

But it is only a week before the convention's opening day that McCain and his team start to seriously consider Palin, after Lieberman and Romney are dismissed. Palin is, in several obvious ways, an appealing candidate. She is female, and McCain would dearly love to draw away from Obama some of the disaffected women who voted for Hillary Clinton in the Democratic primaries. Second, she is young, at forty-four, and an 'outsider' to Washington at a time when conventional politicians are very unpopular. As a social conservative, an enthusiastic hunter and a Pentecostal Christian who is passionately anti-abortion, she would be popular with the Republican base. Finally, she has achieved widespread popularity in her home state by positioning herself as the reformer of a wasteful and corrupt political system. She might form a powerful complement to McCain.

There are some equally obvious problems with picking Palin. The biggest one is her inexperience: she has been a governor for only two years (before that she was the mayor of Wasilla, population 9,000). She comes from a state far from the heartland and has no fame outside it. She has never run for national office and nobody knows how she might react in the intense heat of a presidential campaign. She is not someone McCain knows well – indeed the two have met only once, when they had a fifteen-minute conversation at a Governors' Association meeting in February. For all these reasons she has never been regarded as a serious contender for the ticket – until now.

On Sunday 24 August, as the Democrats gather in Denver, aides arrange a phone call between McCain and Palin, and scrutinise her answers to a lengthy questionnaire they have asked all potential candidates to complete. On Wednesday, as the media's attention is focused on the Democrats, they secretly fly her to Flagstaff, Arizona for a meeting with McCain's top advisers, Steve Schmidt and Mark Salter. The next morning she is taken to McCain's ranch in Sedona, Arizona. McCain offers her some coffee before taking her to his favourite spot: a bend in the creek where there are places to sit in the shadow of a hawk's nest. The two are joined, some time later, by Cindy McCain. After an hour or so Palin returns to the cabin. McCain goes for a walk along the creek with Cindy. On their return he holds a meeting with Schmidt and Salter. After a brief conversation, he says: 'I'm going to offer it to her.'

Almost up until the moment it's announced, the press have no inkling of McCain's decision. When the story emerges, the universal reaction is astonishment. Everybody has a different opinion on this choice but nobody was expecting it. Seasoned political commentators shake their heads at McCain's unpredictability. Democrats pounce on Palin's lack of experience. Some observers wonder whether he has made, in a panic, a mistake he will live to regret. Yet others acclaim it as a masterstroke. Most voters simply ask: who is Sarah Palin?

On Friday 29 August, less than twenty-four hours after Obama's big speech, they get their first chance to find out. Sarah Palin is introduced by her new running mate at a rally at Wright State University in Ohio. She steps up to make a brief speech about herself, emphasising her record as a reforming governor. Viewers on television see a young-looking woman speaking in a distinctive Alaskan accent. To many she looks unlike a politician, resembling instead a mother they might meet at their daughter's school fete. This is no bad thing. Palin pays tribute to Clinton, making transparent the McCain campaign's hope to lure female voters away from Obama. Her short speech wins good reviews, though the main discussion is what her shock selection means for the race, a subject on which commentators are confused and divided.

One group of people are in no doubt what to think or feel. 'There is an electricity going through the social conservative crowd right now,' says James Muffett, the head of Michigan's Citizens for Traditional Values. Conservatives had resigned themselves to being disappointed, or even outraged, by McCain's pick. As it is, many are – literally – weeping with joy. Evangelicals, pro-gun lobbyists and anti-abortion campaigners are beside themselves with excitement. Rush Limbaugh, the popular conservative talk show host, sums it up in an email to his followers that has the subject line 'Palin = Guns, Babies, Jesus.'

At last, John McCain has given his party's conservative base a reason to be enthusiastic about his candidacy.

September 2008

Sarah Palin's convention

When Sarah Palin takes to the stage of the Republican convention on Wednesday 3 September to deliver the biggest speech of her life, she faces a crowd that is at least as nervous as she is. She also faces – via the banks of television cameras trained upon her – a curious audience of voters across the country, half of whom are watching in case she embarrasses herself.

Since her announcement, Palin has been the focus of intense, aggressive scrutiny and criticism. The press do not enjoy being taken by surprise. When the announcement is made they have little to say about Palin except for a few simple facts: she is married to a commercial fisherman and snowmobile champion; she is the mother of five children, the youngest of whom was born four months ago and has Down's syndrome; she was once voted Miss Congeniality in an Alaskan beauty contest; she eats moose stew.

The media suspect that McCain's team cannot have properly vetted a candidate chosen so late in the day, and they throw themselves into doing the job on behalf of their readers, viewers and listeners. Within twenty-four hours of the announcement, dozens of reporters descend on Juneau and Wasilla. Anyone who knows or who has worked with Palin is called and visited and pumped for information, insight and gossip.

The Obama campaign is as thrown as everyone else by McCain's choice of running mate. Its spokesman issues an instant statement dismissing Palin: 'Today, John McCain put the former mayor of a town of 9,000 with zero foreign policy experience a heartbeat away from the presidency.' A few hours later Barack Obama suggests that this hasty response was overly dismissive and offers warmer words to Palin, in a joint statement with Joe Biden.

A rumour bubbles up in the liberal blogosphere: that Palin's baby is in fact her daughter's illegitimate child. It is false, but it pushes another story to the surface just three days after the announcement of Palin's candidacy. The McCain campaign issues a statement to the effect that Sarah Palin's seventeen-year-old daughter, Willow, is pregnant. There is speculation that the news is as much a surprise to the campaign as it is to the public. This revelation, together with stories about Palin's record, such as the suggestion that she tried to ban books from Wasilla library and the fact that she is under investigation by an ethics committee for allegedly trying to pressure officials into firing a state trooper over a family row, generates a sense of frenzied excitement in the media. The natural eagerness of reporters to break big stories is intensified by their sense that McCain's entire candidacy is in jeopardy. The press suspect that his decision to elevate an unknown to the level of potential president without diligent background research may prove to be a disastrous mistake.

Republicans meeting at the convention in St Paul, Minnesota desperately need Palin to deliver a good speech this evening, or, at the very least, not a bad one. They are in need of a boost. The first day of the convention is cancelled after Hurricane Gustav threatens the Louisiana shoreline. With memories of Katrina still fresh in people's minds, McCain deems it unwise to start until the storm has passed. The change of schedule offers him one piece of good news: the wildly unpopular president and vice-president will not now address the convention in person. George W. Bush offers his endorsement of McCain by video link instead, taking care to note that the two have often been in disagreement in the past. The mood in St Paul is flat. It is generally thought that the Democrats had a good week, and the Republicans are nervous that their convention will fare poorly in comparison. The performance of John McCain's running mate has taken on unusual importance.

Rudy Giuliani's keynote speech earlier in the evening gees up the delegates. He excoriates Obama, describing him as the least experienced candidate in 100 years, focusing in particular on his lack of executive experience in order to draw a contrast with Palin.

But now it is up to Palin. In the last few days, Americans have seen the debris of controversy flying around the slight-looking figure who walks out to take her place at the convention podium, but they haven't had a good look at the woman herself. Palin is intently aware of the colourful speculation that surrounds her life and background. In the next forty minutes she must step forward and give her own version of the story.

If she has any nerves, they are not on display. Her voice is steady, her demeanour relaxed as she begins her speech by accepting the party's nomination for vice-president and praising her new boss. Palin introduces her family, who are sitting in the audience: husband Todd, holding the baby, Trig; son Track, soon deploying to Iraq; and daughters Bristol, Willow and Piper (though Willow is not around to receive the applause). The naturalness of Palin's delivery makes these unfamiliar names sound pleasingly eccentric rather than simply odd.

Palin's speaking style is conversational, her language casual: Todd, who she met in high school, is 'still my guy'. Describing herself as 'just your average hockey mom', she says: 'I love those hockey moms. You know they say: "The difference between a hockey mom and a pitbull? Lipstick."' The joke is delivered with perfect timing.

Introducing her parents, Palin emphasises her small-town heritage and upbringing. Quoting words written about Harry Truman, she says: "'We grow good people in our small towns, with honesty and sincerity and dignity." I grew up with those people. They're the people who do some of the hardest work in America . . . They love their country in good times and bad, and they're *always* proud of America.' The last phrase gets the crowd on their feet and waving their McCain–Palin placards; they recognise the dig at Michelle Obama.

Next, Palin turns to the subject of her experience in governing. Critics have pointed out that the gap between being a mayor of a small town and holding office in the White House is vast. Palin returns the fire: 'Since our opponents in this presidential election seem to look down on that experience, let me explain to them what the job involved.' Here she pauses as delegates – who are truly excited now – send up an anticipatory wave of cheers from the floor. 'I guess that being a small-town mayor is sort of like a community organiser – except that you have actual responsibilities.' The crowd whoop with delight at this smackdown of Barack Obama. There is more to come. 'I might add', says Palin, 'that in small towns we don't know quite what to make of a candidate who lavishes praise on working people when they're listening and then talks about how bitterly they cling to their religion and guns when those people aren't listening.'

'*Well*,' says Palin, adjusting her glasses and allowing that word to twang with her rural accent, 'I'm not a member of the permanent political establishment. And I've learned quickly these last few days that if you're not a member in good standing of the Washington elite, then the media consider a candidate unqualified for that reason alone.' The crowd are on their feet and cheering again. Palin continues: 'Now, here's a little newsflash for those reporters and commentators. I'm not going to Washington to seek their good opinion. I'm going to Washington to serve the people of this good country.'

She goes on to talk about her accomplishments as governor, presenting herself as a fearless reformer of Alaska's stale and corrupt political institutions. Then she returns to Obama, a man she derides as having 'authored two memoirs but not a single major law'. What is his plan for the country, she asks, 'when the stadium lights go out and those Styrofoam Greek columns are hauled back to some studio lot'? She contrasts Obama's fine words with McCain's record of service to his country. It is a withering assault, delivered with a light touch.

Palin finishes with a dextrous framing of the election: 'If character is the measure in this election, and hope the theme, and change the goal we share, then I ask you to join our cause. Join our cause and help America elect a great man as the next president of the United States.' With what can only be described as audacity, Palin takes the Obama keywords of hope and change but roots them in the question of character: a sign of the turf on which the McCain campaign now hopes to fight this election.

It is a dazzling performance, blending sarcasm and sincerity, warmth and scorn. Palin's speaking skills far exceed expectations: she is entirely comfortable with the teleprompter; she switches from the declamatory to the conspiratorial with ease; she rolls with the surges of audience excitement rather than let them knock her off her stride. Republicans in the hall and across the country are wild with excitement. They sense that they have witnessed the birth of a star. They're not the only ones vulnerable to Palin's charms; viewers of all political persuasions, or none, are taken with the sheer ebullience of a woman who makes most politicians look stiff, slow witted and mechanical by comparison.

But it is what Palin says, as well as how she says it, that makes such impact. By casting both the media's investigations into her life and her opponents' attacks as a concerted assault by the elites on the values of small-town America, she executes a brilliant counter-move and creates an instant defence against further criticism. By setting about Obama with such gusto she demonstrates a talent for attacking with charm, a highly valued ability in a running mate. Finally, by presenting herself as a gutsy reformer who cannot wait to get stuck into disrupting the comfortable old boys' club of Washington, she promises to be a trusty ally to John McCain.

With one speech, Palin seems to have changed the election. She reverses the whole direction and tenor of the media's coverage of her, and of McCain. Nearly forty million see it on television, more than watched Obama, and the following week massive crowds turn up wherever she appears to speak. In the face of such palpable popular excitement, the press put aside their initial scepticism: Palin's face appears on magazine covers and decorates admiring newspaper profiles. McCain's decision is suddenly acclaimed as a daring gamble that paid off.

Palin's speech has the effect of an electro-magnetic shock on the party's base. Suddenly Republicans everywhere start believing they can win; the 'enthusiasm gap' between Republicans and Democrats, hitherto so pronounced, starts to close. Most importantly, Palin galvanises McCain himself. Whether by accident or design, he has found a running mate who gives him a new rationale for his candidacy: real change, as opposed to Obama's mere rhetoric. This sits awkwardly with 'Country First', which rooted his candidacy in his experience. But now, when McCain cries out to his supporters 'Change is coming!' he appears to believe it. A few days later, his campaign releases an ad presenting McCain and Palin, like a TV detective duo, as 'The Original Mavericks': reformers with records.

In the days and weeks that follow, the McCain campaign manages Palin's public appearances with extreme caution. Except for one inter-view – with ABC's Charlie Gibson – she is not allowed any unscripted contact with reporters. Palin has no record of foreign policy pronouncements and only got a passport in 2006 (she has visited four countries, including Canada, since then). Her vice-presidential debate with Joe Biden is in a few weeks; she has a lot of catching up to do. She gets through the Gibson interview largely unscathed, except when he asks her to comment on 'the Bush doctrine' and she appears not to have a clue what it is. This confirms suspicions amongst Palin's critics that her knowledge of the issues, especially foreign affairs, is sketchy.

Meanwhile, commentators set about trying to understand and characterise the woman behind the phenomenon.

Born in 1964, Sarah Heath grew up in the town of which she was later to become mayor: Wasilla, an old fur-traders' outpost, now absorbed into an expanding Anchorage. She was one of four children raised in a small cabin by her mother Sally and father Chuck, a science teacher and enthusiastic naturalist. The family relied on wild game for their food supply. Together with a neighbouring family, they would hunt for moose – one moose would get both families through the winter. By the age of ten, Sarah was picking off rabbits from the back door, hunting ducks and sniping at ptarmigans on cross-country skis. She was a confident, sparky girl: her mother says she had a swagger from the time she learnt to walk. Though Chuck Heath was not a keen church-goer, Sally was, and she sent her children to Bible camp during the summers. Aged twelve, Sarah asked to be baptised at camp and was dipped into the freezing waters of Lake Beaver. At Wasilla High School she met Todd Palin, the man she was to elope with in 1988.

When Sarah Palin was born, Wasilla was a village of 400 on the edge of a wilderness. During the 1970s Texans and Oklahomans, attracted by the oilfields, started arriving in Wasilla in droves. The new settlers were evangelical Christians with conservative values. These voters formed the core of Palin's support when she entered local politics after a brief career as a TV sportscaster. Palin ran for mayor in 1996 on a platform of gun rights, opposition to abortion and a promise to shake up a complacent political establishment. A campaign pamphlet from this time reads: 'I'm tired of "business as usual" in this town, and of the "Good Ol' Boys" network that runs the show here.'

Palin has always had one eye on the glass ceiling. When she was first running for mayor, her campaign manager suggested that one day she might even become governor. Palin was ahead of her: 'I want to be president,' she replied.

As governor Palin proved herself a tough, driven and highly confident operator, unintimidated by older, more experienced colleagues and political opponents. She relied heavily on a tight circle of family and loyal friends, and particularly on Todd, who was often found in or around her office in Juneau. When she came to power in 2006 Palin actively cleared out a swathe of long-standing state officials, either firing them herself or putting pressure on others to get rid of them (she had performed a similar purge in Wasilla). She showed no hesitation in installing her loyalists in the vacant positions. By the slow-moving standards of Alaskan politics, Palin's arrival was revolutionary. Juneau had never seen anything like it.

It wasn't just the political establishment that Palin set about with such zeal. The big oil companies, who had enjoyed a cosy relationship with previous Alaskan administrations, found themselves dealing with a governor determined to extract a higher price for the right to operate in the state than they were used to paying. She forced them into competitive bids for a new pipeline and imposed a windfall tax on their profits, in the teeth of fierce and well-financed lobbying.

Palin's tenacity was rooted in her confidence that public opinion sided with her. Throughout her political career in Alaska she was highly attuned to the feelings of voters and possessed of a sure populist touch. As mayor it was said she kept a jar on her desk containing pieces of paper bearing the names of all Wasilla's residents. Every week she would pull one out at random and call that person, asking: 'How is the city doing?' Elected governor on a promise to fight corruption and restore transparency to government, one of her first moves was to put the governor's jet up for sale on eBay. 'She hears the mood of the electorate very, very well,' observes an Alaskan historian. Palin was adept at leveraging her popularity: she enjoyed an approval rating of more than 80 per cent in Alaska, and knew how to pressure legislators into doing her bidding. She was never very interested in the mechanism of government or the detail of policy, however. State senate leaders, meeting the governor and her team to discuss a new oil pipeline, were bemused to find her preoccupied with her two BlackBerrys for most of the meeting.

Like the man who has just elevated her to national fame, Palin doesn't have an explicit governing philosophy, and cares little for traditional party politics – she often worked closely with Democrats rather than her own party mandarins when it suited her. She is an instinctive moralist rather than an ideologue, and enjoys the thrill of a crusade against the complacent, the comfortable and the corrupt. In this regard McCain has chosen a woman with similar instincts to his own.

The mania for this Alaskan newcomer now sweeping the country is hardly explicable in conventional political terms, however: something more primal seems to be at work. Palin is a potent combination of cultural archetypes. She is an attractive, feminine woman who shoots moose and talks tough. Her astute self-presentation as a small-town dweller taps into a deep national nostalgia for a time before America was urbanised – but at the same time, she is that most modern of figures, the working mother. She is a comfortingly familiar hockey mom, and a figure redolent of the western pioneer – the cowgirl turned sheriff. She is a staunch social conservative who had the courage and compassion to give birth to and raise a child with Down's syndrome. Palin reaches several different parts of the national psyche at once; the result is a set of powerful emotional responses, positive and negative, that threaten to transform the whole election.

At a rally the week after her triumphant speech, a supporter hoists aloft a McCain placard on which is hand-scrawled 'Guns, God and Lipstick'.

McCain tells his story

It is Thursday night of convention week and John McCain is reaching the closing section of his acceptance speech. The crowd is cheering every line. In the front row of the audience, out of view of the cameras, a man stands up and begins to whirl his hands in circles, urging the speaker on like a conductor exhorting his orchestra to crescendo.

The man is Mark Salter, McCain's chief speechwriter. Salter has been working for McCain for more than twenty years. He has collaborated with his boss on five books about McCain's life and political philosophy (unusually for ghost writers, Salter receives half the royalties). More than anyone else, it is Salter who has crafted McCain's public image.

Salter, 53, is a constant, brooding presence by McCain's side on the campaign trail. He wears Aviator shades and is rarely without a cigarette on the burn. Salter reveres and loves McCain, who for his part knows and trusts Salter more than anyone else in the world save for his wife. The two have spent so much time together that friends say it is hard to tell where one mind ends and the other begins. Salter shares McCain's somewhat fatalistic view of the world and his taste for games of long odds. Both men idolise Robert Jordan in

Hemingway's *For Whom the Bell Tolls*, who fights a futile battle for a noble cause. But Salter lacks his boss's subversive humour or instinctive personal warmth. Campaign staff sometimes express relief when the man known as 'The Shadow' leaves the room.

After McCain returned from Vietnam in 1973 he wrote a long, rambling article about his experiences that offered little in the way of self-reflection or insight. It concluded: 'Now I see more of an appreciation of our way of life. There is more patriotism. The flag is all over the place.' That was before he met Salter. Twenty-six years later, with the help of his co-writer, McCain expressed himself rather more eloquently. The experience of captivity, he wrote in *Faith of My Fathers*, helped him discover that 'I was dependent on others to a greater extent than I had ever realised, but that neither they nor the cause we served made any claims on my identity. On the contrary, they gave me a larger sense of myself than I had had before.' Over the years, Salter's solemn, shapely prose has turned the raw material of McCain's life into a story about the ancient virtues of duty, honour, sacrifice and humility.

Salter has also helped to create and articulate McCain's worldview, which is less about a consistent set of political principles than it is an existential theory: it is what kind of a person you are that counts. As McCain declares in one of his books: 'It is your character, and your character alone, that will make your life happy or unhappy.'

Neither Salter nor McCain have a high regard for the character of Barack Obama. In 2006, McCain was in Europe when news came through that Obama had rescinded a private promise to join McCain's effort to pass an ethics bill (Obama went with a version proposed by Democratic leaders instead). 'Give him the brush-off,' McCain told Salter over the phone, trusting that, as ever, his friend knew what he meant and how to say it. Salter wrote, on McCain's behalf, a letter to the Democrat that began: 'I would like to apologise to you for assuming that your private assurances to me regarding your desire to cooperate . . . were sincere,' and ended: 'I hold no hard feelings over your earlier disingenuousness. Again, I have been around long enough to appreciate that in politics the public interest isn't always a priority for every one of us. Good luck to you, Senator.' McCain didn't see it before Salter sent it – he didn't have to.

Now, of course, Obama stands between McCain and the White House. In an interview with *Newsweek*, Salter says of Obama: 'Yes, he's good onstage. But my guy can't even lift his arms because of his war injuries! McCain always has chosen to devote his life to his country, not himself. My job is to help voters see that.' Salter now desperately hopes that the acceptance speech he has written, the greatest gift he can give his beloved friend and mentor, will help make McCain president.

But a speechwriter can only sit and watch as his work is brought to life – or murdered – by someone else, and McCain, by his own admission, is not a great orator. Tonight, as usual, his rhythms are uneven, his eyes too intently focused on the teleprompter, and he bungles some of his best lines. Salter and the rest of the McCain camp were expecting this but hope that McCain's inexpert delivery will only enhance the impression of rough-hewn authenticity.

McCain pays tribute to Sarah Palin, praising her as a bipartisan reformer who will shake up Capitol Hill: he says, with a grin, that he 'can't wait to introduce her to Washington'. He then describes his own record as one long series of battles – against pork barrel spenders, against corruption, against tobacco companies and drug companies – in which political affiliations come second to the job of upholding America's honour. 'I don't mind a good fight,' says McCain. 'I've had quite a few tough ones in my life.' In a passage met with uncomfortable silence in the hall, he says that the Republicans were 'elected to change Washington, and we let Washington change us. We lost the trust of the American people . . . when we valued our power over our principles.' He bemoans the 'partisan rancour' of Washington politics and says that 'again and again' he has reached across the aisle to solve the nation's problems. 'I have that record and the scars to prove it,' he says. 'Senator Obama does not.'

McCain's speech bases his candidacy not in a set of policies or a vision of good government but in his own character. It portrays him as a battle-scarred Washington warrior who has always put his country before his own or his party's cause. In its final section McCain reaches back to what he describes as the formative experience of his life, telling the story of his experience in Vietnam as a lesson in humility. In Salter's terse, sturdy sentences he sketches a portrait of a cocky young man brought low:

> I liked to bend a few rules and pick a few fights for the fun of it. But I did it for my own pleasure, my own pride. I didn't think there was a cause that was more important than me. Then I found myself falling toward the middle of a small lake in the city of Hanoi, with two broken arms, a broken leg and an angry crowd waiting to greet me. I was dumped in a dark cell and left to die. I didn't feel so tough any more. When they discovered my father was an admiral, they took me to a hospital. They couldn't set my bones properly, so they just slapped a cast on me. And when I didn't get better and was down to about 100 pounds, they put me in a cell with two other Americans. I couldn't do anything. I couldn't even feed myself. They did it for me. I was beginning to learn the limits of my selfish independence.

Now, for the first time in the speech, McCain sounds fully in charge of his material: his delivery is crisp, and his eyes seem to meet those of the watching millions rather than stare at the teleprompter. He tells of how he suffered for refusing the Vietnamese offer of release: 'They worked me over harder than they ever had before, for a long time.' Alluding to his suicide attempt, he admits before a hushed audience that 'they broke me'. He describes how he was saved by the sympathy and encouragement of a fellow prisoner who urged him, via taps on the prison wall, to fight on for his country. 'I fell in love with my country when I was a prisoner in someone else's,' says McCain. 'I was never the same again. I wasn't my own man any more. I was my country's.'

The crowd breaks out into cheers and keeps going as McCain builds to the rousing climax of his speech. 'My country saved me, and I cannot forget it. And I will fight for her as long as I draw breath, so help me God.' In the front row, Salter gets to his feet. 'Fight with me. Fight with me,' says McCain over the cheers of the audience. 'Fight for what's right for our country. Fight for the ideals and character of a free country.' Salter is like a man possessed now, mouthing the words as his boss speaks them, pounding his palm rhythmically with his fist, thrusting it down at the moments of emphasis. 'Stand up,' says McCain, his words barely audible over the noise of the crowd. 'Stand up and fight. Nothing is inevitable here. We're Americans, and we never give up. We never quit. We never hide from history. We make history.'

The audience deliver a long, enthusiastic and genuinely warm ovation. In his own way, McCain has delivered a spellbinding speech this evening. It is rough magic: a call to arms, delivered falteringly at times but with gathering force, by a man whose suffering on behalf of his country is written across his body. From the podium, McCain does not have Obama's control or Palin's charm, but he has an undeniable force of presence. Nobody knows if his emotional appeal to patriotism will be enough to win the election. But this evening, few dispute the power of his story.

Republicans leave St Paul in far better spirits than they arrived. They have discovered, in Sarah Palin, a bona fide political star, and simply by picking her McCain has been elevated in the eyes of many. They are also glad to contrast the heroism of their candidate with what they see as Obama's shallowness. The polls show McCain closing the gap on his opponent. For the first time in this campaign, Republicans start believing they will win.

Lowering the tone

If John McCain's speech saw him hit rhetorical heights, the next couple of weeks see his ads aiming lower. His campaign issues a series of attacks on Barack Obama in quick succession, each bearing a somewhat tenuous relationship with the facts or the rules of fair play.

At a town hall meeting in the working-class town of Lebanon, Virginia, Obama – in one of his slightly clumsy attempts to sound down-home – uses the phrase 'lipstick on a pig' to describe McCain's attempts to position himself as a force for change. The McCain camp pounce on it, claiming that Obama was alluding to Sarah Palin (who joked about pitbulls with lipstick in her convention speech). They denounce him for making a sexist insult, and a full-blown row erupts between the two camps.

The lipstick row is just the beginning. A new ad accuses Obama of wanting children to 'learn about sex before they can read', a claim based on a distorted reading of an education bill sponsored by Obama. Then McCain states that Obama wants 'to raise your taxes' even though he plans a tax cut for 95 per cent of the population. Meanwhile Palin claims that she opposed the 'bridge to nowhere' – a notorious 'earmark' project in Alaska – when every credible report demonstrates that she supported it, at least initially. Some conservatives express their doubts over these tactics. Even Karl Rove, regarded as the most ruthless political strategist of modern times (and reputed to be the besmircher of McCain's reputation in New Hampshire eight years ago) wonders publicly if McCain is stretching the truth too far.

But the campaign team are happy at their success in setting the agenda. Under Steve Schmidt's bullish leadership, they have hit on a tactic of creating daily controversies that distract and unsettle their opponent while allowing them to dominate the news cycles. A Republican consultant describes this approach as the 'ugly frog' strategy: 'Stick that frog right in their face, shake it all around and say: "Here, look at this *big ugly frog*." Then, as they defend themselves and explain the context, real quick grab another ugly frog. Repeat often until they've spent most of the campaign reacting to your agenda.'

Long-time McCain-watchers wonder how he squares these tactics with his earlier promise to run an honourable campaign. How, they ask, could the victim of such brutal tactics in 2000 even begin to go down the same road? But McCain draws different a lesson from his first presidential run. Back then he was beaten by an opponent more ruthless than he was, and he is determined not to be a righteous loser again. What's more, he and his team have little or no regard for the character of their rival. When Obama broke his promise to opt into public financing in June, McCain was furious and frustrated with the failure of the press to give the Democrat a hard enough time. He was also deeply unimpressed by the way Obama backed away from his offer, earlier in the campaign season, to hold a series of town hall debates. From then on, McCain seemed to decide that Obama didn't deserve the full measure of his respect.

Democrats get that familiar feeling

Barack Obama seems uncertain how to respond to John McCain's aggressive tactics. He is not at his best under attack. When Hillary Clinton fixed him with a fierce stare and tore into his record during the primary debates, he often looked hurt – as if bewildered that anyone could think anything but well of him.

He is also somewhat flummoxed by the Palin phenomenon, in many ways reminiscent of the widespread excitement that propelled him to national fame. Should he attack her inexperience and risk provoking explosive counter-attacks from the McCain camp? Or ignore her and hope Palin fever proves short lived?

As McCain moves up in the polls, a panic sets in amongst Democrats. They have seen candidates lose winnable races at this stage of the contest before, and are deeply anxious at the prospect of witnessing the same story again. Four years ago, John Kerry lost the lead he had over George W. Bush after a successful Republican convention. He never regained it. Now, a major Democratic fundraiser expresses the fears of many in the party: 'I'm so depressed. It's happening again. It's a nightmare.'

In private and in public, anxious Democrats urge Obama to wake up to the Republican threat. Fight back, they say. Take McCain on more directly. Attack his character. Beef up your policy message. Be more populist. Show more urgency. Bill Clinton's old advisers suggest, in a series of mostly anonymous press briefings, that Obama should listen to their advice because, unlike him, they've beaten a Republican in a tough race. They remind people that Obama's big political battles – back in Illinois and during the primaries this year – have all been against other Democrats. Perhaps he does not understand how ruthless an opponent can be and how futile it is to rail against the unfairness of it all. 'The McCain campaign said: "Fuck it, we're just going to go out there and say he is going to raise taxes and do all this bad shit,"' says one Clintonite. 'And then you see the reaction from the Obama people saying: "We're not going to be bullied, we're not going to let our record be misconstrued." The second you start hearing that kind of rhetoric, you *are* being bullied and your record *is* being misconstrued.'

But Obama's team – whom some call unflappable, others arrogant and insular – are holding no late-night conference calls or emergency strategy sessions at their Chicago headquarters. They refer their critics back to October 2007, when so many were urging Obama to change his tactics in order to overcome a resurgent Hillary Clinton. They kept their nerve then, stuck with their original plan and came through. 'We have been given up for dead any number of times in this process, so it does stiffen your spine a little bit,' David Plouffe tells the *New York Times*, responding to what he terms the 'hand-wringing and bed-wetting'. Many Democrats are infuriated by his insouciance and by what they regard as the stubbornness and insularity of the Obama camp.

The Obama campaign does make some concessions to its critics, but its attempts to fashion sharper lines of attack can be clumsy. A new ad about McCain points out he doesn't know how to use a computer or send email. 'Things have changed in the last twenty-six years, but John McCain hasn't,' says the announcer, in a less-than-subtle reference to the age of the Republican candidate. 'After one president who was out of touch, we just can't afford more of the same.' The McCain team are quick to point out that their man's wartime injuries make it difficult for him to use a keyboard. In a TV interview, Joe Biden himself repudiates the ad.

In the last thirty years, only one Democrat has won a presidential election – and as criticisms swirl around his head, Obama goes to meet him. He sits down to lunch with Bill Clinton in the former president's office in Harlem, New York. It is the first time the two men have met for a proper conversation. Afterwards, both deny that they discussed anything so base as political strategy. But it is difficult to believe that Clinton didn't advise the younger man on how to make this election about the topic that he focused on so relentlessly in 1992: the economy.

The economy doesn't wait to be asked, however. The next week, it forces its way to centre stage.

Crisis

On the evening of Thursday 18 September, in the office of the House Speaker, Nancy Pelosi, a group of congressional leaders and their aides have just listened to Ben Bernanke, the chairman of the Federal Reserve, and Hank Paulson, the Treasury secretary, explain the nature, scale and urgency of the crisis faced by the US financial system. Outlining the magnitude of the action needed to deal with it, Bernanke, a softly spoken former academic, says: 'If we don't do this, we may not have an economy on Monday.'

He is met by silence. For the time being, nobody can think of anything to say.

The past six months have seen a series of shocks to the US financial system, each presaging further trouble. In March, the investment bank Bear Stearns had to be rescued from collapse by the Federal Reserve. During the summer, the nation's largest mortgage-lenders, Freddie Mac and Fannie Mae, revealed the extent to which the credit crunch had undermined their fundamental stability. In early September, Paulson and Bernanke were forced to lead a government takeover of both. Weeks later, they watched as the epitome of Wall Street's financial solidity, Lehman Brothers, melted into air. Almost simultaneously they ushered another investment bank, Merrill Lynch, into the arms of Bank of America, before striking a deal to rescue the insurance giant AIG.

Few people have read or written more about financial crises than Bernanke. A professor of economics, his first major work was a study of the events leading to the Great Depression, and he specialises in the spiralling dynamics of panicked markets. Writing about them is one thing, however; living them is quite another. As he awoke on the morning of 17 September Bernanke might have been forgiven for imagining he had tumbled down a rabbit hole into one of his books. Reaching out of bed to check his BlackBerry, he received alarming news. Despite the government's swift action over AIG, the money markets were in free fall. Conferring with Paulson that morning, the two agreed that an economic nightmare of historic proportions was about to be unleashed on the nation. Fear was freezing the financial system; banks were refusing to lend to other banks. In a matter of days, businesses across the country would run out of the cash they needed to pay their employees.

That was yesterday. This evening, Bernanke and Paulson propose their radical solution to the lawmakers in Nancy Pelosi's office. First, they sketch the outlines of the impending catastrophe: mass bankruptcies, widespread job losses and a stock market crash. The chain reaction that took place over months in 1929 will now take place in days, they say – unless the government makes a massive, unprecedented intervention. On behalf of the Treasury, Paulson wants to ask Congress for the staggering figure of $700 billion to buy up Wall Street's bad debts. The plan takes up just three pages of A4. Hearing that Bernanke and Paulson want legislation passed within days, the Senate majority leader, Harry Reid, expresses incredulity. 'This is the United States Senate,' he says. 'We can't do it in that time frame'. His Republican counterpart, Senator Mitch McConnell, replies: 'This time we can.'

The next week sees the bailout plan locked into intense negotiations on Capitol Hill, as President Bush, Vice-President Cheney and Paulson press lawmakers to pass a bill, however imperfect, rather than risk a financial apocalypse. For an administration and party that champion free markets, this is foul-tasting medicine. But the alternative seems much worse. In public, Bush warns of a 'painful recession' if the measures aren't passed. In private, he puts it even more bluntly: 'If money isn't loosened up, this sucker could go down.'

McCain gambles, again

On Wednesday 24 September, amidst some reports that an agreement on Paulson and Bernanke's plan might be near, John McCain springs a surprise: he announces the temporary suspension of his campaign and says that he will not attend the first presidential debate, scheduled for a few days' time, if no deal has been reached on the bailout. Declaring that he will make haste to Washington to join his fellow legislators, he says: 'I am calling on the president to convene a meeting with the leadership from both Houses of Congress, including Senator Obama and myself. It is time for both parties to come together to solve this problem.' McCain, advised by Steve Schmidt, has decided that rather than stay at arm's length from the negotiations, he should go all in and give a vivid demonstration of his ability to rise above petty partisan politics in the larger interest of the nation.

Barack Obama, like everyone else, is blindsided by McCain's announcement. So far this week, both candidates have been playing a cautious game. Neither has wanted to seem too enthusiastic about a plan that many Americans view with scepticism. But nor have they wished to be responsible for derailing the agreement and risking economic chaos. On the morning of McCain's announcement,

Obama called him to suggest a joint statement on the crisis that would outline a set of shared principles and conditions for the Treasury proposal. McCain agreed in principle to such a statement. But only a few hours later, and before a final draft was signed off, he appeared on television to make his dramatic announcement.

Just as he did with his choice of running mate and his string of outlandishly negative ads, McCain is risking criticism from all sides to seize the initiative in this race. By instinct, he is a gambler who relishes the drama of a high-stakes game, and he knows that if he plays by the normal rules of these contests, the race will slip away from him. Gambling may have become a rational strategy.

The economy was never McCain's strong suit. On more than one occasion he has cast doubt on his own knowledge of this topic, telling an interviewer with characteristic candour in December 2007 that 'the issue of economics is not something I've understood as well as I should'. Last week he damaged his already suspect credibility on the subject further, when, on the very day that Lehman Brothers collapsed, he declared on the stump that 'the fundamentals of our economy are strong'. He quickly realised his error and the next day told a TV interviewer that the economy was in 'crisis, total crisis', calling for a commission to investigate what had gone wrong. He only succeeded in giving the impression of a man trying everything he can to right an out-of-control aircraft. Obama mocked McCain for not knowing what was going on, in an unsubtle attempt to paint his opponent as old and past it.

With every piece of bad economic news, Obama rises in the polls, and he now holds a small but significant lead over his opponent. McCain, aware that time is running out, clearly feels that he must do something to change the dynamic of the race – and his latest move certainly puts his opponent in a tricky position. Should Obama follow suit, suspend his own campaign, and allow his opponent to look like the leader? Or carry on and risk being accused of putting politics before country? Obama's aides are bombarded with emails from external advisers telling them to fall into line with McCain. But Obama decides instead to call his opponent's bluff. Rejecting McCain's claim that politics should cease until the bailout is agreed, he holds a press conference to say that he will not stop campaigning, has no plans to go to Washington and will be attending the debate. His tone is calm and quizzical rather than heated. He laconically remarks that presidents must be able to focus on more than one thing at a time.

Obama doesn't accuse his opponent of opportunism (he leaves that to his supporters and surrogates) but, not for the first time, McCain's execution of his tactic doesn't help his own cause. He cancels a scheduled appearance on David Letterman's show that night, explaining that he has to dash to Washington. But when Letterman finds out that McCain is actually still in New York giving an interview to the CBS anchor Katie Couric he is furious, and spends the whole of his show mercilessly mocking the senator as a doddering fool trying desperately to reverse his slide in the polls.

Much now depends on what, if anything, McCain will be able to achieve on Capitol Hill. President Bush, at McCain's suggestion, invites both candidates to a bipartisan summit at the White House on Thursday 25 September. An exasperated Obama flies to Washington from Clearwater, Florida, where he has been holed up with key aides in order to prepare methodically for the first presidential debate (his rehearsals took place in a room set up as an exact replica of Friday's venue, with podiums set at precise angles, and sessions scheduled for the evening to match the candidate's natural circadian rhythms; McCain's one preparatory session was arranged between meetings in New York, took place in a makeshift office, and was ended prematurely in order to make time for his surprise announcement).

On television that afternoon, the president is seen surrounded by congressional leaders from both parties, with McCain and Obama at either end of the table. In public, neither candidate says much about the proposed bailout beyond some bland generalities, and everyone pledges to work together in the spirit of bipartisanship. But once the cameras are gone the summit descends into squabbling. Lawmakers on both sides, but particularly Republicans, have deep reservations about the deal – the main one being that it is unpopular with their constituents. Why, ask voters, should we rescue the bankers of Wall Street to save them from their own greedy mistakes?

McCain finds he can make little impact on the debate. Rather than being greeted as a hero, he is given the cold shoulder by his own party's congressmen, who are in no hurry to forgive him for his antagonistic stances towards them in the past, during his crusades to pass ethics and immigration reforms. When the Republican leader in the House admits that he can't muster enough votes to pass the bill, angry shouting breaks out on all sides. Democrat leaders demand to know where McCain stands. He remains uncharacteristically silent, unwilling either to back or to cross his fellow Republicans.

With enormous pressure to reach a deal before the markets open on Monday, discussions continue in an emotionally overwrought atmosphere. At one point, Hank Paulson, a lanky man, is seen down on one knee in front of Nancy Pelosi, begging her not to withdraw her party's support for the package. 'I didn't know you were a Catholic,' says Pelosi. After both candidates leave the meeting that evening, Obama suggests to an interviewer that 'when you inject presidential politics into delicate negotiations, sometimes it's not helpful'.

On Friday, the negotiations appear to be making progress, without the candidates. McCain keeps everyone guessing about his intentions towards the debate, raising the bizarre prospect that Obama will take

to the stage alone. But with only hours to go word comes from the
McCain camp that he will be attending after all. Early on Friday
afternoon a reporter from McCain's pool – one of the few members
of his travelling press corps to keep track of him today – issues the
following dispatch:

> McCain now boarding plane at DC airport with Cindy,
> Salter, Rudy Giuliani, wife Judith, and other aides.
> Heading to Memphis, then motorcade to site. General
> atmosphere is utter confusion.

Presidential debate I: Ole Miss

Steve Schmidt, John McCain's burly, ball-headed adviser, is surrounded
by microphones and cameras, behind which stand a crowd of
reporters shouting questions and jostling each other out of the way.
Schmidt is repeating the same number over and over again. 'Eleven
times! Senator Obama said John McCain was right eleven times . . .
It was a home run for Senator McCain . . . The person who is losing
the debate, the person who is on defence, is the person who says his
opponent is right eleven times.'

Schmidt is in the 'spin tent' after the debate, trying to convince
the press that his man won a clear victory. A few feet away, Obama's
strategist David Axelrod is surrounded by a similar scrum. Even
amidst the tumult he looks as though he has only just woken up.
Unlike his counterpart he tends not to stick to a single phrase or
point. 'I don't think he was too nice . . . There were clear differences
. . . He made a very strong case, absolutely.'

Axelrod is a very different character from Schmidt. His rumpled
clothes, hooded eyes and downturned moustache give him the air of

a bedraggled rodent. If Schmidt can seem like a driven young cop, Axelrod is a veteran detective who has seen too much not to be aware of life's tragic nature. He doesn't have the talent for quickfire sound-bites that Schmidt shares with other top political operatives. Axelrod's value to Obama consists in his talent for crafting the candidate's image and political vision.

Obama and Axelrod met in 1992 when the state senator was thirty years old and coordinating a voter registration drive in Chicago known as Project Vote. Axelrod was already an established player on the Chicago scene, having left his job as lead political reporter for the *Chicago Tribune* to become a successful political consultant. The two didn't become instant friends but liked each other and kept in touch over the following years, and when Obama decided to run for the Senate in 2004 he asked Axelrod to join him. By then, Axelrod had become one of the most respected operatives in the country, having already worked with John Edwards and Hillary Clinton and helped elect the first black governor of Massachusetts, Deval Patrick. But he hadn't yet had the chance to implement his own theory of political campaigns with a candidate he truly believed in.

Axelrod nurtured a belief that in a cynical age, the candidates most likely to succeed would be those who could convincingly demonstrate an authentic connection between who they were and what they believed. Unlike other consultants, he didn't start with a ready-made strategy or slogan and then try to retro-fit his candidate's life and career onto it. Instead, he aimed to craft campaigns that emerged organically from the candidate's biography. In Obama, with his unusual background, independent political instincts and knack for story-telling, Axelrod found his perfect project. He came to believe that Obama's mixed racial identity, rather than being a dis-advantage, might symbolise a more united future for the country. As he said proudly of his candidate in 2007: 'He is his own vision.' He also found a vocation: Axelrod's relationship with his client is not just a professional one. A 1960s liberal who has lacked a true hero ever since Bobby Kennedy was assassinated, Axelrod credits Obama with reviving his idealism.

The marquee in which Schmidt and Axelrod are standing resembles a crowded bazaar. Surrogates for each campaign stand beneath big signs – blue for Obama, yellow for McCain – whilst journalists swarm around them. The big-name supporters draw crowds; others see their audiences expand and dissolve according to their ability to hold the interest of their interlocutors. John Kerry wanders into the tent, looks around, fails to attract much attention and leaves.

Both camps know that presidential debates are often won and lost in the hours and days after the event rather than during it, as the media begin to settle on a story about who performed strongly and who didn't, what the turning points were, and which were the most memorable images. Much can turn on points of style: the first President Bush glancing at his watch towards the end of his debate with Bill Clinton, Al Gore's impatient-sounding sighs during the answers of his opponent, George W. Bush. Such factors loom large after debates in which there are no clear winners, resounding sound-bites or clumsy gaffes – as has been the case this evening.

The debate takes place in an auditorium at the University of Mississippi, otherwise known as 'Ole Miss'. Blacks were barred from attending the college for more than 100 years. In 1962 James Meredith, a black Air Force veteran, attempted to enrol but was refused entry by the university's chancellor, in defiance of a court order to admit him. When Meredith arrived for a fourth attempt to register, he was accompanied by 173 US marshals dispatched by President Kennedy. A crowd of over 2,000 gathered, many of them calling for Meredith to be lynched. The marshals responded with tear gas, and the campus exploded into violence, during which two people were killed. The next day, soldiers occupied the local town as Meredith registered for classes. After graduating Meredith went on to earn a law degree from Columbia University in New York. His son and stepson also attended Ole Miss.

It is a poignant moment, then, when the first black presidential candidate for a major party walks out on to the stage to meet his opponent this evening. The audience applaud both men, though it is the last time they will do so until the end: it has been agreed by the campaigns that clapping, laughter or any other noise be banned during the debate.

Tonight's topic was originally to be national security, but recent events have forced a change of plan, and the opening section is now devoted to the economy. Taking the first question, Obama wears a sober expression as he addresses what he calls 'the worst financial crisis since the Great Depression'. He lists a series of four proposals to protect the taxpayers of 'Main Street' from the worst of a crisis created in Wall Street, finishing his answer by linking the crisis to policies 'promoted by George Bush, supported by Senator McCain'.

McCain's answer contains less detail. After agreeing with Obama that the bailout package should have provision for more oversight, he refers vaguely to the need for 'a number of other essential elements'. He mentions his decision to suspend his campaign to work with 'my Republicans' but doesn't dwell on it, perhaps nervous that last week's surprise move may not have played well with voters.

Throughout the discussion of the financial crisis McCain rarely sounds comfortable. But when the conversation moves to foreign policy he is far more at ease. On Iraq, he argues passionately that the war was mismanaged in the first few years, and recounts his role in supporting last year's troop surge, citing it as evidence of his determination to do the right thing even if it is unpopular at the time.

Obama responds with his sharpest attack of the evening, and the only point at which he addresses his opponent directly:

> John, you like to pretend like the war started in 2007. The war started in 2003 and at the time when the war started you said it was going to be quick and easy. You said we knew where the weapons of mass destruction were. You were wrong. You said we were going to be greeted as liberators. You were wrong. You said that there was no history of violence between Shia and Sunni, and you were wrong.

A more ruthless debater might leave it there, but Obama dissipates the impact of his criticism by adding a paragraph about judgement.

By this point McCain is almost jumping up and down behind his lectern, desperate to interrupt. When he gets his turn, in scathing reference to Obama's description of the surge, he says: 'I'm afraid Senator Obama doesn't understand the difference between a tactic and a strategy.' It is one of several moments this evening when McCain scolds or derides his younger opponent, his exasperated expression seeming to betray his personal feelings about his rival. Throughout the debate he never addresses Obama directly, nor looks him in the eye. It is as if he resents having to share a stage with the younger man. Obama is more emollient in tone, using McCain's first name and frequently mentioning points of agreement.

The audience and viewers at home are confronted by a clear contrast in demeanours and speaking styles. Obama is, as usual, poised and self-contained, though there is an edge of intensity to his speech not seen until now. He talks at a faster pace than he did in his debates with Hillary Clinton; his sentences are shorter. His expressive range is still narrow, though. He smiles rarely, pursing his lips tightly at the end of each answer, and when he is not talking his face and his body are still. He frequently talks into the camera, although he doesn't attempt to make a real emotional connection, Bill Clinton-style, with television viewers.

McCain's face is more mobile: he grins, frowns and grimaces, and opens his eyes wide when in full flow. He waves his hands around despite the limited movement available to his arms. His tone is more varied: angry when he discusses congressional earmarks, gleeful when he accuses Obama of supporting tax breaks for oil companies. He directs all his answers to the moderator and not to the camera. He also relies heavily on material from his stump speeches, which he compresses or occasionally misremembers, with the result that some of his sentences make little sense: 'The average South Korean is 3 inches taller than the average North Korean. A huge gulag.' Obama, who has evidently put much effort into preparing his answers, is more fluent, although his words often blur into a hum of technocratic detail. When McCain takes up a subject – like earmarks or the surge – he returns to it repeatedly and drives home his central point. Obama slides from topic to topic, showing off his comprehensive grasp of the issues but rarely leaving a memorable imprint on any. More than once he refers to 'a whole bunch of things' that need to be mentioned, and mentions them.

The debate ends with neither man having scored a knockout blow, nor any real moments of drama. But Americans have had their first chance to compare the two men up close and draw their conclusions.

In the spin tent, Schmidt and his allies argue that their man demonstrated his firm leadership, incisiveness and depth of foreign policy experience. Obama, they say, came off as a waffler with nothing of substance to say. They cite the many times that Obama agreed with McCain as evidence of their candidate's superior authority. Before the night is out they have produced an ad that edits together every clip of Obama saying McCain was right about something. It ends by asking if Obama is ready to lead and – in case anyone might be uncertain – answering 'No'.

Obama, according to his team, sounded far more in command of his material during the economic discussion and displayed a more presidential bearing throughout. Referring to McCain's refusal to look Obama in the eye, they suggest that the Republican showed himself to be surly and irritable. Their instant TV ad focuses on the fact that Obama used the phrase 'middle class' twelve times, and McCain used it not at all. This is proof, they say, that whilst McCain has much to say about his opponent, he fails to understand and doesn't address the problems of voters.

Amongst experienced observers, there is a consensus that neither candidate scored a clear victory, though they are divided on who had the edge. If anything, a slight majority of pundits call McCain the night's victor. But over the next few days, it becomes clear that the voters saw it differently. In nearly every poll, Obama is declared the winner.

Did the pundits miss something? Obama didn't win all, or even most of the arguments that night. Nor did he introduce compelling new ways of framing the issues at stake. But it appears that he did one big thing well: he looked and sounded presidential.

Most voters, unlike the pundits, have not been following this race closely until now, and many of them have only a vague idea of Obama, from seeing images of him accepting the adulation of crowds or reading emails that describe him as a secret Muslim. The man they saw on Friday night was calm, reasonable, knowledgeable and, for the most part, likeable enough. He addressed voters at home directly. He held the stage next to his more experienced opponent and seemed utterly at home there.

Obama achieved his main goal on Friday night: establishing himself firmly as a safe and plausible alternative to a known quantity.

Ironically, whilst McCain might have won the first debate on tactics, it is Obama who achieved strategic success.

Meltdown

On the morning of Monday 30 September, John McCain is speaking to a crowd of 4,000 students at Capital University in the suburbs of Columbus, Ohio. It is his first public appearance since the debate three days ago. He is on bullish form. After widespread criticism that his dramatic actions of the previous week hindered more than helped progress to an agreement, McCain is eager to claim credit for his role in shaping the bill that will go before the House of Representatives today. 'I put my campaign on hold for a couple days last week to fight for a rescue plan that put you and your economic security first,' he says. In a voice scalding with sarcasm, McCain contrasts his approach with that of his opponent:

> Senator Obama took a very different approach to the crisis
> our country faced. At first he didn't want to get involved.
> Then he was 'monitoring the situation'. That's not leader-
> ship; that's watching from the sidelines . . . I've never been
> afraid of stepping in to solve problems for the American
> people, and I'm not going to stop now.

Within hours, though, it becomes clear that the most urgent problem facing the nation has not been solved. News arrives that the House of Representatives has voted to reject the bailout plan. This triggers a terrifying market decline: the Dow Jones index records its biggest one-day fall ever. The credit markets freeze up even further. The reverberations of this unexpected setback are felt around the world.

Representatives from both sides voted against the bill, but most were Republicans, in defiance of their own president, vice-president and Treasury secretary. Most of those who voted against it have tough re-election races coming up – and they know that the bailout plan is very unpopular with their constituents. Americans across the country are deeply wary of the president's proposal, and some are fiercely hostile to it. A combination of populist sentiment and free-market ideology leads Republican congressmen to risk financial chaos rather than support the bill.

The defeat represents a shocking collapse in the authority of the White House, and of party leaders. It also comes as a shattering blow to McCain's candidacy. Even though he suspended his campaign so dramatically to work with 'my Republicans' to find a resolution, those same Republicans have now torpedoed the agreed plan, thus exposing in the most humiliating fashion his lack of influence within his own party. Even worse, the confidence that McCain displayed in Ohio now makes him look out of touch with events – which is just how the Obama campaign has been trying to portray him.

McCain is still in Ohio when he hears the news. After speaking to Paulson and Ben Bernanke on the phone, he makes a brief statement criticising Obama and calling for bipartisanship at the same time. He boards a plane to Iowa to campaign in a state where polls show him trailing his rival badly. McCain wants this election to be a referendum on his inexperienced rival, but in the last two weeks it has been his own temperament that voters have questioned. He has appeared impetuous, headstrong and erratic at a time when the nation is seeking respite from economic turmoil.

It is five weeks before election day. The nation faces its most severe economic crisis since the Great Depression, and political leaders seem incapable of formulating a response to it. Paulson and congressional leaders vow to return a different version of the bill to the House within days. For now, only one thing is certain: there couldn't be a tougher or more rigorous proving ground for this year's presidential candidates.

October 2008

An excited buzz fills Field House at Washington University, in St Louis, Missouri on the evening of 2 October. The audience of students, staff, reporters and invited guests have come to witness the most anticipated vice-presidential debate in memory.

There is applause as the moderator, Gwen Ifill, takes the stage. Ifill, an African-American woman who delivers lucid political commentary for the public broadcaster PBS, broke her ankle two days earlier and has to hobble to her desk on stage with the help of two burly football players. 'By the way, I fell,' she tells the audience. 'I wasn't pushed.' (She is alluding to Republican complaints about a book she has written that they argue is evidence of her bias towards Barack Obama.) Ifill lays down the rules for the audience. No shouting. No applause. 'Anything you would do at the circus, don't do here.' A hush descends as the hour of 8 p.m. approaches. On television, the networks begin their coverage.

As Sarah Palin stands in the wings, stage right, any nerves she has may be settled by the knowledge that expectations for her performance tonight could hardly be lower. After enjoying two weeks of success, the bloom has come off her candidacy. Palin is still drawing enormous crowds across the country – 60,000 in Florida, just over a week ago – and delivering crowd-pleasing stump speeches to the Republican faithful. But the rest of the country is less impressed. The McCain campaign has been keeping her away from all but the friendliest interlocutors on television. As a result, she has seemed inaccessible to most viewers, and speculation about her ability to handle questioning grows. When the campaign does arrange a major interview – with CBS's Katie Couric – the result of Palin's seclusion proves disastrous. Instead of confidently batting away difficult questions she runs at them full tilt and ends up entangled in a thicket of contradictions, outlandish assertions, non-sequiturs and awkward silences. Even sympathetic Republicans are appalled. As the prominent conservative commentator David Frum puts it: 'I think she has pretty thoroughly – and probably irretrievably – proven that she is not up to the job of being president of the United States.' Her situation isn't helped by the popular success of the comedian Tina Fey's unflattering impersonation of her on *Saturday Night Live*.

This is, in large part, why the nation's interest in tonight's debate is so intense, higher even than in the first presidential debate. Many viewers are expecting, dreading or hoping for a spectacle of humiliation. Others just want to get a good look at the woman they've heard so much about but haven't heard talk very much. If Palin flunks this evening's debate, John McCain – who took such a risk in choosing her – may see his campaign go down with her reputation.

A few days before, Steve Schmidt flew with Palin down to McCain's ranch in Sedona, Arizona, with two aides practised in schooling candidates for debates. They were determined not only that Palin would be more prepared for this than she was for her Couric interview but that she would be in a better frame of mind. The most important thing, McCain tells his staff, is that she should be allowed to let the personality that captivated millions of voters at the convention shine through. Just enjoy yourself, he tells her.

As she waits to take her place opposite her more experienced adversary, Joe Biden, Palin is ready to do just that. She is quite used to low expectations, and adept at turning them to her advantage.

'Please welcome the candidates,' says Ifill. Wearing a black suit, Palin walks out on stage, smiling and blowing a kiss to the audience. As she shakes Biden's hand, viewers at home hear her ask: 'Hey, can I call you Joe?'

Biden takes the first question, on the financial crisis. His tone is firm, measured and low key. As he speaks, Palin looks down at her podium and takes notes. When it's her turn, Palin stares directly into the camera. With a rapid delivery, she tells viewers:

> The best way to figure out what's going on with the American economy is to go to a kids' soccer game on Saturday, and turn to any parent there on the sideline and ask them: 'How are you feeling about the economy?' And I bet you, you're going to hear some fear in that parent's voice.

This illustration of economics by way of a soccer mom vignette establishes Palin's strategy for the whole debate.

Schmidt and his team relax a little as the opening exchanges take place. Palin looks comfortable behind her podium. She speaks quickly but for the most part fluently. Biden is careful, authoritative, somewhat senatorial. Palin is informal, almost chatty. Her speech is deliberately unlike a typical politician's, and is sprinkled with self-conscious colloquialisms ('You betcha . . . Say it ain't so, Joe . . . Gosh darn. . .'). When she does trip over her own words she carries straight on rather than try to correct herself. Her only hint of nerves is a slight shortness of breath to begin with, but as the evening goes on she grows in confidence and starts to display the joy in political combat so much in evidence in her speech to the convention.

It is rare to see a politician so extravagantly expressive in close-up. Palin's smile is rarely absent, although it is just as likely to suggest disbelief or the imminent approach of a joke at her opponent's expense as it is warmth. Her head cocks from side to side as she talks; her thumb gestures jauntily over her shoulder; she shimmies her shoulders on the delivery of a particularly arch line. Explaining McCain's 'fundamentals of the economy are strong' remark as being a reference to America's tireless workforce, Palin says: '*That's* what John McCain meant,' and accompanies her assurance with a wink to the camera. Candidates in vice-presidential debates do not, in general, wink. Seasoned debate-watchers note its deployment with the excitement of tennis commentators observing a particularly unorthodox backhand.

This isn't the only way in which Palin plays fast and loose with the normal rules. She declares independence from the questions themselves. 'I may not answer the questions in the way the moderator or you want to hear,' she tells Biden. 'But I'm going to talk straight to the American people.' At one point, asked to respond to Biden's diagnosis of the subprime mortgage crisis, she demurs and chooses to discuss her favoured topic of energy policy instead.

All of which is evidence of Palin's considerable nerve. Despite her agile performance, however, there is a sense in which Palin is not fully present this evening, that she is a little too inside her script to be wholly attuned to the atmosphere in the room – something illustrated by the debate's single most memorable moment.

Biden knows that he is not the star of the show this evening. In fact, he knows that if he is, it will mean bad news. If commentators believe that Palin might melt in the heat of tonight's debate, they are even more confident that Biden will make at least a couple of his famous gaffes and that he won't be able to restrain himself from unleashing a bombastic broadside on his junior opponent. As it is, Biden puts in a quiet but well-judged performance. He keeps his answers to the point and for the most part free of political jargon. He doesn't attempt to bully Palin as many predicted he would. Instead, he smiles warmly at her as she jabs at him and Barack Obama, as if watching a favourite niece perform in a school play.

In one of the last answers of the night, Biden tells voters suffering hard times that he knows something of what they're going through. He explains that although he has been a senator for a long time his life has not always been comfortable. Referring to the car crash that killed his first wife and badly injured his two sons, he says: 'I know what it's like to have a child you're not sure is gonna' – here he chokes on his words, clenches his fist – 'is gonna make it.' Biden regains his composure and finishes his answer. The evening's one moment of genuine emotion hangs in the air. But Palin doesn't adjust her tone. She rattles on in the same quickfire, smiling style, repeating that McCain is a 'maverick', as she has done several times tonight already.

It is a flaw in a performance which, in context, was strong – or at least not as weak as some predicted. Palin's answers, whilst superficial and often confused on detail, are delivered with verve and confidence, and the next day's reports focus on her success at getting through the debate without succumbing to the sort of deadly muddle that made her Couric interview so notorious. Some commentators, especially conservative ones, call her the night's victor.

But as the polls come in the public's verdict is, once again, that the Democrat won. Americans were charmed by Palin – but they believed in Biden.

Going negative

In the weeks following the first presidential debate, it transpires that the financial crisis – along with the bailout saga – marked something of a watershed in the race. Barack Obama has opened up a significant lead in national polls and gained ground in all the swing states. The McCain campaign, in a move that stuns many in his party, announces that it is withdrawing advertising and other activity from Michigan, which up until now was regarded as one of the Republican's key targets. With only a few weeks to go, John McCain finds himself in severe trouble.

He knows it, but seems uncertain how to respond. This puts him in a foul mood. A tape of an interview with a newspaper editorial board shows him bristling with indignation at their questions and offering biting, sardonic responses. On the Senate floor, where both candidates are present to vote on a revised bailout bill, Obama crosses to the Republican side and extends a hand to McCain. He receives a cold welcome. McCain barely turns to greet him and makes it clear he has no wish to keep his rival's company for even a few moments. Obama beats a quick retreat.

In language reminiscent of that used by Hillary Clinton's campaign after her Iowa loss, sources in McCain's campaign tell the press that from now on 'the gloves are off'. They intend, they say, to turn the last few weeks of the campaign into a punishing interrogation of Obama's character, paying particular attention to his associations with shady characters such as William Ayers.

Ayers is a professor of education at the University of Illinois and used to live in Hyde Park, the same Chicago neighbourhood as Obama. As a prominent liberal activist, Ayers's path crossed with Obama's on several occasions as the latter made his way up through local politics. The two men served on the board of a charitable foundation devoted to education reform and Ayers donated to Obama's state senate re-election campaign. Ayers has an unsavoury history, however. He is a former member of the Weathermen, a radical leftist organisation formed in 1969 which violently opposed the Vietnam War. Ayers and his wife, Bernadine Dohrn, were involved in several acts of domestic terrorism, though they were never successfully prosecuted. They have since been flatly unrepentant. 'I don't regret setting bombs; I feel we didn't do enough,' Ayers told the *New York Times* in 2001.

Clinton raised Obama's association with Ayers in the run-up to Pennsylvania's primary. Now McCain's campaign is using the same tactic as a way of planting doubts about Obama's background and character. New McCain ads ask 'Who is Barack Obama?' and raise his connection with Ayers. On the stump in Nebraska, Sarah Palin goes even further, asking her audience why Obama is 'palling around with terrorists'. Obama's campaign responds by playing down the extent of the relationship and by arguing that McCain is trying to distract voters from his lack of anything to say about the economic crisis. Meanwhile, it rolls out a retaliation in the form of an ad about McCain's involvement in the Keating Five scandal, the financial corruption case from 1989 that was a low point – and a turning point – in McCain's career.

As the campaigns snipe, the markets convulse. Two days before the second presidential debate the country reverberates to the sound of another thunderous stock market crash as Wall Street expresses its lack of confidence in the newly passed bailout bill to rescue the banking system.

Presidential debate II: the town hall

John McCain's town hall meetings in New Hampshire 2000, reprised in the autumn of 2007, have become the stuff of political legend. Talking to voters in the round, taking questions, telling jokes and starting arguments, McCain was at his best, invigorated and invigorating. His campaign team hope that the second of the presidential debates, to be held in a town hall format, will play to the strengths of their candidate.

But on the night of 7 October, before an audience at Belmont University in Nashville, Tennessee, McCain might be forgiven for not feeling in his element. The organisers have contrived to create a stilted affair. Unlike the boisterous crowds that McCain thrives on, tonight's audience is quiet, cowed by the strictness of the rules: each question pre-submitted, and no follow-ups allowed. Tom Brokaw, NBC's familiar, Moses-voiced anchor, is tonight's moderator and makes matters worse by asking long questions and repeatedly requesting that the candidates keep their answers short.

One reason for the debate's sobriety is the gloominess of the nation's economic situation. Wall Street continues to suffer shocks, and markets around the world tumble and collapse.

Barack Obama and John McCain reflect, in their different ways, the national mood. Both are subdued, though McCain is edgier, taking advantage of the candidates' freedom to move around by roaming restlessly across the stage. When stationary he takes notes compulsively as Obama talks, his face flickering with incredulity or scorn like the gauge on a high-pressure container of frustration. His annoyance can spill over into his answers. 'There was an energy bill on the floor of the Senate loaded down with goodies, billions for the oil companies,' he says at one point. 'And it was sponsored by Bush and Cheney. You know who voted for it?' Pointing at Obama – without looking at him – he says: 'That one.'

Obama is more fluent and emits less emotional heat than his opponent. When McCain is talking he sits perfectly still on his stool, one foot resting on its crossbar, the other on the floor, arranging his face into a picture of careful attention, or ironic amusement when his opponent is on the attack. Although he addresses the questioners directly he makes no real attempt to engage with them; McCain is more likely to get up close to the audience, at one point shaking the hand of a chief petty officer and thanking him for his service. Obama's one moment of real emotional connection, pre-prepared but nonetheless powerful, comes in a discussion about health insurance when he recalls his mother's struggle with cancer.

McCain insists throughout that he is the candidate with a record of bipartisanship, and presents himself as the seasoned veteran who will see America through its current troubles. Obama talks more directly and in more detail about the plight of 'the middle class' and takes every opportunity to pair McCain's name with that of George W. Bush. Neither candidate seeks to detonate the campaign's most explosive materials. McCain doesn't mention William Ayers; Obama makes no reference to the Keating Five. Each strives to portray the other as the riskier choice for uncertain times. McCain, in an unusual position for a Republican, criticises Obama for being too bellicose in his rhetoric about Pakistan. Obama responds by reminding the audience that McCain once jokingly called on America to 'bomb bomb bomb, bomb bomb Iran'.

As with the first debate there are no moments of crystallising confrontation, though their physical and temperamental differences are accentuated by the format. More than once during the debate McCain says that the nation needs a 'steady hand at the tiller', but his movements, body language and tone convey instability. His peram- bulations give the impression of a turbulent mind, and the cameras, often filming him from behind, ruthlessly highlight his age: the round body and stiff gait, the soft pink pate beneath strands of white hair. His opponent appears sleek and languid by comparison and, most importantly, calm. With his body language Obama communicates reassurance to viewers intensely anxious about the nation's fortunes. This, combined with his persistent focus on 'the middle class', does much to convince them that he, rather than McCain, is the man to see the country through its current crisis. As the polls come in they show that the majority of viewers regard Obama as the evening's clear winner.

In the town hall meetings of New Hampshire a year ago McCain was able to work closely with his audiences, building conversations between voters with different opinions, engendering an atmosphere of mutual respect for opposing views, all the while injecting his own antic humour into the event. Tonight's strict format allows no room for that tonight. McCain seems hemmed in, cramped and crabbed by restrictions, in a way that embodies something about his relationship with his whole campaign.

Caught in a trap

On 9 October, two days after the second presidential debate, John McCain is holding his own town hall meeting in a sports centre gym in Waukesha, Wisconsin, and calls on a member of the audience to ask a question. 'I'm mad, I'm really mad,' says the man. 'It's not the economy. It's the socialist taking over our country.' McCain starts to respond but the man interrupts him. 'Let me finish please. When you have an Obama, Pelosi and the rest of the hooligans up there gonna run this country, we've got to have our head examined. It's time that you two who are representing us, and we are mad.' The man's syntax is mangled by his fury but the sentiment is clear. McCain is silenced as the crowd breaks into a chant: 'USA! USA!'

Normally it is the candidate who attempts to fire up the crowd. At McCain's events, these days, it is the other way around. Though he sets about Barack Obama with alacrity, questioning his connection to William Ayers and deriding his inexperience, the crowds demand more. They shout out the names of Rev. Wright (whom McCain has declared out of bounds, perhaps nervous of the political storm that using Wright to attack Obama might invoke, perhaps believing that most voters are weary of that name) and ACORN, a housing advocacy group that also leads voter registration drives that benefit Democrats, which is being investigated for irregularities.

McCain has taken to asking 'Who is the real Barack Obama?' in an attempt to raise anxieties that his opponent's moderate exterior conceals a more radical politician. But the question touches on deeper fears. When he asked it of a crowd in Albuquerque, New Mexico, a few days before the Waukesha meeting, somebody in the audience called out 'Terrorist!' McCain frowned momentarily and carried on. At Sarah Palin's rallies there have also been reports of people crying 'Terrorist!' and 'Traitor!' and even 'Kill him!'. Liberal bloggers with cameras have goaded attendees of McCain's and Palin's rallies into rabid, racist diatribes against the Democrat candidate and posted the resulting videos on YouTube. The media – also a target of Republican fury – have been putting the spotlight on this extremist element in McCain's support. Unaligned voters considering which side to join are being confronted with a deeply unattractive picture of McCain's followers.

McCain now finds himself at the mercy of contradictory forces, caught between the necessity of keeping his core supporters energised and the need to prevent their anger from poisoning his whole campaign. It is a conflict that goes to the heart of his struggle to reconcile his instincts with those of his party in this race.

In 1970, when McCain was in captivity, the president of the American National Students Association was a man named David Ifshin. At a time when students across the country were demanding that America withdraw its troops from Vietnam, Ifshin went further than most. He travelled to Hanoi and made a speech in which he called US pilots 'war criminals' and urged US troops to turn against the war. The speech was broadcast repeatedly into the cells of the Hanoi Hilton for the edification of the prisoners of war held there, McCain amongst them. For McCain, and most Americans, Ifshin's actions were repugnant and very close to treason.

Ifshin never repented his opposition to the war but as he grew older he came to regret the speech he made in Hanoi. He developed a richer appreciation for his own country and its people, coming to believe in their essential goodness and generosity. He moved into the political mainstream, becoming an adviser to the Democrat Walter Mondale during his unsuccessful run for the presidency in 1984. Ronald Reagan's campaign team was eager to use Ifshin to discredit Mondale, and asked McCain to make a speech denouncing him. McCain did so but afterwards felt great remorse. He had sworn to himself after his attempted suicide in prison that he would never question the integrity of anybody else's decisions or statements about the war. After his return to America he was frequently asked about anti-war protestors and always refused to condemn them.

In 1985, McCain and Ifshin happened to find themselves at the same Washington meeting. Ifshin approached McCain, who immediately said: 'I'm sorry I gave that speech. I didn't even know you.' Ifshin replied: 'You're apologising to me? I've been wanting to apologise to you for years. I feel terrible about that speech I gave in Hanoi.'

The two became firm friends. They returned to Vietnam together to do charitable work and to further the reconciliation of that country with their own. When Bill Clinton was attacked by Republicans because of his own ties to Ifshin, McCain spoke up for his friend. Ifshin became fatally ill with cancer in 1996 and McCain visited him regularly in hospital. That same year, he was called upon to give a eulogy at Ifshin's funeral. His voice breaking, he said: 'David taught me a lot about the meaning of courage.'

McCain is unusual in being an ex-PoW who has never seemed

resentful of the American left for its opposition to the Vietnam War. In a reflective interview for this month's issue of the *Atlantic* he recalls that when he was released he was concerned above all with his country's morale. He worried about the treatment of returning soldiers ('the only heroes were the PoWs, and in all due respect to us, that's not the object of warfare, to get captured') and about the divisions that the war opened up amongst his fellow citizens. He was right to be anxious; the political and cultural legacy of the Vietnam War was a corrosive one. The estrangement between those who fought in Vietnam and those who didn't, and those who supported the war and those who opposed it, has shaped and inflamed the national debate ever since. McCain's capacity for friendship with those on both sides is rare.

The same spirit of generosity has informed McCain's approach to politics. One of his first real friends in Washington after he was elected to the House was his fellow Arizonan congressman Mo Udall, a Democrat. He was one of the only visitors to Udall's hospital bedside when the older man was struck with Parkinson's disease in the last years of his life. McCain went on to forge strong personal friendships and productive working relationships with Democrats in the Senate. He often relied on them when unpopular with his own colleagues. For most of his career McCain has been unafraid of picking a fight with his own party on issues, such as campaign finance, on which he disagreed with it. In McCain's 'character first' view of the world, which side you are on counts for only so much. He is, proudly, a patriot rather than a partisan.

In a year when Republicans are deeply unpopular, McCain's ability to think beyond partisan politics should be an advantage. But when he won the nomination he became head of a party that was angry, fearful and in no mood to compromise with those on the centre ground. If he hadn't already realised that, he surely did after being rudely disabused of the idea that Joe Lieberman might be his running mate. In this election McCain can't be the man who reached out his hand to Ifshin or Udall. His party is demanding, in the most unequivocal terms, that he pick sides.

At the Waukesha meeting a local African-American radio host and McCain supporter named James T. Harris stands up. 'It's absolutely vital that you take it to Obama, that you hit him where it hurts. We have all these shady characters surrounding him,' bellows Harris. 'I am begging you, sir. Take it to him.' The crowd roar their approval. In response, McCain tries to steer an uneasy course away from personal attacks and to lift the tone of the conversation. 'Yes, I'll do that,' he replies. 'But I also, my friends, want to address the greatest financial challenge of our lifetime with a positive plan for action that Senator Obama and I have. We need to restore hope and trust and confidence in America and have Americans know that our best days are ahead of us.' The crowd are unimpressed. As they file out some fling insults at reporters, whilst others express their anger at the positive coverage of Obama. 'I can't stand to look at him, I don't trust him,' says one woman of the Democratic candidate.

The next day, at a town hall meeting in Lakeville, Minnesota, McCain starts off with his old verve and pep, and the crowd respond enthusiastically. Then a supporter takes the microphone and tells him: 'We want to see a real fight at the next debate. We want a strong leader for the next four years.' McCain doesn't make a rousing promise to do just that. Instead, whilst acknowledging how glad he is to see the 'energy' of his supporters, he declares: 'I respect Senator Obama and his accomplishments.' There are boos at the very mention of his opponent's name. McCain, visibly annoyed, stops them. 'I want everyone to be respectful.' Later, another man stands up and says: 'We are scared. We're scared of an Obama presidency.' McCain, his eyes downcast, replies: 'I have to tell you, he is a decent person, and a person that you do not have to be scared of as president of the United States.' To shouts of dismay from the crowd, McCain then says: 'Now look, if I didn't think I'd be a heck of a lot better president I wouldn't be running.' A woman takes the microphone. 'I've read about Obama,' she says. 'I can't trust him. He's a. . . an Arab.' McCain shakes his head and takes back the microphone from her. 'No, no, ma'am. He's a decent family man with whom I happen to have some disagreements.' There is applause at his reply but much of the energy in the room has drained away, never to return. For the rest of the meeting McCain looks uncomfortable, his eyes fixed on the ground or darting around the hall as if wary of settling on any one supporter. At times, he looks hunted.

Racists for Obama

A canvasser knocks on a door in Washington, Pennsylvania and a woman answers. The caller asks her who she is planning to vote for. She is unsure and asks her husband, who is in another room watching television. He yells back: 'We're voting for the nigger!' The woman turns back to the canvasser. 'We're voting for the nigger,' she says, brightly.

Barack Obama's racial identity has been a central theme of this election, sometimes explicitly, other times more subtly. It is both a barrier and a boon to the Democratic candidate. It has undoubtedly made it harder for him to gain the support of those voters who feel uncomfortable with the idea of a black president. But it has drawn black voters to his side with greater commitment than they showed to previous Democrat nominees, and his colour, as David Axelrod foresaw, acts as a powerful signifier to all voters that he represents change.

The encounter above, reported to the popular election website

Politico, is one of a number of anecdotes that indicate a phenomenon nobody had predicted: voters who dislike the idea of a black president elected nonetheless declaring for Obama. A key factor is the economic crisis. These voters believe in Obama's ability to manage it more than they do McCain's. Racism has become a luxury they can't afford. An Obama volunteer campaigning in Fishtown, a white working-class area of Philadelphia, reports: 'I was blown away by the outright racism, but these folks are undecided. They would call him racist names and then say they don't know what to do because of the economy.' Another factor is the sheer unpopularity of McCain's party. A GOP consultant reports an older white male of firm conservative tendencies saying of Obama: 'I'm gonna hate him the moment I vote for him. He's gonna be a bad president. But I won't ever vote for another goddamn Republican.'

Of course, the relationship of voters to race has always been more nuanced than commentators often allow. 'They've all got one black friend,' says a Democratic congressman from a white working-class district of his more unreconstructed constituents. 'And they won't stop talking about their black friend.' Perhaps in this election, he muses, 'that's Obama'.

Presidential debate III: table talk

On 13 October, two days before the final presidential debate, John McCain and Sarah Palin take to the stage at a rally in Virginia Beach, Virginia to the theme from *Rocky*, just as Hillary Clinton did when she was on the ropes back in April.

McCain's advisers, speaking to the press the day before, told them that the campaign was 'hitting the reset button'. This week will see the unveiling of a new McCain – or at least the old McCain redux: a scrappy, happy warrior on the comeback trail. The focus from now on will be the candidate's experience and mettle. As McCain puts it this morning in his new stump speech: 'What America needs now is a fighter, someone who puts all his cards on the table and trusts the judgement of the American people.'

Concerned that the anger of supporters at their events is threatening to overwhelm their campaign, both McCain and Palin have toned down their speeches. There are fewer references to William Ayers or Barack Obama's 'extreme' position on abortion: the kinds of issue that fire up their supporters but so far seem to be leaving most voters unmoved. Palin alludes to the need to convert the seething frustrations of her party's base into more positive messages when she says: 'Ladies and gentlemen, let John McCain turn anger into action.' McCain then gives the crowd his analysis of where the contest stands:

> Let me give you the state of the race today. We have twenty-two days to go. We're six points down. The national media has written us off. Senator Obama is measuring the drapes . . . But they forgot to let you decide. My friends, we've got them just where we want them.

This is perilously close to self-satire. It is barely three weeks until election day and McCain's campaign still hasn't recovered from the setback his candidacy suffered when the financial crisis hit. Surveys suggest that voters now judge Palin to be unready for the job of vice-president. McCain trails Obama by increasing margins in national polls and in key states, such as Florida, that he must win if he is to achieve victory. That McCain is appearing in Virginia this morning and North Carolina later on is evidence enough of his difficulties: these southern states are usually solid for the Republicans. But Obama is pouring visits, staff and advertising dollars into the former

Confederacy and is catching or even beating McCain in many polls there. McCain's campaign is beset by critics in the media and in his own party. Enemies denounce him for the supposed negativity of his campaign. Friends call on him to hit Obama harder. Few outside his camp are optimistic about his prospects.

McCain has been counted out before, though. He survived his captivity, learned to fly again when doctors told him it would be impossible, and forced himself back into contention in this race after everyone else had consigned him to history. Understandably, then, he has a deep faith in his ability to come back. But he knows that the third presidential debate represents one of his last chances to do so. He also knows that attacks on Obama are unlikely to be enough to win. He must somehow find a way of leading the conversation about the economy.

The debate is held at Hofstra University on Long Island, New York, and is moderated by the veteran newsman Bob Schieffer. The two candidates sit across a table from each other. Both men look weary this evening. The dynamic between them is similar to the last two debates; slightly exaggerated, if anything. Obama is placid to the point of detachment, McCain tenser and more pugnacious.

The Republican is clearly out to puncture his opponent's calm. He jabs at Obama at every opportunity, making a particularly effective attack on him for his knack of eloquently evading a question. He is more convincing on economic issues than in previous encounters and better prepared for Obama's attempt to portray him as the heir of George W. Bush. 'I am not President Bush,' he says with feeling. 'If you wanted to run against President Bush, you should have run four years ago.' Once again, McCain barely bothers to hide his dislike of Obama. It is there in every sigh, shrug and mirthless smile.

McCain drops the name of Joe Wurzelbacher into the discussion. Wurzelbacher, a self-employed plumber, had confronted Obama at a campaign event days before and engaged him in an argument over whether, as a small businessman, he would have to pay more taxes under a Democratic administration. McCain now uses the story of 'Joe the Plumber' to attack his rival on this issue. Obama responds in kind and the two keep up a back-and-forth about Joe the Plumber throughout the evening. It is one of the first times in any debate that McCain has succeeded in setting the terms of the economic discussion.

Meanwhile, Obama seeks to present himself as the candidate most focused on the 'big challenges' and to seem amused rather than upset by his opponent's attacks. He is not quite as serenely self-contained as in the previous debates, however. His smiles at McCain's attacks can look like smirks, his shakes of the head as symptoms of irritation, and his responses to McCain's sallies are, by even his previous standards, flabby. At times he appears bored by the event, by his opponent's arguments and by himself. Just as in his last debate with Hillary Clinton, Obama comes dangerously close to giving the impression that he doesn't think he should have to endure this nonsense any more.

McCain loses much of the momentum he has been building when Schieffer asks the candidates about negative campaign tactics. It is a question clearly inspired by the Republican focus on Ayers and ACORN and the overheated responses of some of their supporters. McCain, rather than making light of rough tactics on both sides and returning to the offensive on tax, decides to play the part of the wounded party. He complains at length about Obama's negative advertising and protests ardently against Obama's refusal to repudiate John Lewis, the congressman and civil rights hero (McCain cited him as an inspiration at Rick Warren's Saddleback forum) for his recent remarks.

Lewis, an Obama supporter, accused the McCain campaign of

'sowing hatred' and compared the atmosphere at its events to that created by George Wallace, the segregationist and former presidential candidate, whose rabble-rousing spawned terrible violence in 1963. The comparison was unfair and inflammatory and McCain is hurt by it. But Obama has already distanced himself from the remarks and Lewis himself has said he went too far. Having set out with the intent of unsettling his opponent, McCain succeeds only in unsettling himself by dwelling on Lewis.

So far, Obama hasn't taken the opportunity to raise the reports of ugly behaviour amongst McCain's supporters. But by persisting with his own grievance McCain forces a discussion of them. Almost reluctantly, after prompting from the moderator, Obama turns to McCain and points out that Lewis made his comments after accounts of people at McCain–Palin events 'shouting, when my name came up, things like "Terrorist!" and "Kill him!"'. The tension of the debate is ratcheted up by these explosive words. Having dropped them into McCain's lap, Obama makes a swift and well-practised move to the political high ground, presenting himself once more as the candidate most eager to get beyond 'tit-for-tat politics' and on to issues voters care about – the economy being foremost amongst them.

An exasperated McCain doesn't follow him, at least not at first. He returns to his outrage over Lewis, then raises Ayers – rather half-heartedly – and ACORN. Even as he does so he seems to realise that he has been left behind by his fleet-footed opponent. He concludes his response with a passage that captures something of the current confusion of his campaign: 'All the details need to be known about Senator Obama's relationship with [Ayers] and with ACORN and the American people will make a judgement. And my campaign is about getting this economy back on track, about creating jobs, and a brighter future for America.'

A hero endorses

It is 1999. John McCain is on the original Straight Talk Express bus, touring New Hampshire as he attempts to build support for his renegade primary campaign against the Republican front-runner, George W. Bush. He is surrounded by journalists who have been told they can ask the senator anything they like. Question after question is fired at him and he answers with candour and directness, cracking jokes to his entranced audience at every opportunity. The session, like previous sessions, goes on for a while and as reporters run out of serious questions they move on to more frivolous ones. Favourite tree? 'Cottonwood.' Favourite word? 'Principle.' Favourite dead hero? 'Julius Caesar.' (McCain is a fan of Gibbon's *Decline and Fall of the Roman Empire*.) Favourite living hero? 'Colin Powell. Served his country. A wonderful man.'

Nine years later, on 19 October 2008, Colin Powell, Vietnam veteran, general and former Republican secretary of state, is asked by Tom Brokaw on the Sunday morning TV show *Meet the Press* to say who he is supporting for the presidency. Will it be John McCain, his old friend and ally, the man to whom he contributed money as a gesture of solidarity after everyone wrote his candidacy off in 2007? Or Barack Obama, whom he observed closely during the campaign and got to know more recently?

Powell declares for Obama and explains why in a seven-minute answer of uninterrupted fluency and passion. It includes some quietly devastating criticisms of his old friend.

'I found that he was a little unsure as to how to deal with the economic problems that we were having,' Powell says of McCain, with deadly understatement, adding that McCain doesn't seem to have a 'complete grasp' of the situation. He moves on to Sarah Palin. 'I don't believe she's ready to be president of the United States, which is the job of the vice-president,' Powell says. 'And so that raised some question in my mind as to the judgement that Senator McCain made.' He criticises the McCain campaign and his own party generally for the substance and tenor of their attacks on Obama and – though he makes no explicit link between McCain and the rumours – says he is troubled by suggestions that Obama is 'a Muslim and he might be associated with terrorists'. He goes on to make a heartfelt defence of American Muslims, pointing out that there are Muslims amongst the American dead at Arlington Military Cemetery.

Powell concludes by saying that after taking time to observe both men during their campaigns, he believes that it is Obama who meets 'the standard of being a successful president, being an exceptional president. I think he is a transformational figure.'

Without evident anger or malice, Powell has administered a punishing assault on McCain's candidacy. It's as if he has applied his own doctrine of military intervention to politics: that if an attack is embarked upon it should be made after careful planning and then with overwhelming force and the intention to devastate.

On the same day, the Obama campaign announces that it raised an astonishing $150 million in September from a donor army whose membership now stands at over three million. This gives Obama an unprecedented financial advantage over his rival in the last two and a half weeks of the campaign.

McCain fights on

In the last weeks of October John McCain continues to campaign with indefatigable energy. On the stump he hurls attack after attack at his opponent, in the hope that if he can raise enough doubts about Barack Obama in the minds of wavering voters then he might yet create an upset. He ridicules what he suggests is Obama's presumption: 'We just learned in the newspaper today Senator Obama's inaugural address is already written,' he says, citing a *New York Times* story on both candidates' transition planning. 'My friends, when I pull this thing off, I have a request for my opponent. I want him to save that manuscript from his inaugural address and donate it to the Smithsonian. They can put it right next to the Chicago paper that said "Dewey defeats Truman".' Obama's spokesman denies there is any such manuscript.

The collective memory of Harry S. Truman's surprise 1948 victory is reliably summoned by trailing candidates, though McCain does so with apparent conviction. He betrays no hint of resignation in public or – according to his aides – in private. He believes that his attacks on Obama's taxation policy in particular are gaining traction. These days McCain is joined on the trail by Joe the Plumber, now a celebrity in his own right. Both McCain and Palin invoke the name of Joe and others like him ('Tito the Builder', 'Rose the Teacher') to warn voters about what they allege will be the punitive effects of Obama's tax regime. Seizing on Obama's comment to Joe that he wanted to 'spread the wealth around', McCain and Palin accuse their opponent of 'socialism'.

At the same time they paint Obama and his supporters in the media as creatures of the elite who look down their noses at ordinary Americans. At a North Carolina fundraiser on 16 October Sarah Palin says: 'We believe that the best of America is in these small towns that we get to visit, and in these wonderful little pockets of what I call the real America, being here with all of you hard-working, very patriotic, very pro-America areas of this great nation.' Joe Biden, on behalf of the Obama campaign, bemoans Palin's resort to 'the politics of division'. A week later, in a joint interview with Palin on NBC, McCain is even more specific about where the elites are located. 'In our nation's capital and New York City . . . I know what a lot of these elitists are. The ones that she [Palin] never went to a cocktail party with in Georgetown . . . [They] think that they can dictate what they believe to America rather than let Americans decide for themselves.'

Their populist attacks are undermined by news that the Republican National Committee spent $150,000 in high-end New York department stores on a new wardrobe for Palin after she was appointed to the ticket. Although Palin herself claims she had nothing to do with the purchases, her image as an ordinary 'hockey mom' takes a battering.

Obama pays a visit

Presidential candidates do not usually take a break from campaigning two weeks before election day. But when Barack Obama hears that his grandmother's cancer is so advanced that unless he visits her immediately he may never get the chance to see her alive again, he quickly assents. His greatest regret, he once told an interviewer, was not making time to visit his mother shortly before she died in 1995. Now, on Thursday 23 October, he takes a nine-hour flight across six time zones, from Indianapolis to Honolulu. His grandmother's eighty-sixth birthday is on Sunday.

Much about Obama dazzles: his oratory, charm and evident intelligence. But in the brilliant glare of his arrival on the national scene, his more prosaic attributes were obscured. As much as anything else, Obama has set himself on a course to the White House through his capacity for hard work, attention to detail and self-discipline. If he learnt those habits from anyone, he did so in large part from his grandmother.

Compared to her husband and daughter, Madelyn Dunham does

not seem to have been a dreamer. Her most dramatic moment may have been in 1940 when she married her fellow Kansan Stanley Dunham without her parents' blessing or permission. While her husband was away during World War II, she stayed at home to raise their daughter Stanley Ann and worked on a bomber assembly line in Wichita. After the war she followed her husband as he struck out west on a restless search for a bigger, more colourful life than he could have in small-town Kansas. They travelled to California, to Washington state and then, finally, to Hawaii.

As his grandson tells it, Stanley Dunham never quite found the satisfaction he sought, and ended up a mediocre salesman unhappy with his lot, no better off than he might have been in Kansas; just a long way from home. Ann shared her father's wanderlust but she too found her big dreams confounded by reality (the theme is echoed by the story of Obama's father, who ended his days adrift and depressed, having turned to drink after breaking ties with members of his tribe in Kenya).

In Hawaii, Madelyn found a job as a secretary in a bank to help pay for the keep of her grandson, and quietly worked her way up through the ranks, eventually becoming one of the first female bank vice-presidents in the state. She battled the ingrained sexism of her workplace with sheer application, competence and determination. For much of this time she was also raising her grandson; when the fourteen-year-old Barack declined to follow his mother to Indonesia it was to stay in Hawaii with his grandparents. 'Toot' (the Hawaiian word for 'grandparent' is *tutu*) had as much, if not more, to do with shaping Barack Obama's character and values than either of his parents.

This Thursday, Obama visits his grandmother in her apartment, the one he grew up in. She is nearly blind now and suffers from osteoporosis; her back is severely hunched. She can hardly have imagined, when raising a black child in the white suburbs of Hawaii, that he would not only prosper in America but become a nominee for president. This year, she has been following the fantastical journey of the grandson she calls 'Bear' closely, having undergone a corneal transplant in order to watch him on television. She surely wants nothing more than to be around to see how that journey concludes.

Closing time

On Monday 27 October, with just over a week to go, the two candidates shadow each other in their travels across the fiercely contested states of Ohio and Pennsylvania. John McCain continues to focus on the issue of taxation, convinced that it is helping him narrow the gap with his opponent. In Dayton, Ohio he reads to the crowd the transcript of a newly discovered radio interview that Barack Obama gave seven years ago. In the extract Obama appears to suggest that he is in favour of 'redistributive change'. 'Senator Obama is running to be redistributionist in chief,' says McCain. 'I'm running to be commander in chief.'

With polls still showing him in the lead, Obama returns to the lofty themes of unity and change with which he launched his candidacy. 'We are one week away from changing America,' he tells a crowd of 15,000 in Pittsburgh. 'In one week, you can put an end to the politics that would divide a nation just to win an election, that tries to pit region against region, city against town and Republican against Democrat, that asks us to fear at a time when we need hope. In one week's time, at this defining moment in history, you can give this country the change we need.'

In an unprecedented move, on 29 October Obama's campaign runs a thirty-minute prime-time 'infomercial' on most of the major networks and cable channels. Combining vignettes of voters suffering financial hardship with stories about the candidate's life, it is a predictably well-crafted piece of propaganda and is watched by more than thirty million Americans. It is a sign of how flush with funds the Obama campaign is that they are able to produce and air such a film.

The two vice-presidential nominees are also campaigning hard, although in their different ways they are both causing some problems for their running mates. Sarah Palin continues to attract large crowds wherever she appears. Although the polls suggest she has become part of the reason McCain lags behind Obama, the fascination with her, at least amongst Republicans, persists. Some leading activists, resigned to McCain's defeat, talk of her with enthusiasm as a future star and potential nominee for 2012. Palin does little to discourage such chatter, suggesting that she disagrees with her running mate on certain points, such as the decision to withdraw from Michigan. In a week that candidates usually devote to making final arguments she makes policy speeches in order to address the widespread perception that she lacks substance.

Joe Biden is keeping a relatively low profile. He speaks at lower-key events than Palin's, sometimes to crowds that number in the hundreds, in small towns populated by the white working-class voters who have been wariest of Obama. For a politician whose off-the-cuff pontifications are legendary, Biden is sticking remarkably closely to his scripts and keeping his distance from reporters. The Obama campaign doesn't like unpredictability and it is notoriously hard to know what Biden might say next when he is speaking freely. Opportunities for him to do so, therefore, are being strictly rationed. This doesn't prevent him from raiding the cupboard now and again. Speaking at a fundraising dinner in Seattle, Biden says:

> Mark my words: it will not be six months before the world
> tests Barack Obama like they did John Kennedy . . .
> Remember, I said it standing here, if you don't remember

anything else I said. Watch – we're going to have an international crisis, a generated crisis, to test the mettle of this
guy.

In a matter of days Biden's comments are the subject of a McCain TV
ad and McCain himself brings them up repeatedly on the stump to
attack the notion that Obama is ready to be president. 'I think that
Joe sometimes engages in rhetorical flourishes,' responds a bemused
Obama, who clearly wishes he wouldn't.

On the last night of October the governor of California joins
McCain at a rally in Columbus, Ohio. Arnold Schwarzenegger's wife
has endorsed Obama and he himself appeared to express reservations
about McCain's running mate in a recent interview. But he has a
strong relationship with McCain and tonight a crowd of 10,000 turn
out to hear one of the party's biggest stars declare his support for the
Republican candidate in characteristic style. 'He needs to do something about those skinny legs!' says Schwarzenegger of Obama. 'We're
going to make him do some squats. And then we're going to give him
some biceps to beef up those scrawny arms. If only we could do
something about putting some meat on his ideas.'

The Democrats roll out their own celebrity this evening: Al
Gore holds rallies in Fort Lauderdale and West Palm Beach, Florida.
Gore has not made a political visit to Florida since the recount of that
state's presidential vote in 2000 was ended, along with his hopes for
the White House, by the Supreme Court. His return is heavy with
significance for the Democrats, for whom the memory of 2000 still
burns with injustice and regret. 'Take it from me,' Gore tells his
audiences, 'every vote matters.'

Like most Democrats, the Obama campaign is in thrall to the
symbolic power of Florida. They don't need to win it this year in
order to achieve overall victory; a combination of other states more

favourable to the Democrats will deliver them a majority in the electoral college. But they are putting an immense effort into doing so. For months they have been flooding Florida with resources, including a massive advertising campaign and thousands of volunteers. Obama has sent two of his top field generals to the state, including Steve Hildebrand, the director of his ground organisation for the Iowa caucus. Two nights ago Obama staged a midnight rally in Kissimmee, Florida, with Bill Clinton, who offered a rousing endorsement of the nominee. Obama was visibly chilly. He wanted to wear a coat, but on seeing that Clinton wasn't wearing one he left his behind.

It was in Florida, eight years ago, that George W. Bush was handed the keys to the White House. Obama and his team believe that a win in this state will enable their party, and the whole country, to put the Bush years behind them and start anew.

4 November 2008

End of the road

In the final days of the campaign, the two candidates cut very different figures. One is entertaining his staff and roaring with laughter at his own jokes. The other is subdued and smiles rarely.

It may seem surprising that John McCain is the one who appears more optimistic as the day of decision approaches. He is, after all, thought by most commentators to be heading for defeat on Tuesday 4 November. He also presides over an increasingly fractious team. For the last few weeks, the Straight Talk Express has not been filled with happy passengers. As often happens in a losing campaign, the candidate's advisers are blaming each other for their situation. There are reports of a stand-up row between Mark Salter and McCain spokesperson Nicole Wallace. Some aides are already speaking to the press, off the record, in an attempt to get their story across first and defend their corner. Much of the backbiting is aimed at Sarah Palin. Unnamed McCain aides are quoted calling her a 'diva' and a 'wacko'. An in-depth *New York Times* article, published on 26 October, details the disagreements within the McCain camp over the last six months and contains many anonymous quotes from staffers. On the day it's published some in McCain's team wonder if they should hide it from him. But he finds a copy and, after reading it for a few minutes, shakes his head. 'I'm very disappointed,' he says.

McCain's spirits often seem to rise in inverse proportion to the likelihood of his political success, however. His favourite saying is 'It's always darkest before it's completely black'. He relishes any fight for what seems to be a lost cause. He also genuinely believes that there is a chance, albeit a small one, that he can pull off an upset on 4 November. He is encouraged by polling data that show him closing the gap in some key states, including Pennsylvania, where his campaign has been concentrating its resources in the last few weeks. In these closing days McCain exhibits his old sense of fun. His friend and fellow senator Lindsey Graham, who accompanies him on this final stretch, has taken to referring to Barack Obama's running mate as 'Joe the Biden'. McCain finds this inexplicably hilarious and begins using the same phrase on the stump. His staff catch their candidate's demob-happy mood and begin to make light of their differences. On the campaign bus, Salter and Steve Schmidt stage a mock boxing match for the amusement of the press – although Schmidt accidentally clips Salter's Aviator glasses, bruising his eye socket. Afterwards, Salter points to his small wound and explains: 'Vicious staff in-fighting.'

On Monday 3 November, the last full day of campaigning, McCain embarks on a hectic twenty-hour odyssey across the country, starting in Florida and travelling to seven states. After getting back to his hotel in Miami at 1.30 a.m. the night before, McCain has his first event at 9.30 a.m. in Tampa. He speaks to a few hundred supporters in a parking lot but rips into a truncated version of his stump speech as if addressing a much bigger gathering. 'With this kind of enthusiasm, this kind of intensity, we will win Florida,' he roars, his voice hoarse. He might be referring to himself as much as to his audience.

McCain seems to determined to have a good time. At his next

stop, in Blountville, Tennessee, he makes a speech in an aircraft hangar to a crowd of thousands. Wandering from his prepared remarks, he brings up Tina Fey's impersonation of his running mate (McCain was on *Saturday Night Live* himself two days ago). 'I really believe that Sarah Palin and Tina Fey were separated at birth,' he muses. 'I really do.' Moving onto the attack, he accuses his opponent of being from 'the far-left lane of American politics'. It is quite a show; McCain's 72-year-old body is clearly coursing with adrenaline. To raucous cheers, he declares: 'The Mac is back!'

On the same day, McCain gives similar performances in Pennsylvania, Indiana, New Mexico, Nevada and his home state, Arizona, often throwing in new jokes. In Roswell, New Mexico, famous for its supposed extra-terrestrial sightings, he announces that he has won 'the alien endorsement'. In Las Vegas he yells: 'What happens in Vegas stays in Vegas!' At every stop he concludes by declaring: 'I am an American and I choose to fight!' By the end of the day his voice is raw and broken but other than that he seems to be in better shape than most of the travelling press.

The man judged by most to be the likely victor on Tuesday is not in a triumphal mood. The lines on Obama's face are etched with more definition than they were when he began his campaign for the presidency, nearly two years ago, and his hair is now dappled with grey. He is happy to be reaching the end of what is perhaps the longest and most gruellingly competitive race ever undertaken by a political candidate. But he seems burdened by the thought that he might win.

It has always been hard to read Obama's feelings from his face. Even his friends sometimes describe him as inscrutable. But aides note that he doesn't smile as much as he used to. He already seems to be thinking about what happens after Tuesday. Either he or McCain will face problems of an urgency and magnitude that few new presidents have to deal with. Obama has been in touch with Hank Paulson, the Treasury secretary, regularly since mid-September, and talks to congressional leaders about possible next steps on the financial crisis.

The thought of how his family's life will be transformed should he win may also be weighing on him. On Halloween he leaves the campaign trail for a few hours. He takes Sasha to a friend's party in the family's Chicago neighbourhood, and the press pool that have followed him scramble to get pictures. He shows a rare flash of anger when a camera crew gets too close. 'That's enough,' he says. 'You've got a shot. Leave us alone.' Obama and his daughter break into a jog and leave the press behind – for now.

On Saturday evening he addresses 20,000 of his local team leaders around the country on a conference call from his mobile phone. Slouched in a leather seat in the front cabin of his campaign plane he gives them a pep talk before they set about the final, crucial task of getting the remaining voters out to the polls on election day (about a third of registered voters have voted early, thanks in part to the efforts of this volunteer army). The plane is resting on the tarmac in Missouri. As Obama talks he knows that a few miles away thousands of people are streaming into a stadium to see him at a late-night rally, each of them bright with expectation.

The yearning optimism of the huge crowds that turn out at every stop is a worry as well as an inspiration. 'What if I disappoint people?' he asks his adviser and friend Valerie Jarrett, as he has done several times during the campaign. Instead of demoralising him, the prospect that he might not live up to people's expectations seems to drive him on. 'It's what gives him the energy to keep getting up every day,' says Jarrett. In the midst of all this, Obama carries the knowledge that his beloved grandmother is close to death.

He spends this last weekend flying to battleground states across three time zones, including Nevada, Colorado, Missouri and Ohio.

He has honed his stump speech to thirty minutes, about half of what it has been for most of the campaign, and doesn't vary it from state to state except for the name he calls out as a greeting. There is little joy in his demeanour in these waning days – the only time aides see him genuinely perk up is when Michelle brings their daughters to meet him as he gets off the plane in Colorado on Saturday.

His performances on the stump are as accomplished as ever. He has hit on a new line that admonishes and excites his audience at the same time. At the mention of McCain, they jeer. 'You don't need to boo,' says Obama. 'Just vote.' But he doesn't neglect to attack McCain, either, seizing on the endorsement he received on Saturday 1 November from Dick Cheney – possibly the only politician more unpopular than George W. Bush.

Whilst not exactly coasting, his diary is lighter than it was in the run-up to his big primary battles with Hillary Clinton. Obama is not a morning person, and though his schedule always includes a 45-minute workout at the gym he tends not to hold public events early in the day. On Sunday his first event is at 1 p.m., in Columbus, Ohio. But he keeps going until late into the night. The same day he joins Bruce Springsteen for an evening rally in a rain-soaked Cleveland, where he tells the crowd: 'Don't believe for a second this election is over. Don't think for a minute that power concedes. We have to work like our future depends on it in these last few days, because it does.' He then travels to Cincinnati for a stadium event at 9.30 p.m. before flying to Jacksonville, Florida for a rally the following morning. He arrives at his hotel at 1.35 a.m., when, as usual, he chats to aides and checks his email before turning in.

At around 8 a.m. on Monday he receives the call he must have hoped wouldn't come for at least another couple of days. Madelyn Dunham has not been able to hold out any longer against her illness. The woman who did so much to raise him has died.

Forty minutes later Obama emerges from his hotel to make his regular trip to the gym. On his return he makes a few phone calls and is briefed by his aides on the day ahead. Following his event in Florida he will make just two more stops: North Carolina and Virginia. Speaking in Jacksonville this morning he betrays little sense of being shaken by his grandmother's death except when, ten minutes into his address, he begins a sentence with the words 'Here in Ohio—'. People in the crowd call out to him and he corrects himself. 'Florida! I've been travelling too much.'

After arriving in North Carolina, his team informs the press about Obama's grandmother, explaining that they wanted to get through part of the day before making the news public. On his way to the University of North Carolina, where he is due to speak, Obama stops off at the local campaign headquarters to shake hands with volunteers and make calls to voters in the presence of the media. He seems to be in good spirits, though his mood is fragile. One of the people he phones raises the subject of health care at home. Turning his back on the press, Obama says, softly: 'Obviously this is happening to my own family. . . my grandmother stayed at home until recently.' When he turns around his face looks drawn and glum.

Entering the field near the university where his rally will be held he finds a crowd of 90,000 waiting for him. They are drenched after a thunderous downpour but happy to see their candidate. Obama begins his speech by talking about his grandma: 'She died peacefully in her sleep with my sister at her side and so there's great joy as well as tears. She has gone home.' Haltingly, he says: 'I'm not going to talk about it too long because it's hard to talk about.' But he describes a little of his grandmother's life, calling her a 'quiet hero'. There are many quiet heroes in this crowd and across the country, he says. 'They're not famous. Their names aren't in the newspaper. But each and every day they work hard. They sacrifice for their families. That's what America's about.' As he speaks, a tear falls down his cheek. He reaches inside his pocket, pulls out a white handkerchief and wipes his eyes before carrying on with the rest of his speech.

That evening Obama holds the last major rally of his campaign, on the site of an old fairground in Manassas, Virginia. His crowds have swelled even more in recent weeks and tonight traffic is backed up for miles on the main highway to the venue – some simply abandon their cars at the side of the road and walk rather than risk missing him. Nearly 100,000 make it to the venue.

After delivering his stump speech, Obama delights his audience by reprising a story that was a staple of his appearances during the primaries but which he hasn't told for months. It is the tale of how, in the early part of his campaign in 2007, he travelled to Greenwood, South Carolina, at the request of a local congress-woman who promised to endorse him if he did. He was in a bad mood that day, he says. The polls showed him lagging Clinton and the press contained only bad news about his campaign. After an unwelcome early start he arrived at the venue to find just a handful of supporters there to greet him. While dutifully shaking hands with them all, he encountered a small black woman in a big church hat who, grinning at him intently, called out 'Fired up!'. He was startled to hear everyone in the hall repeat the cry. Then the woman said 'Ready to go!' and again the small crowd followed suit. As the call and response continued, a local staffer identified the woman as Edith Childs, a city councilwoman, and explained to Obama that her chant was something of a local tradition. Bemused at first, Obama joined in and within a couple of minutes was feeling 'fired up' himself, for the first time in days. The chant subsequently became a mantra for him and his campaign during the run-up to Iowa. It was how he used to finish every speech.

Tonight he tells the story brilliantly, lingering tenderly over its details, describing Childs's hat with a flamboyant sweep of his hand. He concludes:

> That's how this thing started. It shows you what one voice can do. One voice can change a room; and if it can change a room, it can change a city; and if it can change a city, it can change a state; and if it can change a state, then it can change a nation; and if it can change a nation, it can change a world.

He finishes by engaging the crowd in the same call and response:

'Are you fired up, Virginia?'

'Fired up!'

'Are you ready to go?'

'Ready to go!'

'Fired up!'

'Fired up!'

'Ready to go!'

'Ready to go!'

'LET'S GO CHANGE THE WORLD!' he shouts, and the crowd sends up an affirmation that can be heard for miles.

Afterwards, as the audience cheers, Obama stands alone at the front of the stage under the spotlights for several minutes longer than usual, arms by his sides, his slender figure absorbing the acclaim. Storing it up, perhaps.

Election day

Finally, the day itself. All over the country the signs are that people are turning out to vote in massive numbers. There are long queues outside polling stations in every state.

For the candidates election day is a time of strange uncertainty. Both know that the polls predict a victory for the Democrat. Both know that the polls have been wrong before. Now, with the campaign virtually over, they can do very little to affect the outcome. Along with the rest of the country, they can vote. . . and wait.

John McCain casts his ballot in a church near his home in Phoenix, Arizona, with Cindy at his side. He then gets on a plane and heads out for two final campaign stops, in Colorado and New Mexico. McCain's election day tradition is to watch a movie and his staff arrange for a flat-screen television and DVD player to be set up on his plane. But as it lands safely in Albuquerque that afternoon – following an aborted first attempt that terrifies the travelling press – McCain has yet to find time for the film. After this last stop he heads back home to Arizona.

Barack Obama votes at his local polling station in Hyde Park, Chicago, accompanied by his wife and daughters. Afterwards he jokes to reporters that Michelle took too long for his liking. 'I had to check who she was voting for,' he says. After one last campaign call in Indianapolis he returns to Chicago, where his friends and advisers have arranged a game of basketball. This was an election day ritual for Obama throughout the primaries. The only times he didn't follow it were in January, on the days of the New Hampshire and Nevada votes. He lost both.

Election night

On Tuesday evening Barack Obama has dinner at home with his family before sitting down to watch the election unfold on television. Later he plans to travel the short distance to Chicago's Grant Park, where, win or lose, he will address his supporters when the outcome is known. The park, surrounded by high-rise buildings, is already starting to fill up with thousands of his followers. A stage has been set up. Two sheets of bullet-proof glass stand on either side of the lectern.

John McCain watches the election in the Biltmore Hotel in Phoenix, where he and Cindy celebrated their wedding twenty-eight years ago. In the hotel ballroom hundreds of well-wishers gather to watch the results on a giant screen and to be entertained by the country singer Hank Williams Jr. In the meantime 'I'm Still Standing' by Elton John blasts out from the speakers. Outside, on the hotel lawn, a stage has been erected in the shadow of the desert mountains, awaiting the moment when McCain steps out to make his victory or concession speech.

As usual the TV networks call each state's results as they come in that evening based on a combination of early returns and exit polls. The first results are predictable: Kentucky goes to McCain, Vermont to Obama. But the evening's first truly significant news comes at about 7.30 p.m. Eastern Standard Time, and it isn't the result of a state. Vigo County in western Indiana is known as one of the nation's most reliable electoral bellwethers, having backed the winning candidate in every election since 1960. Although all the votes have yet to be counted, it is reportedly leaning towards Obama. The other news from Indiana is that there is no news from Indiana, which in recent elections has been a reliably Republican state (George W. Bush won it by twenty points in 2004). If the TV networks aren't calling it yet, that's because it is close – an ominous sign for McCain.

Shortly after 8 p.m. the networks call Pennsylvania for Obama. This is a hammer blow to McCain's remaining hopes. His campaign threw everything into winning there, despite polls showing Obama ahead by a large margin. Until now McCain was optimistic that he might pull out a last-ditch victory that would set him on course to win the entire election.

Obama leaves home with his family and makes his way to a hotel near Grant Park, where he joins a few of his closest advisers to watch the rest of the results. He can hear the noise of more than 100,000 supporters following the night's events on giant screens in the park. At 9.30 p.m. the large swing state of Ohio is called for Obama, cutting off McCain's last narrow path to victory. A cheer goes up in the park. But it is not full throated. Democrats have seen their candidates lose too many times not to feel nervous. In Phoenix, however, the crowd gathered in the Biltmore ballroom know that their candidate stands on the verge of defeat. The organisers of McCain's party turn off the election night broadcast and play music instead. In his Chicago hotel suite Obama turns to David Axelrod and says: 'So it looks like we're going to win this thing, huh?'

At 10 p.m. more results come in, including Utah and Mississippi, which vote for McCain. But Iowa – the state where it all began for Obama – goes to the Democrat. Then, shortly before 11 p.m., the networks call Virginia for Obama. He and his team are thrilled. Always conscious of history, they wanted badly to win this state in part because of its profound symbolic importance. The constitution was born there; Richmond was the capital of the Confederacy and a major centre of the slave trade; no Democratic presidential candidate has won Virginia since Lyndon Johnson. A few minutes later the Obama campaign savours victory in a state of more recent electoral significance: Florida.

The verdict

There is no longer any ambiguity about tonight's outcome. Barack Obama has won a resounding victory in the electoral college and become the first Democrat since Jimmy Carter to win a majority of the popular vote. Just after 11 p.m., when polls close on the reliably

Democratic west coast, the networks announce unanimously that Obama will be the next president of the United States.

There is a moment's silence in Grant Park as Obama's supporters process news they can scarcely comprehend. Then the park explodes with a roar of delight that shakes the surrounding buildings. The cheers are sent up far into the night sky, where they meet and mingle with others from across the land – from New York to Georgia to Colorado and California. They are joined by cheers from even further afield: Hawaii, Nairobi and Jakarta, and from the millions of people around the world who have been willing on the progress of this most unlikely candidate for America's highest office.

Nobody is cheering louder than African-Americans, nor is anyone quite as moved. In the streets of Harlem and the churches of Atlanta, joyful tears are shed by those who remember segregation and those who have learnt about it from their parents. They weep in part for their ancestors, raised in slavery, who could only dream of such a day. Children laugh and cry at something amazing, without quite knowing why.

All over the world, people of every colour and stripe try to grasp the scarcely credible truth: a man named Barack Hussein Obama, son of a Kenyan who herded goats and a Kansan with no connections to wealth or power, will be America's forty-fourth president.

The final speeches

At 11.18 p.m. John McCain steps out on to the stage in the chilly Arizonan night. He has made a phone call to Barack Obama to congratulate him on his victory and now he seems resigned and at ease and perhaps even a little relieved as he embarks on his concession speech. Cindy stands to his right. On his left are Sarah Palin, looking somewhat shell shocked, and her husband Todd.

McCain begins by acknowledging that 'the American people have spoken, and they have spoken clearly'. He says: 'A little while ago, I had the honour of calling Senator Barack Obama to congratulate him on being elected the next president of the country we both love.' At this first mention of his opponent the crowd boos. McCain raises his hands. 'Please,' he says. 'Please.' The crowd is silenced not only by his evident determination to carry on but by the power of the stately sentences crafted for him by Mark Salter.

The Republican pays unstinting tribute to his opponent:

> In a contest as long and difficult as this campaign has been, his success alone commands my respect for his ability and perseverance. But that he managed to do so by inspiring the hopes of so many millions of Americans who had once wrongly believed that they had little at stake or little influence in the election of an American president is something I deeply admire and commend him for achieving.

Calling it 'an historic election', McCain then reaches back into the past to convey the length of the journey travelled:

> A century ago, President Theodore Roosevelt's invitation of Booker T. Washington to dine at the White House was taken as an outrage in many quarters. America today is a world away from the cruel and prideful bigotry of that time. There is no better evidence of this than the election of an African-American to the presidency of the United States.

Some in the crowd greet this passage with cheers and applause. McCain goes on to reaffirm his congratulations to Obama and to

commiserate with him on the loss of his grandmother. He calls on the
country to unite behind the new president. 'Whatever our differences,'
he says, 'we are fellow Americans. And please believe me when I say
no association has ever meant more to me than that.'

Next, he addresses the raw feelings of his supporters: 'It's natural,
tonight, to feel some disappointment. But tomorrow we must move
beyond it and work together to get our country moving again. We
fought as hard as we could. And though we fell short, the failure is
mine, not yours.'

After thanking his family, his campaign team and the people of
Arizona for their support, he finishes with a version of the words with
which he has been ending his speeches since the convention, their
meaning suddenly transformed by tonight's result:

> I wish Godspeed to the man who was my former opponent
> and will be my president. And I call on all Americans, as
> I have often in this campaign, to not despair of our present
> difficulties, but to believe, always, in the promise and
> greatness of America, because nothing is inevitable here.
> Americans never quit. We never surrender. We never hide
> from history. We make history.

It is a speech worthy of the moment, and also of the man.
McCain has rarely appeared at his best during the last few months:
the generosity of his character diminished, the scale of his achieve-
ments in public life obscured, by his struggle to lead a party he has
usually been happiest running against. Tonight he has no compunction
about quieting the sourer elements in his audience. This thoughtful,
magnanimous speech reminds America, and the world, of just how
distinguished an opponent Obama has overcome.

Obama himself watches McCain's speech in his hotel room before being driven to Grant Park. Minutes later, introduced as 'the next first family of the United States', Barack, Michelle, Malia and Sasha Obama take to the stage to accept the noisy congratulations of their euphoric supporters.

At almost exactly midnight, Obama steps up to the lectern to make his first speech as president-elect. There is nothing by way of formal introduction. He charges straight in: 'If there is anyone out there who still doubts that America is a place where all things are possible, who still wonders if the dream of our founders is alive in our time, who still questions the power of our democracy, tonight is your answer.' A thunderous roar of agreement rolls out across the vast crowd in front of him. 'It's the answer', he continues, alluding to a phrase coined by Martin Luther King, 'that led those who've been told for so long by so many to be cynical and fearful and doubtful of what we can achieve to put their hands on the arc of history and bend it once more toward the hope of a better day.' After King comes an echo of Sam Cooke: 'It's been a long time coming, but tonight . . . change has come to America.'

Obama pays full tribute to McCain, who has, he says, been 'extraordinarily gracious' in defeat. After thanking his wife and telling his daughters that they have 'earned the new puppy that's coming with us to the White House', he pays tribute to his campaign team, singling out David Plouffe and David Axelrod. Then he says to the crowd: 'I will never forget who this victory truly belongs to. It belongs to you.' He admits that he was 'never the likeliest candidate for this office' and recalls the beginnings of his candidacy, twenty-one long months ago, in a passage that celebrates the breadth of popular participation in his campaign and ends with Abraham Lincoln's famous definition of democracy.

We didn't start out with much money or many endorsements. Our campaign was not hatched in the halls of

Washington; it began in the backyards of Des Moines and the living rooms of Concord and the front porches of Charleston. It was built by working men and women who dug into what little savings they had to give five dollars and ten dollars and twenty dollars to the cause. It drew strength from the young people who rejected the myth of their generation's apathy, who left their homes and their families for jobs that offered little pay and less sleep. It drew strength from the not-so-young people who braved the bitter cold and scorching heat to knock on the doors of perfect strangers; from the millions of Americans who volunteered and organised, and proved that, more than two centuries later, a government of the people, by the people and for the people has not perished from this earth. This is your victory.

As he turns towards the future, his tone is grave, even sombre:

Even as we celebrate tonight, we know the challenges that tomorrow will bring are the greatest of our lifetime – two wars, a planet in peril, the worst financial crisis in a century . . . I will ask you join in the work of remaking this nation the only way it's been done in America for 221 years – block by block, brick by brick, calloused hand by calloused hand.

Then Obama does a rare thing for a winning presidential candidate. He pays tribute not just to his opponent, but to his opponent's party:

Let's remember that it was a man from this state who first carried the banner of the Republican Party to the White

House – a party founded on the values of self-reliance,
individual liberty and national unity. Those are values that
we all share. And while the Democratic Party has won a
great victory tonight, we do so with a measure of humility
and determination to heal the divides that have held back
our progress.

Addressing those whose support he didn't earn, he says: 'I may not
have won your vote tonight, but I hear your voices, I need your help,
and I will be your president too.'

Obama returns, as he finishes, to the theme that underpinned his
speech about race in Philadelphia back in March: 'That's the true genius
of America – that America can change. Our union can be perfected.'

He weaves his peroration around the story of Ann Nixon Cooper,
a voter from Atlanta who is 106 years old. She was born, he says, 'just
a generation past slavery . . . when someone like her couldn't vote for
two reasons – because she was a woman and because of the colour of
her skin'. He lists the challenges that Nixon Cooper has lived through
over the last hundred years and the ways in which her country has met
them. From female suffrage to the Great Depression and the New
Deal, to the Second World War and the civil rights movement and the
end of communism. Like McCain, Obama borrows a phrase from his
campaign that, now it is over, resonates anew: he appends each example of national overcoming with the softly intoned words 'Yes we can'.

Obama's purpose tonight is not simply to congratulate the nation on
its achievement. It is to ask Americans to believe that their current
problems can also be overcome. His final paragraph looks to the future,
quoting the nation's founding motto, and invoking Lincoln once more:

This is our moment. This is our time: to put our people
back to work and open doors of opportunity for our kids;

to restore prosperity and promote the cause of peace; to reclaim the American dream and reaffirm that fundamental truth – that out of many, we are one; that while we breathe, we hope, and where we are met with cynicism and doubt and those who tell us that we can't, we will respond with that timeless creed that sums up the spirit of a people: yes we can.

Together, these two speeches act as a bracing rebuke to those who have lost faith in the ability of the United States to set an inspiring example to the world. Stirring and eloquent, each of them wreathed in the history and poetry of their country yet utterly of their moment, they form a fitting conclusion to the spirited, fervent, all-encompassing debate that the country has sustained over the past twelve months.

Now for the hard part

As Barack Obama is driven back to the home in which he and his family will live for less than three more months he might be reflecting that it is only eight years since Bobby Rush handed him an electoral drubbing in his own backyard, and only four since left the Illinois statehouse to launch a career in national politics.

More likely, his mind is turning to the question of how to meet the vast hopes of the people in Grant Park and across the whole of America. In a TV interview given the day before the election, Obama expressed the sense of responsibility he felt towards his supporters, in words that now describe a wider obligation:

There are times when you're shaking hands after a rally and you look out over the crowd and people are telling their stories: 'I lost my job' or 'my wife has ovarian cancer but she's out there campaigning for you'. You hear those stories and you feel an enormous sense of obligation and responsibility to really just work your heart out for folks.

Obviously there's a historic dimension – you know, when a ninety-year-old African-American woman just grabs my hand and won't let go and says: 'I am so proud.' I think about what an African-American woman's gone through over the course of her ninety-year life, and it moves me. Deeply. But it's not just a sense of the history made because of race. There is also just this overwhelming feeling of humility and gratitude where you say: 'Boy, I really better come through for folks if I win this thing. Because they really need it.'

Epilogue

The vanquished and the victor

John McCain

What if John McCain had asserted his authority over his party more forcefully – by selecting Joe Lieberman as his running mate, for example? By proving his independence from the Republicans, he might have set a different course. But he would just as likely have provoked a violent schism in the party and suffered an even worse defeat. To paraphrase Tony Blair on John Major, Obama was able to lead his party; McCain had to follow his.

That being a Republican was so much of a handicap in 2008 was due in large part to the unprecedented unpopularity of the incumbent president. On 5 November, McCain might have been reflecting that George W. Bush had beaten him for a second time.

But if McCain was dealt a poor hand the truth is he played it badly. He and his campaign proved themselves incapable of settling on a coherent story about why their man should be president and why their opponent should not. Instead, they told several (leader versus celebrity, patriot versus careerist, conservative versus socialist) and voters heard none with any clarity. McCain's failure to offer a convincing answer to the central question of a presidential bid – why you? – reflected the core problem with his candidacy.

In the dying weeks of McCain's campaign many of his admirers complained that the 'real McCain' – the McCain of New Hampshire 2000, of Straight Talk and No Surrender – was being obscured. In reality, there was always a mismatch between McCain's brand of politics and the office he sought and this election exposed it ruthlessly. McCain made his name as a maverick. But mavericks do not necessarily make for great presidents. Mavericks divide, presidents unite; mavericks agitate, presidents reassure; mavericks disrupt, presidents keep order. McCain's choice of Sarah Palin as a running mate and the suspension of his campaign during the bailout negotiations were, in their daring and sense of theatre, his most characteristic moments. They were also the decisions that did most damage to his candidacy.

John McCain's other big problem, of course, was his opponent.

Barack Obama

Running against Barack Obama must be enormously frustrating. Nothing seems to throw the man off his monotonous rhythm. He takes few risks. Rather than seek the match-winning gambit, he waits and waits for his opponents to undo themselves, as Hillary Clinton did in the weeks before Iowa and later during the sniper fire affair, and as John McCain did over the bailout.

When Obama did make bold moves, as with his decision to make a foreign tour, or to speak at Invesco Field, or to air a thirty-minute infomercial in prime time, he and his team executed them with such scrupulous care, thought, and attention to detail that they didn't seem, in retrospect, to have been risky at all. When thinking big, he never forgot to think small.

Clinton can at least claim to have disrupted the younger man's composure. In the long primary battle, Obama seemed at times unsettled and bewildered by her tenacity, her fierce refusal to lie down and the brilliance with which she and her husband found new ways to needle him. McCain never got as close to seriously unnerving his opponent.

Obama's strength as a candidate was rooted in his exceptional emotional self-control, allied to judiciously applied charisma. In *Dreams from My Father* he recalls that as a young black man in a white society he learnt that it would do him good to always smile and to make 'no sudden moves'. Whether learnt or innate, this was the defining feature of the political identity he cultivated in the 2008 election contest and it sometimes frustrated his supporters nearly as much as his opponents. It was there in all three debates with McCain. Obama never reached for a killer line or embarked on a surprise attack but was content to grind out draws or points victories. It was there in his refusal to heed the million pieces of advice he received, when running against Clinton and McCain, to get angry, to show his teeth, to scrap and to kneecap. Most importantly, it was evident in his restrained response to the melodrama of McCain's campaign suspension. Come November, voters who first noticed him for his speeches came to trust that beneath the brilliant oratory was a highly competent, steady and reliable operator.

It was Obama's fortune to inherit the audacity to dream and the cool determination to prevail. It was his genius to fuse them into a political persona that reassured even as it inspired.

Appendix I

Primaries, delegates and superdelegates

Each presidential candidate is formally chosen by a majority vote of delegates at their party's national convention. Candidates seek to maximise the number of delegates from each state that will vote for them.

Delegates used to be chosen by local party bosses and activists striking deals at the convention in the proverbial smoke-filled rooms. But the second half of the last century saw the popular vote of party members become increasingly important, in the form of primaries. A primary allows members of the public who are registered supporters of a particular party to participate in the nomination process. Their vote now decides who the state's delegates will back at the convention. The primary season is therefore a race to win the most delegates, by way of the popular vote.

Primaries in both parties have evolved organically and somewhat haphazardly, and the voting rules in different states are notoriously inconsistent and arcane. Some states hold 'closed primaries', in which only those registered earlier in the year as Democrats or Republicans can vote. Others hold 'open primaries', in which a registered voter may vote in any party's primary regardless of party affiliation (voters can register and vote as independents as well as Democrats or Republicans).

A few states don't hold primaries at all, but caucuses instead.

Caucuses are small-scale meetings held across the state (in Iowa, caucus meetings are held in each of 1,781 precincts). Participation tends to be limited to more committed party activists (though there was a massive and successful effort by the campaigns this year to bring new participants into the process). On the basis of the results of these caucuses, delegates are sent to county conventions to elect delegates to state conventions, who choose the national convention delegates. Some states, like Texas, employ a mixture of primaries and caucuses. In this book 'the primary season' and 'primaries' have some-times been taken to refer to both primaries and caucuses for the purposes of simplicity.

The overall size of a state's delegation depends on the size of the state population and also on factors such as its past support for each party's candidates in federal elections and levels of turnout in previous primaries. When it comes to determining how many of each state's delegates should go to which candidate, the parties apply different standards. In most Republican primaries the rule is 'winner takes all': the candidate with the most votes wins all the delegates from that state. In the Democratic Party the delegates are elected on a propor-tional basis. Candidates receiving a minimum 15 per cent of the vote obtain a share of the state's delegates corresponding to their share of the vote (this partly explains why the Obama–Clinton battle stayed so close for so long).

The primary season traditionally lasted from February till June but it has become increasingly 'front loaded' as party officials seek an early and conclusive result and individual states jostle for an early date (and therefore more influence – the early states, especially Iowa, New Hampshire and South Carolina, have enormous influence over the outcome, due to the exposure and momentum that winning candidates can gain there. Michigan and Florida thought they deserved more of a say, which is why they moved their primaries up the calendar this year). 'Super Tuesday' in early February, when a large number of states hold primaries or caucuses on the same day, is often decisive. Once one candidate establishes a clear lead there is a snowballing effect as funds and endorsements flow towards the front-runner and other candidates are forced to drop out, having lost the backing of their donors.

Delegates elected via the primaries and caucuses are known as 'pledged delegates'. The Democratic Party introduced 'superdelegates' in 1982 after party officials became nervous that the unmediated will of primary voters risked producing election-losing prospects. Superdelegates were created to restore a measure of power over the process to party insiders. They include all of the party's members in Congress, various party officials and former office holders – essentially, the party establishment. They make up about a fifth of total delegates, and they can vote for whom they wish. The winning candidate must win an absolute majority of all delegates, pledged and super. This year that meant winning 2,118 delegates.

Historically superdelegates haven't had much of a decision to make. One candidate usually wins such an overwhelming number of pledged delegates that the others drop out and the superdelegates simply swing behind the emergent nominee. In 2008 things were different, as they were in so many other respects.

Appendix II

Concession and victory speeches

John McCain

My friends, we have come to the end of a long journey. The American people have spoken, and they have spoken clearly.

A little while ago, I had the honour of calling Senator Barack Obama to congratulate him on being elected the next president of the country that we both love. In a contest as long and difficult as this campaign has been, his success alone commands my respect for his ability and perseverance. But that he managed to do so by inspiring the hopes of so many millions of Americans who had once wrongly believed that they had little at stake or little influence in the election of an American president is something I deeply admire and commend him for achieving.

This is an historic election, and I recognise the special significance it has for African-Americans and for the special pride that must be theirs tonight.

I've always believed that America offers opportunities to all who have the industry and will to seize it. Senator Obama believes that, too. But we both recognise that, though we have come a long way from the old injustices that once stained our nation's reputation and denied some Americans the full blessings of American citizenship, the memory of them still had the power to wound.

A century ago, President Theodore Roosevelt's invitation of Booker T. Washington to dine at the White House was taken as an outrage in many quarters. America today is a world away from the cruel and prideful bigotry of that time. There is no better evidence of this than the election of an African-American to the presidency of the United States.

Let there be no reason now for any American to fail to cherish their citizenship in this, the greatest nation on Earth.

Senator Obama has achieved a great thing for himself and for his country. I applaud him for it, and offer him my sincere sympathy that his beloved grandmother did not live to see this day. Though our faith assures us she is at rest in the presence of her creator and so very proud of the good man she helped raise.

Senator Obama and I have had and argued our differences, and he has prevailed. No doubt many of those differences remain.

These are difficult times for our country. And I pledge to him tonight to do all in my power to help him lead us through the many challenges we face. I urge all Americans who supported me to join me in not just congratulating him, but offering our next president our good will and earnest effort to find ways to come together to find the necessary compromises to bridge our differences and help restore our prosperity, defend our security in a dangerous world, and leave our children and grandchildren a stronger, better country than we inherited. Whatever our differences, we are fellow Americans. And please believe me when I say no association has ever meant more to me than that.

It's natural, tonight, to feel some disappointment. But tomorrow, we must move beyond it and work together to get our country moving again. We fought as hard as we could. And though we fell short, the failure is mine, not yours.

I am so deeply grateful to all of you for the great honour of your support and for all you have done for me. I wish the outcome had been different, my friends. The road was a difficult one from the outset, but your support and friendship never wavered. I cannot adequately express how deeply indebted I am to you.

I'm especially grateful to my wife, Cindy, my children, my dear mother and all my family, and to the many old and dear friends who have stood by my side through the many ups and downs of this long campaign. I have always been a fortunate man, and never more so for the love and encouragement you have given me.

You know, campaigns are often harder on a candidate's family than on the candidate, and that's been true in this campaign. All I can offer in compensation is my love and gratitude and the promise of more peaceful years ahead.

I am also, of course, very thankful to Governor Sarah Palin, one of the best campaigners I've ever seen, and an impressive new voice in our party for reform and the principles that have always been our greatest strength, her husband Todd and their five beautiful children for their tireless dedication to our cause, and the courage and grace they showed in the rough and tumble of a presidential campaign. We can all look forward with great interest to her future service to Alaska, the Republican Party and our country.

To all my campaign comrades, from Rick Davis and Steve Schmidt and Mark Salter, to every last volunteer who fought so hard and valiantly, month after month, in what at times seemed to be the most challenged campaign in modern times, thank you so much. A lost election will never mean more to me than the privilege of your faith and friendship.

I don't know what more we could have done to try to win this election. I'll leave that to others to determine. Every candidate makes mistakes, and I'm sure I made my share of them. But I won't spend a moment of the future regretting what might have been.

This campaign was and will remain the great honour of my life, and my heart is filled with nothing but gratitude for the experience and to the American people for giving me a fair hearing before deciding that Senator Obama and my old friend Senator Joe Biden should have the honour of leading us for the next four years.

I would not be an American worthy of the name should I regret a fate that has allowed me the extraordinary privilege of serving this country for a half a century. Today, I was a candidate for the highest office in the country I love so much. And tonight, I remain her servant. That is blessing enough for anyone, and I thank the people of Arizona for it.

Tonight, more than any night, I hold in my heart nothing but love for this country and for all its citizens, whether they supported me or Senator Obama.

I wish Godspeed to the man who was my former opponent and will be my president. And I call on all Americans, as I have often in this campaign, to not despair of our present difficulties, but to believe, always, in the promise and greatness of America, because nothing is inevitable here.

Americans never quit. We never surrender. We never hide from history. We make history.

Thank you, and God bless you, and God bless America.

Barack Obama

If there is anyone out there who still doubts that America is a place where all things are possible, who still wonders if the dream of our founders is alive in our time, who still questions the power of our democracy, tonight is your answer.

It's the answer told by lines that stretched around schools and churches in numbers this nation has never seen, by people who waited three hours and four hours, many for the first time in their lives, because they believed that this time must be different, that their voices could be that difference.

It's the answer spoken by young and old, rich and poor, Democrat and Republican, black, white, Hispanic, Asian, Native American, gay, straight, disabled and not disabled – Americans who sent a message to the world that we have never been just a collection of individuals or a collection of red states and blue states. We are, and always will be, the United States of America.

It's the answer that led those who've been told for so long by so many to be cynical and fearful and doubtful about what we can achieve to put their hands on the arc of history and bend it once more toward the hope of a better day.

It's been a long time coming, but tonight, because of what we did on this date, in this election, at this defining moment, change has come to America.

A little bit earlier this evening, I received an extraordinarily gracious call from Senator McCain. Senator McCain fought long and hard in this campaign. And he's fought even longer and harder for the country that he loves. He has endured sacrifices for America that most of us cannot begin to imagine. We are better off for the service rendered by this brave and selfless leader.

I congratulate him; I congratulate Governor Palin for all that they've achieved. And I look forward to working with them to renew this nation's promise in the months ahead.

I want to thank my partner in this journey, a man who campaigned from his heart and spoke for the men and women he grew up with on the streets of Scranton and rode with on the train home to Delaware, the vice-president-elect of the United States, Joe Biden.

And I would not be standing here tonight without the unyielding support of my best friend for the last sixteen years, the rock of our family, the love of my life, the nation's next first lady, Michelle Obama.

Sasha and Malia, I love you both more than you can imagine. And you have earned the new puppy that's coming with us to the White House. And while she's no longer with us, I know my grandmother's watching, along with the family that made me who I am. I miss them tonight, and know that my debt to them is beyond measure.

To my sister Maya, my sister Auma, all my other brothers and sisters, thank you so much for all the support that you've given me. I am grateful to them.

And to my campaign manager, David Plouffe, the unsung hero of this campaign, who built the best political campaign, I think, in the history of the United States of America. To my chief strategist, David Axelrod, who's been a partner with me every step of the way. To the best campaign team ever assembled in the history of politics. You made this happen, and I am forever grateful for what you've sacrificed to get it done.

But above all, I will never forget who this victory truly belongs to. It belongs to you. It belongs to you.

I was never the likeliest candidate for this office. We didn't start with much money or many endorsements. Our campaign was not hatched in the halls of Washington; it began in the backyards of Des Moines and the living rooms of Concord and the front porches of Charleston. It was built by working men and women who dug into what little savings they had to give five dollars and ten dollars and twenty dollars to the cause. It drew strength from the young people who rejected the myth of their generation's apathy, who left their homes and their families for jobs that offered little pay and less sleep. It drew strength from the not-so-young people who braved the bitter cold and scorching heat to knock on doors of perfect strangers, and from the millions of Americans who volunteered and organised and proved that more than two centuries later a government of the people, by the people and for the people has not perished from the Earth. This is your victory.

Now, I know you didn't do this just to win an election. And I know you didn't do it for me. You did it because you understand the enormity of the task that lies ahead. For even as we celebrate tonight, we know the challenges that tomorrow will bring are the greatest of our lifetime – two wars, a planet in peril, the worst financial crisis in a century. Even as we stand here tonight, we know there are brave Americans waking up in the deserts of Iraq and the mountains of Afghanistan to risk their lives for us. There are mothers and fathers who will lie awake after the children fall asleep and wonder how they'll make the mortgage or pay their doctors' bills or save enough for their child's college education.

There's new energy to harness, new jobs to be created, new schools to build, and threats to meet, alliances to repair.

The road ahead will be long. Our climb will be steep. We may not get there in one year or even in one term. But, America, I have never been more hopeful than I am tonight that we will get there. I promise you: we as a people will get there.

There will be setbacks and false starts. There are many who won't agree with every decision or policy I make as president, and we know the government can't solve every problem. But I will always be honest with you about the challenges we face. I will listen to you, especially when we disagree. And, above all, I will ask you to join in the work of remaking this nation the only way it's been done in America for 221 years – block by block, brick by brick, calloused hand by calloused hand.

What began twenty-one months ago in the depths of winter cannot end on this autumn night. This victory alone is not the change we seek. It is only the chance for us to make that change. And that cannot happen if we go back to the way things were. It can't happen without you, without a new spirit of service, a new spirit of sacrifice.

So let us summon a new spirit of patriotism, of responsibility, where each of us resolves to pitch in and work harder and look after not only ourselves but each other. Let us remember that, if this financial crisis taught us anything, it's that we cannot have a thriving Wall Street while Main Street suffers.

In this country, we rise or fall as one nation, as one people. Let's resist the temptation to fall back on the same partisanship and pettiness and immaturity that has poisoned our politics for so long. Let's remember that it was a man from this state who first carried the banner of the Republican Party to the White House, a party founded on the values of self-reliance and individual liberty and national unity. Those are values that we all share. And while the Democratic Party has won a great victory tonight, we do so with a measure of humility and determination to heal the divides that have held back our progress.

As Lincoln said to a nation far more divided than ours, we are not enemies but friends. Though passion may have strained, it must not break our bonds of affection.

And to those Americans whose support I have yet to earn, I may not have won your vote tonight, but I hear your voices, I need your help, and I will be your president, too.

And to all those watching tonight from beyond our shores, from parliaments and palaces, to those who are huddled around radios in the forgotten corners of the world: our stories are singular, but our destiny is shared, and a new dawn of American leadership is at hand. To those who would tear the world down: we will defeat you. To those who seek peace and security: we support you. And to all those who have wondered if America's beacon still burns as bright: tonight we proved once more that the true strength of our nation comes not from the might of our arms or the scale of our wealth, but from the enduring power of our ideals: democracy, liberty, opportunity and unyielding hope.

That's the true genius of America – that America can change. Our union can be perfected. What we've already achieved gives us hope for what we can and must achieve tomorrow.

This election had many firsts and many stories that will be told for generations. But one that's on my mind tonight's about a woman who cast her ballot in Atlanta. She's a lot like the millions of others who stood in line to make their voice heard in this election, except for one thing: Ann Nixon Cooper is 106 years old.

She was born just a generation past slavery; a time when there were no cars on the road or planes in the sky; when someone like her couldn't vote for two reasons – because she was a woman and because of the colour of her skin. And tonight, I think about all that she's seen throughout her century in America – the heartache and the hope; the struggle and the progress; the times we were told that we can't, and the people who pressed on with that American creed: yes we can.

At a time when women's voices were silenced and their hopes dismissed, she lived to see them stand up and speak out and reach for the ballot. Yes we can.

When there was despair in the Dust Bowl and depression across the land, she saw a nation conquer fear itself with a New Deal, new jobs, a new sense of common purpose. Yes we can.

When the bombs fell on our harbour and tyranny threatened the world, she was there to witness a generation rise to greatness and a democracy was saved. Yes we can.

She was there for the buses in Montgomery, the hoses in Birmingham, a bridge in Selma, and a preacher from Atlanta who told a people that 'we shall overcome'. Yes we can.

A man touched down on the moon, a wall came down in Berlin, a world was connected by our own science and imagination. And this year, in this election, she touched her finger to a screen and cast her vote, because after 106 years in America, through the best of times and the darkest of hours, she knows how America can change.

Yes we can.

America, we have come so far. We have seen so much. But there's so much more to do. So tonight, let us ask ourselves: if our children should live to see the next century; if my daughters should be so lucky to live as long as Ann Nixon Cooper, what change will they see? What progress will we have made?

This is our chance to answer that call. This is our moment. This is our time: to put our people back to work and open doors of opportunity for our kids; to restore prosperity and promote the cause of peace; to reclaim the American dream and reaffirm that fundamental truth – that out of many, we are one; that while we breathe, we hope. And where we are met with cynicism and doubt and those who tell us that we can't, we will respond with that timeless creed that sums up the spirit of a people: yes we can.

Thank you. God bless you. And may God bless the United States of America.